RATIONALITY

Main s:
Wolve

E8·50

Robert Scott Library
St Peter's Square

KEY CONCEPTS IN THE SOCIAL SCIENCES

RATIONALITY

EDITED BY BRYAN R. WILSON

BASIL BLACKWELL

© in this collection, Basil Blackwell 1970
Reprinted 1974, 1977, 1979, 1981, 1984, 1985, 1986

Basil Blackwell Ltd
108 Cowley Road, Oxford OX4 1JF, UK

ISBN 0 631 09900 X

Printed in Great Britain by
Billing & Sons Limited, Worcester

CONTENTS

ACKNOWLEDGEMENTS

Thanks are due to the authors and publishers of the essays included in this volume for permission to reprint material of which they hold the copyright. The original provenance is indicated at the beginning of each paper. J. H. M. Beattie's paper 'On Understanding Ritual' has not been published previously.

A Sociologist's Introduction

BRYAN R. WILSON

From their beginnings the sociological sciences have been variously but inescapably involved in the discussion of rationality. Comte, Hobhouse and, in different ways, Marx and Durkheim, all hankered, with greater or lesser self-consciousness, for a rational ethic—for patterns of social regulation that utilized the findings of scientific social enquiry, which some of them saw as convergent with the laws of history itself. The views of the nineteenth-century sociologists engendered controversy that arose in considerable measure from their attempt to adopt consciously rational procedures for the analysis of data that had, in the humanities, formerly been discussed in normative terms as the stuff of literature and history, vital to the preservation and transmission of cultural values. Abandoning the earlier historicism in which the development of society was identified with the development of Reason, and emphasizing an empirical approach—whether realist or intellectualist—the early sociologists put less than tentative feet on the soggy ground that they took to be terra firma. Only their successors, Pareto and, more particularly, Max Weber, were able to distanciate themselves from the optimism that the earlier espousal of rationality had induced. Weber, studying the development of rationality in western science, economy and social organization, sought to make explicit the point at which the value freedom demanded by scientific rationality could be fully operative in social enquiry. Of the classical sociologists, he came closest to recognizing the limitations of rational procedures of enquiry and understanding. But he did not raise doubts about the criteria of rationality itself. Since Weber, sociologists have had no excuse for being unaware of the problem of ethical neutrality in social enquiry, but they have not allowed the persisting uncertainties concerning the value-freedom of their approach overmuch to inhibit their empirical investigations, their attempts to comprehend other cultures, and their interpretation of behaviour that is not self-evidently purposive and that might, in their terms, readily be regarded as non-rational. Functionalist analysis, in particular, permitted sociologists to avoid the facile optimistic rationalism of their—intellectual, if not strictly chronological—predecessors (some of whom, it must be remembered, were still writing in the 1920s and 1930s). The explanation of social phenomena in terms of the ends that they subserved, and of the specific operation of social institutions by reference to their inter-dependence, made it unnecessary to pay much attention to the inten-tions of the actors except as a foil to add cogency to the latent functions which sociological analysis might then reveal. Functionalism was an approach that justified the study of non-rational behaviour by reference to the not so irrational 'hidden hand' by which all things worked to sustain each other. It is not necessary here to discuss the degree to which functionalism, in recognizing the extensiveness of the non-rational in society, sought to retreat from the rationalistic value-judgments implicit or explicit in earlier sociological theories; nor the measure to which it represented an imposition by investigators on their data of concepts of rational operation which they saw as latent in society, even though they did not prevail in the minds of men. Simpler peoples might not be able to explain how their societies worked, nor religious men the real import of their religiosity, but in each case their non-rational acts and their false beliefs were necessary to sustain a certain internally coherent pattern of order. The philosophical problems involved in translating the meanings and the reason of one culture into the language of another, and of explaining super-empirically-oriented beliefs in scientific terms, were not solved by functionalism. They were evaded. Other forms of sociological analysis neglected these issues no less: the use of statistical techniques was often accompanied by mindless lack of interest in the philosophical assumptions involved in social enquiry.

Occasionally, of course, nagging doubts about the philosophical status of sociological knowledge were raised. The sociologist has not always had a ready answer (even though he has increasingly had the dubious assurance of the growing fashionability of his approach) when challenged by, say, a theologian to explain how a non-religious man might hope to understand religious activity. In simpler, less abstract, ways, savages may have asked similar questions of anthropologists. But in recent years these questions have been raised more pertinently and more challengingly by philosophers. The problem of the culture-boundedness of meaning; of the universality of the criteria of rationality as it has developed in Western society; of the comprehensibility of ritual acts—have come into the full focus of a many-sided debate conducted between philosophers, sociologists and anthropologists. The issues go to the very core of what a social science is and can claim to do. Social scientists will not, of course, wait for the conclusions of the debate (if such there could be) or even for interim agreements, before they continue with their chosen tasks, but there is a real possibility that they will pursue those tasks with more sophistication, and that they might make fewer unwarranted or dubious assumptions, if they are acquainted with the arguments that have gone on about the possibility and plausibility of the goals that they set themselves.

The principal contributions to this continuing debate are gathered together in this volume: it has proceeded from different quarters and with somewhat different, albeit always related, foci. The papers have been ordered in this volume very broadly in chronological sequence: all except that of Beattie have appeared before.

It is not my intention, as editor of this book and as a sociologist who has not been involved in this debate, either to summarize the arguments that others can better put for themselves, or to enter the lists myself. It might be deemed permissible, however, for me to make some passing comments on some of the issues that, in the following pages, are handled at greater length and with greater philosphical dexterity than I can command. It is at once striking that it is sociology (and under sociology I subsume anthropology) rather than history that has given rise to this particular set of controversies. Other cultures raise, more pointedly than do other periods, the question of how we are to understand the beliefs and actions of other men.[1]

Yet, if one may change the scene from a primitive culture to a mediaeval society, there is a sense in which it may be said that no one but a mediaeval man could possibly understand mediaeval society. But there is also a sense, and the statement is no less comprehensible to us, in which we may say that mediaeval man had little or no chance of ever understanding mediaeval society—and certainly far less prospect of doing so than has modern man. Obviously to make this latter statement is to claim that there are ways of interpreting the data about one culture into the terms employed in another, and the implication is that these are in some respects more comprehensive methods than

[1] A not dissimilar issue arises once the attempt is made to understand religion in neutral, non-normative terms.

have been available either in earlier periods of history or in other cultures. This is the claim on which social science, despite cultural relativism, despite the unwillingness to label other cultures as 'primitive', necessarily rests. Even Peter Winch, who raises doubts about this view, is obliged in his essay, 'Understanding a Primitive Society' to refer to the Zande as applying something very like our technical concept 'perhaps in a more primitive form'.[1] Since technology is itself the application of rational procedures, a judgement of the primitiveness of technology seems to me to imply a judgement about rationality, and concedes something to the idea that the criteria of rationality in western society may be properly applied more widely, even if it does not establish them as *the* universally valid criteria of rationality. The only explanations that *we* can have of other cultures will necessarily depend on the rules of logic as we know and use them.

The two apparently contradictory statements above about understanding mediaeval society rest on two different meanings of the word 'understand'. A modern man, even of heightened sensitivity (and it is sensitivity and not intellect which is perhaps most at issue) might remain bewildered—might never wholly understand—a mediaeval society to which he was transplanted. He might never come fully to share the expectations and assumptions common to men in that society. It is in this sense that mediaeval society is understandable only to mediaeval man.

But it is doubtful whether, even over the distance of centuries within a given continuing society, or even as between, say, our own and a very different culture, there are not many forms of behaviour and many statements which a contemporary sociologist might not readily understand. This is an issue which Hollis takes up in his paper 'The Limits of Irrationality'. Going further than this, the sociologist has also the opportunity of examining social processes, and forms of behaviour in many different cultures. He has, and on this sociology at least may rest a considerable part of its case, the benefit of comparison. Beneath the particularities of a given cultural content, there may be discernible similarities of sequence in social processes: by observing such similarities and cases in which similarities might be expected the sociologist has a procedure for understanding another culture or another epoch unavailable to the men who participate in that culture or that period. Clearly, such comparative procedures depend on a range

[1] See below, p. 103.

of empirical data, an established logic of enquiry, and a sustained discourse among investigators.

To have put the matter in these terms omits mention of the extent to which mediaeval men (or primitive men) have their own accumulated body of interpretative constructs. These may appear in the form of proverbs, precepts, moral tales or myths. Such items, and the categories that they employ, are, however, rarely found as exclusively explanatory constructs. We know from empirical investigation that they are used to summon behaviour as much as to explain it. Explanation as such and in isolation is not a focus of concern in primitive societies. In general, it has been the other attributes of interpretative constructs that has attracted the attention of the sociologist—their use in ordering the chaos of everyday experience; in reassuring men about events and actions; in facilitating their pursuit of goals and purposes. Horton sees the activities of the diviner in Africa as not so different from those of scientists in the Western world, and relates much of the difference to the personal style of African societies. That difference may relate to the more limited opportunity for empirical observation of the African diviner (when compared with the western scientist) but it reflects also the consequence of that limitation, in a less developed objectivity, in a lesser prospect of abstract thought, and, in consequence, a lesser likelihood of distinguishing factual and evaluative elements, and of separating emotional from cognitive orientations. This last consideration is relevant to the role of interpretative constructs in simple societies as devices that summon behavioural response together with particular cognitions. That the categories of other cultures are not always translatable into our own is the burden of argument in some of these papers. That they are derived from a much more limited range of experience, from less comparative opportunity and are expressed in much more concrete terms, must I think also be conceded. It is because the sociologist has a wider range of data, has become conscious of the importance of eliminating emotional and evaluative elements in his concepts and has a tradition of enquiry that uses such concepts and provides models of analysis, that he is in a better position than mediaeval man or primitive man to understand mediaeval and primitive society. He, after all, makes the attempt to understand other societies. They do not. His wider tolerance, his intellectual curiosity, and his willingness to criticize his own procedures are his initial advantages over men in other cultures. Other societies to them—but not to him—are bizarre, laughable and 'ununderstandable'.

The attitudes of the western investigator are aspects of the cultural relativism that he has inherited as part of the posture of value-freedom that he has attempted to adopt in approaching other cultures. Part of the greater likelihood of understanding other cultures that he enjoys, when compared with men from those cultures, arises from the fact that cultural relativism is a possible perspective in his culture but not in theirs. What must be acknowledged, however, is that cultural relativity has its own inherent bounds precisely because of this. Other cultures are made understandable by ordering their concepts, beliefs, activities according to the premises of the tradition of Western social science. It cannot be escaped that the tolerance, ethical neutrality and detached curiosity about other cultures arise as the products of a particular culture at a certain stage of its development.

There are, then, limits to be set to the claim that western man understands another culture better than have other men, and better, in particular, than do the participants in it. Understanding an alien society by the procedures of social science may, indeed, partly preclude the possibility of understanding it by that inner empathy that, in general, lifelong participants in a society spontaneously manifest. It may—although this is scarcely the burden of discussion here—imply more: not only may it preclude this empathic understanding of another culture; it may even affect that type of understanding of one's own. If one learns to relate personal experience to a set of abstract categories these may become—and for some intellectuals appear to become—necessary constructs for them even for them to interpret their own world. Intellectual apprehension may then be gained at the cost of some degree of empathy and sensitivity. It must be conceded that social scientists do not always appear to the man-in-the-street to behave wholly comprehendingly even in their own culture.

The distinction between rational understanding and empathic understanding is well-established in social science. Western man increasingly comprehends his own culture by systematic observation, the conscious process of creating well-defined categories and employing them in accordance with equally conscious logical principles. As the fullest embodiment of these procedures, the social sciences seek to order knowledge systematically in value-free, emotionally-neutral, abstract propositions. Such value-freedom—in the degree to which it is ever attainable—contradicts the value-commitment that an empathic understanding of society demands. Emotional involvement in and evaluation of persons, objects and activities are precisely the first order experience common in all societies: they are practically the totality of experience in most societies. Only in advanced western societies is the detached and systematic approach to social (and perhaps also to natural) phenomena at all commonly adopted—or adoptable. It is in this society that the dilemma of how to understand the world arises as an intellectual problem, and in this sort of society that men are aware that 'knowing' in one way may partially preclude, or at least compromise, 'knowing' in another way. The dilemma of knowing what rational procedures can yield, and yet being aware of what they also eclipse has been central to sociology since Max Weber saw the blossoming of rationality in the west as simultaneously the blight of man's capacity for a different type of comprehension of the world, and of the realization of his potential within it.

Comparison of the scientific procedures of western society with the beliefs and actions of men in primitive societies is the central focus of discussion in these pages. The ghost of Lévy-Bruhl, who sought to distinguish modern man's logicality from the 'pre-logical' mentality of primitive man, is, for several writers in this book, the thing to be exorcised. No one disputes that advanced societies are so largely because of the rational and empirical orientations that have become incorporated into their technical equipment, material culture and social organization. The thought-processes of western man may not be typically more rational, but he does live in a more controlled environment, and the control is achieved by the employment of formally rational procedures of thought and action in certain significant, indeed dominant, sections of the social system. It is to be expected that he should, even if only to work the machines, have come to embrace a similar logic to that which machines (including social 'machines') incorporate, and by which his life is in so many ways regulated. There remain areas of social activity where the norms of rationality may not be invoked, or only partially invoked. These areas may command a diminishing proportion of man's energy, resources and time: faced with the impress of instrumental rationality, the complexity, 'richness' and vigour of their poetic, symbolic, artistic character may have declined. Those institutions that organize action towards ultimate ends or promote activity that is justified in terms of its intrinsic quality (which Max Weber, to distinguish it from traditional or purely affectual action, labelled evaluatively rational [*wertrational*] action), are those that are threatened by the increasing dominance in society of formally rational procedures.[1]

Most evidently, religious activity, the ends of which are not susceptible to empirical verification, are most affected. Those some-time assertions of western religious systems that have become testable by rational empirical enquiry and that have been falsified (such as special creation or the relations of the sun, moon and planets) have largely been abandoned. The super-empirical propositions remain, weakened perhaps by the impact of rational tests on those supportive tenets that have been falsified. Just how rational religious men are must be first assessed in terms of the internal consistency of their beliefs (and within the theological tradition of Christianity it has been a major enterprise to establish the internal consistency of at least the theological propositions themselves) and secondly, how consistent these beliefs are with the general secular (including scientific) beliefs which also inform the actions of religious men in any given culture. It is likely, in advanced societies, where the social and physical milieux are increasingly dominated by formally rational prescriptions, that most religious believers maintain beliefs and undertake acts that reveal some degree of inconsistency. Without seeking to stand Lévy-Bruhl on his head, this particular inconsistency between rational procedures in some spheres, and the commitment to contradictory super-empirical goals in others, may appear less evident in simple societies.

Beyond this, however, is it an obligation of the sociologist to judge whether the beliefs of primitive man or religious man are rational? There is, in the fact that he investigates at all, an implied commitment to the rational procedures that his discipline embraces. This is the sociologist's inbuilt bias, but a bias that he feels, on the evidence of the effectiveness of rational procedures in his own culture—if on no higher ground—that he can justify. But going beyond this implication—that

[1] Weber distinguished between *wertrational* action (evaluatively rational action) and *zweckrational* action (purposive or instrumental action). The former was action taken to realize particular values that were self-justifying: the latter was procedurally rational action to attain interim ends that were themselves always to be justified as the means to further ends. Thus, ritual action was of the former, economic action of the latter, type. *Zweckrationalität* characterized the mode of operation of modern capitalism and bureaucracy. The contrast of the two types and the growing dominance of *Zweckrationalität* emerges clearly in Weber's essay, *The Protestant Ethic and the Spirit of Capitalism* (1904, English translation, by Talcott Parsons, London: Allen and Unwin, 1930.)

in using rational standards alien to the social groups he investigates he makes an implicit judgement of the inadequacy of the explanations which these groups offer about their own beliefs and activities—need he judge more explicitly? It seems to me that it is only in his methodological agnosticism in using rational procedures that the sociologist need be involved in making judgments. He selects problems for enquiry and chooses methods: both entail evaluations. Beyond this is it not imperative that he makes no further explicit judgements? The initial judgements he cannot eschew. This is his 'cultural' inheritance, and the mandate of his profession—albeit an inheritance that allows him latitude to be critical of his own procedures, self-conscious about his thought processes, and aware of precisely those dilemmas which his activity as a sociologist create for him.

Need he, however, presuppose that the ultimate natural order is to be explained only according to the rational principles known to him? May he not accept rational procedures as the best that he knows as a mode of explanation? That these procedures could ever be shown to be less adequate than others, he may not believe: but he need not actually disbelieve it either. At this point he may remain neutral. He may see religion as a human projection, and he need not decide whether this projection might conform to a supernatural order.[1] If he were a theologian of the religion in question then he must believe in that ultimate convergence: if he were a theologian of another religion working on comparative symbolics, then he would have to dispute it and treat the religion in question as erroneous. The sociologist need do neither. For his purposes religion must be seen in relation to the circumstances of those who establish it and maintain it, but he does not rule out the possibility that religious ideas could converge with ultimate reality. He need not regard his rational procedures as being more than the best way we know of investigating. Here I pursue a line that falls between the positions taken between Winch and MacIntyre in the papers in this volume.[2]

In examining the social circumstances in which beliefs are held, the sociologist will not ignore the believers' own explanations of the

---

[1] This position is set forth with great cogency by Peter L. Berger, *The Sacred Canopy*, New York: Doubleday, 1968.

[2] In considering this point I have had the benefit of seeing an unpublished draft paper by Alasdair MacIntyre, *Rationality as a Sociological Category*, in which MacIntyre disputes the argument that the sociologist can in fact adopt a position of neutrality of the type that is here defended.

origin and provenance of his faith and practice. The more difficult case arises, and it is very much a starting point for some of the papers in this volume, when internal contradiction is found between propositions within a belief system, or when categories are used which make no sense to the investigator. The sociologist may say, using his own criteria, that mutually contradictory propositions cannot rationally be believed at the same time, *providing that he understands the sense in which they are asserted*. Several papers address themselves precisely to this problem. Are statements found in an alien belief-system appropriately subject to sociological scrutiny? Winch sees the anthropologist making category mistakes when he deals with primitive views of witchcraft as if they were quasi-scientific views. But the similarity of procedures of men in simple and advanced societies is elaborately argued by Horton.

If the rationality found in simple societies and in western societies does show considerable convergence, we have already noted that the application of rational principles is far less extensive in simple society. There is, however, another side of this matter to be taken into account which may be of more importance to sociologists than to philosophers. As Gellner argues, statements may be socially effective and powerful precisely because they are not strictly rational, and there is, even in advanced societies, some willingness to credit the non-rational with this type of power. A religious system deals in such power, and the religious may not seek—may indeed resist—analysis of their propositions by purely rational procedures. If the sociologist were to insist on imposing categories of rationality explicitly to judge belief systems, he might from certain points of view blind himself to the social and psychological operation and potency of non-rational propositions. Gellner makes evident the importance of ideal norms in society, even though they embody statements that are rarely (or never?) true and exhort conduct which is not, by western standards, rational. The need that men have for pretence may itself set a limit to the utility of strictly intellectual orientations in seeking to understand society. Concepts are not always rigorous and precise, and do not always carry well-defined meanings: they may, indeed, be important precisely because of the strategic ambiguities that they embrace. It has been a merit of functionalist analysis to recognize this, but clearly functionalism has greatest cogency as a mode of explanation where latent functions can be revealed. It is not distinguishable as a form of explanation where rational action occurs in accordance with internal beliefs. When functions are specified in advance and—given perfect knowledge and control—when consequences are predicted and appropriate action mounted, as occurs, at least as an ideal, in economic systems of western society, there are no latent functions to uncover. If society increasingly embraces rational techniques, and the findings that emerge from rational processes of enquiry—as, in its increasing use of technology, in quantification and planning, it appears to do—then latent functions become a less significant phenomenon. As sociological enquiry itself uncovers and publicizes latent functions it may also be that the impress of this reasoning affects social processes even though the investigators sought only to discover them and not to cause their amendment. How far men can rationally plan facilities to meet all their demands for gratification is not an issue with which we need here be concerned. Ultimate goals and values do not fit into the instrumental means-ends-means schema of the self-perpetuating circle that characterizes formal rationality. Sociologists may indeed make category mistakes if they seek to relate ritual acts to the rational categories of action with which they are acquainted. More significant, socially, however, is that in doing so they may also render the categories employed by the ritualists eventually untenable—even for men in simpler societies. They will, by western standards, have made them into 'rational' men. They will also have destroyed a process of thought and action that had, in its pristine state, some internal code of meaning of its own, derived from its own social context. What was done was understandable empathically, poetically, mystically, and could not be communicated in a set of rational propositions.

The point made by Winch, and by Jarvie and Agassi, that it is essential to seek to view the world as much as possible from the standpoint of primitive men themselves when they are the object of study, and in some measure to hold in abeyance, to put it no more strongly, the inbuilt categories that the investigator normally employs, is certainly a *sine qua non* of sociological enquiry in its early stages. It can, however, never be all that there is to such enquiry. If comparison is to be made and if explanation is to occur by the relation of particular social processes and phenomena to more general propositions, at certain points the categories of the investigator must come into play. Once we have had regard to this contextual rationality, as Lukes calls it—the acts that seem appropriate according to the beliefs that are held in the situation—our own best methods (to make no greater claim for them than that) which are empirical and rational procedures of science

—must be used if *we* are to understand these social processes. Understanding primitive society, in this sense, is incompatible with being a primitive because to be one is to cease to be an anthropologist, since anthropology operates according to norms and values that do not inhere in primitive society. To understand such a society in its own terms is not to explain anthropologically but to become completely assimilated socially. An approximation to assimilation, as a limited procedure, may be an extremely important aid to the anthropologist's eventual task, but it is difficult to see that it in any sense exhausts that task, and carried too far it appears to preclude the possibility of that task's being accomplished.

All Souls College
July 1969   B.R.W.

I

The Idea of a Social Science

PETER WINCH

The Investigation of Regularities

A follower of Mill might concede that explanations of human behaviour must appeal not to casual generalizations about the individual's reaction to his environment but to our knowledge of the institutions and ways of life which give his acts their meaning. But he might argue that this does not damage the fundamentals of Mill's thesis, since understanding social institutions is still a matter of grasping empirical generalizations which are logically on a footing with those of natural science. For an institution is, after all, a certain kind of uniformity, and a uniformity can only be grasped in a generalization. I shall now examine this argument.

A regularity or uniformity is the constant recurrence of the same kind of event on the same kind of occasion; hence statements of uniformities presuppose judgments of identity. But this takes us to an argument, according to which criteria of identity are necessarily relative to some rule: with the corollary that two events which count as qualitatively similar from the point of view of one rule would count as different from the point of view of another. So to investigate the type of regularity studied in a given kind of enquiry is to examine the nature of the rule according to which judgments of identity are made in that enquiry. Such judgments are intelligible only relatively to a given mode of human behaviour, governed by its own rules.[1] In a

This chapter is reprinted in abridged form from pp. 83–90, 111–16, 123–36 of Professor Winch's book of the same title—London: Routledge and Kegan Paul, 1958; (New York: Humanities Press).

[1] Cf. Hume: *A Treatise of Human Nature*, Introduction—"'Tis evident, that all the sciences have a relation, greater or less, to human nature; and that however wide any of them may seem to run from it, they still return back by one passage or another.'

physical science the relevant rules are those governing the procedures
of investigators in the science in question. For instance, someone with
no understanding of the problems and procedures of nuclear physics
would gain nothing from being present at an experiment like the
Cockcroft-Walton bombardment of lithium by hydrogen; indeed
even the description of what he saw in those terms would be unintelligible to him, since the term 'bombardment' does not carry the
sense in the context of the nuclear physicists' activities that it carries
elsewhere. To understand what was going on in this experiment he
would have to learn the nature of what nuclear physicists do; and this
would include learning the criteria according to which they make
judgments of identity.

Those rules, like all others, rest on a social context of common
activity. So to understand the activities of an individual scientific
investigator we must take account of two sets of relations: first, his
relation to the phenomena which he investigates; second, his relation
to his fellow-scientists. Both of these are essential to the sense of saying
that he is 'detecting regularities' or 'discovering uniformities'; but
writers on scientific 'methodology' too often concentrate on the first
and overlook the importance of the second. That they must belong to
different types is evident from the following considerations.—The
phenomena being investigated present themselves to the scientist as an
object of study; he observes them and notices certain facts about them.
But to say of a man that he does this presupposes that he already has a
mode of communication in the use of which rules are already being
observed. For to notice something is to identify relevant characteristics,
which means that the noticer must have some *concept* of such characteristics; this is possible only if he is able to use some symbol according
to a rule which makes it refer to those characteristics. So we come
back to his relation to his fellow-scientists, in which context alone he
can be spoken of as following such a rule. Hence the relation between
N and his fellows, in virtue of which we say that N is following the
same rule as they cannot be simply a relation of observation: it cannot
consist in the fact that N has noticed how his fellows behave and has
decided to take that as a norm for his own behaviour. For this would
presuppose that we could give some account of the notion of 'noticing
how his fellows behave' *apart from* the relation between N and his
fellows which we are trying to specify; and that, as has been shown, is
untrue. To quote Rush Rhees: 'We see that we understand one another,
without noticing whether our reactions tally or not. *Because* we agree

in our reactions, it is possible for me to tell you something, and it is possible for you to teach me something'.[1]

In the course of his investigation the scientists applies and develops the concepts germane to his particular field of study. This application and modification are 'influenced' both by the phenomena *to* which they are applied and also by the fellow-workers *in participation with* whom they are applied. But the two kinds of 'influence' are different. Whereas it is on the basis of his observation of the phenomena (in the course of his experiments) that he develops his concepts as he does, he is able to do this only in virtue of his participation in an established form of activity with his fellow-scientists. When I speak of 'participation' here I do not necessarily imply any direct physical conjunction or even any direct communication between fellow-participants. What is important is that they are all taking part in the same general kind of activity, which they have all *learned* in similar ways; that they are, therefore, *capable* of communicating with each other about what they are doing; that what any one of them is doing is in principle intelligible to the others.

Understanding Social Institutions

Mill's view is that understanding a social institution consists in observing regularities in the behaviour of its participants and expressing these regularities in the form of generalizations. Now if the position of the sociological investigator (in a broad sense) can be regarded as comparable, in its main logical outlines, with that of the natural scientist, the following must be the case. The concepts and criteria according to which the sociologist judges that, in two situations, the same thing has happened, or the same action performed, must be understood *in relation to the rules governing sociological investigation*. But here we run against a difficulty; for whereas in the case of the natural scientist we have to deal with only one set of rules, namely those governing the scientist's investigation itself, here *what the sociologist is studying*, as well as his study of it, is a human activity and is therefore carried on according to rules. And it is these rules, rather than those which govern the sociologist's investigation, which specify what is to count as 'doing the same kind of thing' in relation to that kind of activity.

[1] Rush Rhees, 'Can there be a private language?' *Proceedings of the Aristotelian Society*, Supplementary Volume XXVIII.

An example may make this clearer. Consider the parable of the Pharisee and the Publican (*Luke*, 18, 9). Was the Pharisee who said 'God, I thank Thee that I am not as other men are' doing the same kind of thing as the Publican who prayed 'God be merciful unto me a sinner'? To answer this one would have to start by considering what is involved in the idea of prayer; and that is a *religious* question. In other words, the appropriate criteria for deciding whether the actions of these two men were of the same kind or not belong to religion itself. Thus the sociologist of religion will be confronted with an answer to the question: Do these two acts belong to the same kind of activity?; and this answer is given according to criteria which are not taken from sociology, but from religion itself.

But if the judgments of identity—and hence the generalizations—of the sociologist of religion rest on criteria taken from religion, then his relation to the performers of religious activity cannot be just that of observer to observed. It must rather be analogous to the participation of the natural scientist with his fellow-workers in the activities of scientific investigation. Putting the point generally, even if it is legitimate to speak of one's understanding of a mode of social activity as consisting in a knowledge of regularities, the nature of this knowledge must be very different from the nature of knowledge of physical regularities. So it is quite mistaken in principle to compare the activity of a student of a form of social behaviour with that, of, say, an engineer studying the workings of a machine; and one does not advance matters by saying, with Mill, that the machine in question is of course immensely more complicated than any physical machine. If we are going to compare the social student to an engineer, we shall do better to compare him to an apprentice engineer who is studying what engineering—that is, the activity of engineering—is all about. His understanding of social phenomena is more like the engineer's understanding of his colleagues' activities than it is like the engineer's understanding of the mechanical systems which he studies.

This point is reflected in such common-sense considerations as the following: that a historian or sociologist of religion must himself have some religious feeling if he is to make sense of the religious movement he is studying and understand the considerations which govern the lives of its participants. A historian of art must have some aesthetic sense if he is to understand the problems confronting the artists of his period; and without this he will have left out of his account precisely what would have made it a history of *art*, as opposed to a rather puzzling external account of certain motions which certain people have been perceived to go through.

I do not wish to maintain that we must stop at the unreflective kind of understanding of which I gave as an instance the engineer's understanding of the activities of his colleagues. But I do want to say that any more reflective understanding must necessarily presuppose, if it is to count as genuine understanding at all, the participant's unreflective understanding. And this in itself makes it misleading to compare it with the natural scientist's understanding of his scientific data. Similarly, although the reflective student of society, or of a particular mode of social life, may find it necessary to use concepts which are not taken from the forms of activity which he is investigating, but which are taken rather from the context of his own investigation, still these technical concepts of his will imply a previous understanding of those other concepts which belong to the activities under investigation.

For example, liquidity preference is a technical concept of economics: it is not generally used by business men in the conduct of their affairs but by the economist who wishes to *explain* the nature and consequences of certain kinds of business behaviour. But it is logically tied to concepts which do enter into business activity, for its use by the economist presupposes his understanding of what it is to conduct a business, which in turn involves an understanding of such business concepts as money, profit, cost, risk, etc. It is only the relation between his account and these concepts which makes it an account of economic activity as opposed, say, to a piece of theology.

Again, a psychoanalyst may explain a patient's neurotic behaviour in terms of factors unknown to the patient and of concepts which would be unintelligible to him. Let us suppose that the psychoanalyst's explanation refers to events in the patient's early childhood. Well, the description of those events will presuppose an understanding of the concepts in terms of which family life, for example, is carried on in our society; for these will have entered, however rudimentarily, into the relations between the child and his family. A psychoanalyst who wished to give an account of the aetiology of neuroses amongst, say, the Trobriand Islanders, could not just apply without further reflection the concepts developed by Freud for situations arising in our own society. He would have first to investigate such things as the idea of fatherhood amongst the islanders and take into account any relevant aspects in which their idea differed from that current in his own society. And it is almost inevitable that such an investigation would lead to

some modification in the psychological theory appropriate for explaining neurotic behaviour in this new situation.

These considerations also provide some justification for the sort of
historical scepticism which that underestimated philosopher, R. G.
Collingwood, expresses in *The Idea of History*.[1] Although they need
not be brought to the foreground where one is dealing with situations
in one's own society or in societies with whose life one is reasonably
familiar, the practical implications become pressing where the object
of study is a society which is culturally remote from that of the
investigator.

Max Weber: Verstehen and Causal Explanation

It is Max Weber who has said most about the peculiar sense which the
word 'understand' bears when applied to modes of social life. The first
issue on which I mean to concentrate is Weber's account of the
relation between acquiring an 'interpretative understanding' (*deutend
verstehen*) of the meaning (*Sinn*) of a piece of behaviour and providing
a causal explanation (*kausal erklären*) of what brought the behaviour in
question about and what its consequences are.

Now Weber never gives a clear account of the *logical* character of
interpretative understanding. He speaks of it much of the time as if it
were simply a psychological technique: a matter of putting oneself in
the other fellow's position. This has led many writers to allege that
Weber confuses what is simply a technique for framing hypotheses
with the logical character of the evidence for such hypotheses. Thus
Popper argues that although we may use our knowledge of our own
mental processes in order to frame hypotheses about the similar
processes of other people, 'these hypotheses must be tested, they must
be submitted to the method of selection by elimination. (By their
intuition, some people are prevented from even imagining that anybody can possibly dislike chocolate).'[2]

Nevertheless, however applicable such criticisms may be to Weber's
vulgarizers, they cannot justly be used against his own views, for he is
very insistent that mere 'intuition' is not enough and must be tested by
careful observation. However, what I think can be said against Weber
is that he gives a wrong account of the process of checking the validity

---

[1] London: Oxford University Press, 1946, passim.

[2] Karl Popper, *The Poverty of Historicism*, London: Routledge and Kegan Paul,
1949. Section 29.

of suggested sociological interpretations. But the correction of Weber takes us farther away from, rather than closer to, the account which Popper, Ginsberg, and the many who think like them, would like to substitute.

Weber says:

> Every interpretation aims at self-evidence or immediate plausibility (*Evidenz*). But an interpretation which makes the meaning of a piece of behaviour as self-evidently obvious as you like cannot claim *just* on that account to be the causally *valid* interpretation as well. In itself it is nothing more than a particularly plausible hypothesis.[1]

He goes on to say that the appropriate way to verify such an hypothesis is to establish statistical laws based on observation of what happens. In this way he arrives at the conception of a sociological law as 'a statistical regularity which corresponds to an intelligible intended meaning'.

Weber is clearly right in pointing out that the obvious interpretation need not be the right one. R. S. Lynd's interpretation of West Indian voodoo magic as 'a system of imputedly true and reliable causal sequences' is a case in point;[2] and there is a plethora of similar examples in Frazer's *The Golden Bough*. But I want to question Weber's implied suggestion that *Verstehen* is something which is logically incomplete and needs supplementing by a different method altogether, namely the collection of statistics. Against this, I want to insist that if a proffered interpretation is wrong, statistics, though they may suggest that that is so, are not the decisive and ultimate court of appeal for the validity of sociological interpretations in the way Weber suggests. What is then needed is a better interpretation, not something different in kind. The compatibility of an interpretation with the statistics does not prove its validity. Someone who interprets a tribe's magical rites as a form of misplaced scientific activity will not be corrected by statistics about what members of that tribe are likely to do on various kinds of occasion (though this might form *part* of the argument); what is ultimately required is a *philosophical* argument like, e.g., Collingwood's in *The Principles of Art*.[3] For a mistaken interpretation of a form of social activity is closely akin to the type of mistake dealt with in philosophy.

Wittgenstein says somewhere that when we get into philosophical difficulties over the use of some of the concepts of our language, we

---

[1] Max Weber, *Wirtshaft und Gesellschaft*, Tübingen: Mohr, 1956. Chapter 1.
[2] R. S. Lynd, *Knowledge for What?* Princeton, 1945, p. 121.
[3] London: Oxford University Press, 1938. Book 1, Chapter IV.

are like savages confronted with something from an alien culture. I am simply indicating a corollary of this: that sociologists who misinterpret an alien culture are like philosophers getting into difficulties over the use of their own concepts. There will be differences of course. The philosopher's difficulty is usually with something with which he is perfectly familiar but which he is for the moment failing to see in its proper perspective. The sociologist's difficulty will often be over something with which he is not at all familiar; he may have no suitable perspective to apply. This may sometimes make his task more difficult than the philospher's, and it may also sometimes make it easier. But the analogy between their problems should be plain.

Some of Wittgenstein's procedures in his philosphical elucidations reinforce this point. He is prone to draw our attention to certain features of our own concepts by comparing them with those of an imaginary society, in which our own familiar ways of thinking are subtly distorted. For instance, he asks us to suppose that such a society sold wood in the following way: They 'piled the timber in heaps of arbitrary, varying height and then sold it at a price proportionate to the area covered by the piles. And what if they even justified this with the words: "Of course, if you buy more timber, you must pay more"?'[1] The important question for us is: in what circumstances could one say that one had *understood* this sort of behaviour? As I have indicated, Weber often speaks as if the ultimate test were our ability to formulate statistical laws which would enable us to *predict* with fair accuracy what people would be likely to do in given circumstances. In line with this is his attempt to define a 'social role' in terms of the probability (*Chance*) of actions of a certain sort being performed in given circumstances. But with Wittgenstein's example we might well be able to make predictions of great accuracy in this way and still not be able to claim any real understanding of what those people were doing. The difference is precisely analogous to that between being able to formulate statistical laws about the likely occurrences of words in a language and being able to understand what was being *said* by someone who spoke the language. The latter can never be reduced to the former; a man who understands Chinese is not a man who has a firm grasp of the statistical probabilities for the occurrence of the various words in the Chinese language. Indeed, he could have that without knowing that he was dealing with a language at all; and anyway, the knowledge

[1] Ludwig Wittgenstein, *Remarks on the Foundations of Mathematics*, Oxford: Blackwell, 1956. Chapter I, pp. 142–51.

that he was dealing with a language is not itself something that could be formulated statistically. 'Understanding', in situations like this, is grasping the *point* or *meaning* of what is being done or said. This is a notion far removed from the world of statistics and causal laws: it is closer to the realm of discourse and to the internal relations that link the parts of a realm of discourse. The notion of *meaning* should be carefully distinguished from that of *function*, in its quasi-causal sense.

To give an account of the meaning of a word is to describe how it is used; and to describe how it is used is to describe the social intercourse into which it enters.

If social relations between men exist only in and through their ideas, then, since the relations between ideas are internal relations, social relations must be a species of internal relation too. This brings me into conflict with a widely accepted principle of Hume's: 'There is no object, which implies the existence of any other if we consider these objects in themselves, and never look beyond the ideas which we form of them'. There is no doubt that Hume intended this to apply to human actions and social life as well as to the phenomena of nature. Now to start with, Hume's principle is not unqualifiedly true even of our knowledge of natural phenomena. If I hear a sound and recognize it as a clap of thunder, I already commit myself to believing in the occurrence of a number of other events—e.g. electrical discharges in the atmosphere—even in calling what I have heard 'thunder'. That is, from 'the idea which I have formed' of what I heard I *can* legitimately infer 'the existence of other objects'. If I subsequently find that there was no electrical storm in the vicinity at the time I heard the sound I shall have to retract my claim that what I heard was thunder. To use a phrase of Gilbert Ryle's, the word 'thunder' is theory-impregnated; statements affirming the occurrence of thunder have logical connections with statements affirming the occurrence of other events. To say this, of course, is not to reintroduce any mysterious causal nexus *in rebus*, of a sort to which Hume could legitimately object. It is simply to point out that Hume overlooked the fact that 'the idea we form of an object' does not just consist of elements drawn from our observation of that object in isolation, but includes the idea of connection between it and other objects. (And one could scarcely form a conception of a language in which this was not so.)

Consider now a very simple paradigm case of a relation between actions in a human society: that between an act of command and an act of obedience to that command. A sergeant calls 'Eyes right!' and his men all turn their eyes to the right. Now, in describing the men's act in terms of the notion of obedience to a command, one is of course committing oneself to saying that a command has been issued. So far the situation looks precisely parallel to the relation between thunder and electrical storms. But now one needs to draw a distinction. An event's character as an act of obedience is *intrinsic* to it in a way which is not true of an event's character as a clap of thunder, and this is in general true of human acts as opposed to natural events. In the case of the latter, although human beings can think of the occurrences in question only in terms of the concepts they do in fact have of them, yet the events themselves have an existence independent of those concepts. There existed electrical storms and thunder long before there were human beings to form concepts of them or establish that there was any connection between them. But it does not make sense to suppose that human beings might have been issuing commands and obeying them before they came to form the concept of command and obedience. For their performance of such acts is itself the chief manifestation of their possession of those concepts. An act of obedience itself contains, as an essential element, a recognition of what went before as an order. But it would of course be senseless to suppose that a clap of thunder contained any recognition of what went before as an electrical storm; it is our recognition of the sound, rather than the sound itself, which contains that recognition of what went before.

Part of the opposition one feels to the idea that men can be related to each other through their actions in at all the same kind of way as propositions can be related to each other is probably due to an inadequate conception of what logical relations between propositions themselves are. One is inclined to think of the laws of logic as forming a *given* rigid structure to which men try, with greater or less (but never complete) success, to make what they say in their actual linguistic and social intercourse conform. One thinks of propositions as something ethereal, which just because of their ethereal, non-physical nature, can fit together more tightly than can be conceived in the case of anything so grossly material as flesh-and-blood men and their actions. In a sense one is right in this; for to treat of logical relations in a formal systematic way is to think at a very high level of abstraction, at which all the anomalies, imperfections and crudities which characterize men's actual intercourse with each other in society have been removed. But, like any abstraction not recognized as such, this can be misleading. It may make one forget that it is only from their roots in this actual flesh-and-blood intercourse that those formal systems draw such life as they have; for the whole idea of a logical relation is only possible by virtue of the sort of agreement between men and their actions which is discussed by Wittgenstein in the *Philosophical Investigations*. Collingwood's remark on formal grammar is apposite: 'I likened the grammarian to a butcher; but if so, he is a butcher of a curious kind. Travellers say that certain African peoples will cut a steak from a living animal and cook it for dinner, the animal being not much the worse. This may serve to amend the original comparison'.[1] It will seem less strange that social relations should be like logical relations between propositions once it is seen that logical relations between propositions themselves depend on social relations between men.

What I have been saying conflicts, of course, with Karl Popper's 'postulate of methodological individualism' and appears to commit the sin of what he calls 'methodological essentialism', Popper maintains that the theories of the social sciences apply to theoretical constructions or models which are formulated by the investigator in order to explain certain experiences, a method which he explicitly compares to the construction of theoretical models in the natural sciences.

> This use of models explains and at the same time destroys the claims of methodological essentialism . . . It explains them, for the model is of an abstract or theoretical character, and we are liable to believe that we see it, either within or behind the changing observable events, as a kind of observable ghost or essence. And it destroys them because our task is to analyze our sociological models carefully in descriptive or nominalist terms, viz. *in terms of individuals*, their attitudes, expectations, relations, etc.—a postulate which may be called 'methodological individualism'.[2]

Popper's statement that social institutions are just explanatory models introduced by the social scientist for his own purposes is palpably untrue. The ways of thinking embodied in institutions govern the way the members of the societies studied by the social scientist behave. The idea of war, for instance, which is one of Popper's examples, was not simply invented by people who wanted to *explain* what happens when societies come into armed conflict. It is an idea which provides the criteria of what is appropriate in the behaviour of members of the conflicting societies. Because my country is at war

[1] R. G. Collingwood, *The Idea of History*, op. cit. p. 259.
[2] Karl Popper, op. cit. Section 29.

there are certain things which I must and certain things which I must not do. My behaviour is governed, one could say, by my concept of myself as a member of a belligerent country. The concept of war belongs *essentially* to my behaviour. But the concept of gravity does not belong essentially to the behaviour of a falling apple in the same way: it belongs rather to the physicist's *explanation* of the apple's behaviour. To recognize this has, *pace* Popper, nothing to do with a belief in ghosts behind the phenomena. Further, it is impossible to go far in specifying the attitudes, expectations and relations of individuals without referring to concepts which enter into those attitudes, etc., and the meaning of which certainly cannot be explained in terms of the actions of any individual persons.[1]

Discursive and Non-Discursive 'Ideas'

In the course of this argument I have linked the assertion that social relations are internal with the assertion that men's mutual interaction 'embodies ideas', suggesting that social interaction can more profitably be compared to the exchange of ideas in a conversation than to the interaction of forces in a physical system. This may seem to put me in danger of over-intellectualizing social life, especially since the examples I have so far discussed have all been examples of behaviour which expresses *discursive* ideas, that is, ideas which also have a straightforward linguistic expression. It is because the use of language is so intimately, so inseparably, bound up with the other, non-linguistic, activities which men perform, that it is possible to speak of their non-linguistic behaviour also as expressing discursive ideas. Apart from the examples of this which I have already given in other connections, one needs only to recall the enormous extent to which the learning of any characteristically human activity normally involves talking as well: in connection, e.g., with discussions of alternative ways of doing things, the inculcation of standards of good work, the giving of reasons, and so on. But there is no sharp break between behaviour which expresses discursive ideas and that which does not; and that which does not is sufficiently like that which does to make it necessary to regard it as analogous to the other. So, even where it would be unnatural to say that a given kind of social relation expresses any ideas of a discursive nature, still it is closer to that general category than it is to that of the interaction of physical forces.

[1] Cf. Maurice Mandelbaum, 'Societal Facts', British Journal of Sociology, VI, 4, 1955.

Consider the following scene from the film *Shane*. A lone horseman arrives at the isolated homestead of a small farmer on the American prairies who is suffering from the depredations of the rising class of big cattle-owners. Although they hardly exchange a word, a bond of sympathy springs up between the stranger and the homesteader. The stranger silently joins the other in uprooting, with great effort, the stump of a tree in the yard; in pausing for breath, they happen to catch each other's eye and smile shyly at each other. Now any explicit account that one tried to give of the kind of understanding that had sprung up between these two, and which was expressed in that glance, would no doubt be very complicated and inadequate. We understand it, however, as we may understand the meaning of a pregnant pause (consider what it is that makes a pause *pregnant*), or as we may understand the meaning of a gesture that completes a statement. 'There is a story that Buddha once, at the climax of a philosophical discussion . . . took a flower in his hand, and looked at it; one of his disciples smiled, and the master said to him, "You have understood me".'[1] And what I want to insist on is that, just as in a conversation the point of a remark (or of a pause) depends on its internal relation to what has gone before, so in the scene from the film the interchange of glances derives its full meaning from its internal relation to the situation in which it occurs: the loneliness, the threat of danger, the sharing of a common life in difficult circumstances, the satisfaction in physical effort, and so on.

It may be thought that there are certain kinds of social relation, particularly important for sociology and history, of which the foregoing considerations are not true: as for instance wars in which the issue between the combatants is not even remotely of an intellectual nature (as one might say, e.g., that the crusades were), but purely a struggle for physical survival as in a war between hunger migrants and the possessors of the land on which they are encroaching.[2] But even here, although the issue is in a sense a purely material one, the form which the struggle takes will still involve internal relations in a sense which will not apply to, say, a fight between two wild animals over a piece of meat. For the belligerents are *societies* in which much goes on besides eating, seeking shelter and reproducing; in which life is carried on in terms of symbolic ideas which express certain attitudes as between

---

[1] R. G. Collingwood, *The Principle of Art*, op. cit., p. 243.
[2] This example was suggested to me by a discussion with my colleague, Professor J. C. Rees, as indeed was the realization for the necessity for this whole section.

man and man. These symbolic relationships, incidentally, will affect, the character even of those basic 'biological' activities: one does not throw much light on the particular form which the latter may take in a given society by speaking of them in Malinowski's neo-Marxist terminology as performing the 'function' of providing for the satisfaction of the basic biological needs. Now of course, 'out-group attitudes' between the members of my hypothetical warring societies will not be the same as 'in-group attitudes'. Nevertheless, the fact that the enemies are *men*, with their own ideas and institutions, and with whom it would be possible to communicate, will affect the attitudes of members of the other society to them—even if its only effect is to make them the more ferocious. Human war, like all other human activities, is governed by conventions; and where one is dealing with conventions, one is dealing with internal relations.

The Social Sciences and History

This view of the matter may make possible a new appreciation of Collingwood's conception of all human history as the history of thought. That is no doubt an exaggeration and the notion that the task of the historian is to re-think the thoughts of the historical participants is to some extent an intellectualistic distortion. But Collingwood is right if he is taken to mean that the way to understand events in human history, even those which cannot naturally be represented as conflicts between or developments of discursive ideas, is more closely analogous to the way in which we understand expressions of ideas than it is to the way we understand physical processes.

There is a certain respect, indeed, in which Collingwood pays insufficient attention to the manner in which a way of thinking and the historical situation to which it belongs form one indivisible whole. He says that the aim of the historian is to think the very same thoughts as were once thought, just as they were thought at the historical moment in question.[1] But though extinct ways of thinking may, in a sense, be recaptured by the historian, the way in which the historian thinks them will be coloured by the fact that he has had to employ historiographical methods to recapture them. The medieval knight did not have to use those methods in order to view his lady in terms of the notions of courtly love: he just thought of her in those terms. Historical research may enable me to achieve some understanding of what was

[1] R. G. Collingwood, *The Idea of History*, op. cit., Part V.

involved in this way of thinking, but that will not make it open to me
to think of *my* lady in those terms. I should always be conscious that
this was an anachronism, which means, of course, that I should not be
thinking of her in just the same terms as did the knight of his lady.
And naturally, it is even more impossible for me to think of *his* lady
as he did.

Nevertheless, Collingwood's view is nearer the truth than is that
most favoured in empiricist methodologies of the social sciences, which
runs somewhat as follows—on the one side we have human history
which is a kind of repository of data. The historian unearths these
data and presents them to his more theoretically minded colleagues
who then produce scientific generalizations and theories establishing
connections between one kind of social situation and another. These
theories can then be applied to history itself in order to enhance our
understanding of the ways in which its episodes are mutually connected.
I have tried to show, how this involves minimizing the importance of
ideas in human history, since ideas and theories are constantly developing and changing, and since each system of ideas, its component
elements being interrelated internally, has to be understood in and for
itself; the combined result of which is to make systems of ideas a very
unsuitable subject for broad generalizations. I have also tried to show
that social relations really exist only in and through the ideas which
are current in society; or alternatively, that social relations fall into the
same logical category as do relations between ideas. It follows that
social relations must be an equally unsuitable subject for generalizations
and theories of the scientific sort to be formulated about them. Historical explanation is not the application of generalizations and theories
to particular instances: it is the tracing of internal relations. It is like
applying one's knowledge of a language in order to understand a
conversation rather than like applying one's knowledge of the laws
of mechanics to understand the workings of a watch. Non-linguistic
behaviour, for example, has an 'idiom' in the same kind of way as has
a language. In the same kind of way as it can be difficult to recapture
the idiom of Greek thought in a translation into modern English of a
Platonic dialogue, so it can be misleading to think of the behaviour of
people in remote societies in terms of the demeanour to which we are
accustomed in our own society. Think of the uneasy feeling one often
has about the authenticity of 'racy' historical evocations like those in
some of Robert Graves's novels: this has nothing to do with doubts
about a writer's accuracy in matters of external detail.

idiom

The relation between sociological theories and historical narrative is less like the relation between scientific laws and the reports of experiments or observations than it is like that between theories of logic and arguments in particular languages. Consider for instance the explanation of a chemical reaction in terms of a theory about molecular structure and valency: here the theory *establishes* a connection between what happened at one moment when the two chemicals were brought together and what happened at a subsequent moment. It is only *in terms of the theory* that one can speak of the events being thus 'connected' (as opposed to a simple spatio-temporal connection); the only way to grasp the connection is to learn the theory. But the application of a logical theory to a particular piece of reasoning is not like that. One does not have to know the theory in order to appreciate the connection between the steps of argument; on the contrary, it is only in so far as one can already grasp logical connections between particular statements in particular languages that one is even in a position to understand what the logical theory is all about. Whereas in natural science it is your theoretical knowledge which enables you to explain occurrences you have not previously met, a knowledge of logical theory on the other hand will not enable you to understand a piece of reasoning in an unknown language; you will have to learn that language, and that in itself *may* suffice to enable you to grasp the connections between the various parts of arguments in that language.

Consider now an example from sociology. Georg Simmel writes:

> The degeneration of a difference in convictions into hatred and fight occurs only when there were essential, original similarities between the parties. The (sociologically very significant) 'respect for the enemy' is usually absent where the hostility has arisen on the basis of previous solidarity. And where enough similarities continue to make confusions and blurred outlines possible, points of difference need an emphasis not justified by the issue but only by that danger of confusion. This was involved, for instance, in the case of Catholicism in Berne ... Roman Catholicism does not have to fear any threat to its identity from external contact with a church so different as the Reformed Church, but quite from something as closely akin as Old-Catholicism.[1]

Here I want to say that it is not *through* Simmel's generalization that one understands the relationship he is pointing to between Roman and Old Catholicism: one understands that only to the extent that one

[1] Georg Simmel, *Conflict*, Glencoe: Free Press, 1955. Chapter I.

understands the two religious systems themselves and their historical relations. The 'sociological law' may be helpful in calling one's attention to features of historical situations which one might otherwise have overlooked and in suggesting useful analogies. Here for instance one may be led to compare Simmel's example with the relations between the Russian Communist Party and, on the one hand, the British Labour Party and, on the other, the British Conservatives. But no historical situation can be understood simply by 'applying' such laws, as one applies laws to particular occurrences in natural science. Indeed, it is only in so far as one has an *independent* historical grasp of situations like this one that one is able to understand what the law amounts to at all. That is not like having to know the kind of experiment on which a scientific theory is based before one can understand the theory, for there it makes no sense to speak of understanding the connections between the parts of the experiment except in terms of the scientific theory. But one could understand very well the nature of the relations between Roman Catholicism and Old Catholicism without ever having heard of Simmel's theory, or anything like it.

2

Concepts and Society

ERNEST GELLNER

1. This paper is concerned with the application of Functionalism to the interpretation of concepts and beliefs.

Concepts and beliefs are themselves, in a sense, institutions amongst others: for they provide a kind of fairly permanent frame, as do other institutions, independent of any one individual, within which individual conduct takes place. In another sense, they are correlates of *all* the institutions of a society: and to understand the *working* of the concepts of a society is to understand its institutions.[1] Hence, a discussion of the application of Functionalism to interpretation (of concepts and beliefs), rather than Functionalism as such, is not really much of a restriction of the subject-matter.

Concepts and beliefs are, of course, of particular concern to social anthropology. Sociology can sometimes be a matter of ascertaining facts within an institutional framework which is taken for granted. The anthropologist can virtually never take anything for granted in this way. But anthropology is also the discipline most associated with Functionalism. The connection is not fortuitous.

This paper was first given as a talk to a Conference of the Society for the Philosophy of Science held at Oxford during the summer of 1958, and was first published in *The Transactions of the Fifth World Congress of Sociology*, 1962. Some aspects of the argument have since been expanded in 'The New Idealism' in I. Lakatos and A. Musgrave (eds.), *Problems in the Philosophy of Science*, Amsterdam: North Holland Pub. Co., 1968.

[1] It is however very important not to misunderstand this point. For it is *not* true to say that to understand the concepts of a society (in the way its members do) is to understand the society. Concepts are as liable to mask reality as to reveal it, and masking some of it may be a part of their function. The profoundly mistaken doctrine that to understand a society is to understand its concepts has a certain vogue and has recently been revived and argued, for instance, in Mr. P. Winch's *The Idea of a Social Science*, London, 1958. Some of the reasons why this view is false are discussed below.

2. Nevertheless the problem of the *interpretation* of concepts is almost as important within sociology—in the narrower sense in which it excludes Social Anthropology. For instance, the problem which is one of the mainsprings of sociological theory and which remains at the very centre of sociology—the question concerning the impact of theological doctrines on the emergence of economic rationality—hinges in large part on how one *interprets* the relevant theological concepts and arguments. Is one merely to take what the recorded theological text says and explicitly recommends? In that case, the connection seems very tenuous. Or is one to take what the text says *and* interpret its meaning, for the people influenced by it, in the light of what they actually *did*? In that case, the explanation of behaviour in terms of doctrine risk becoming vacuous and circular. There must, one hopes, be some middle way, which allows interpretation, which allows some but not all of the context to be incorporated into the meaning of the concept, thus avoiding both an unrealistic literal-minded scholasticism, and yet also escaping circularity of explanation. The problem concerns the rules and limits of the invocation of social *context* in interpreting the participants' concepts.

Consider as an example one of the most recent contributions to this debate, Professor Kurt Samuelsson's *Religion and Economic Action*.[1] This work is an onslaught on the Weberian thesis. '. . . our scrutiny of Puritan doctrine and capitalist ideology . . . has rendered untenable the hypothesis of a connection between Puritanism and capitalism . . .' (p. 153). Samuelsson employs a battery of arguments to support his conclusion, and some of these are highly relevant to the present theme. For one, he refers (p. 153) to '. . . the impossibility, in the last resort, of correlating concepts as broad and vague as those in question.' Here he seems to mean primarily the sociologist's own concepts (Puritanism, capitalism), but indirectly the alleged breadth and vagueness of these reflects the vagueness of Puritan or capitalist notions themselves. But it would be an absurd requirement to restrict sociological interpretation to clear and distinct concepts: these are historically a rarity, and there is nothing to make one suppose that vague and broad notions, whose logical implications for conduct are ill-determined, do not in fact have a powerful and specific impact on actual behaviour. We are faced here with the unfortunate need to *interpret* just what the concepts in question meant to the participants—and the problems connected with such interpretation are the theme of the present paper.

[1] London, 1961: Swedish edition, *Ekonomi och Religion*, Stockholm, 1957.

Samuelsson is not content with a declaration of the impossibility 'in the last resort' of establishing such correlations at all, but also specifically tries to refute the correlation by adducing contrary evidence. This counter-evidence largely consists, reasonably enough, of examining just what the Puritans actually said, and the kind of conduct they actually commended. Considering this, Samuelsson concludes (p. 41) that 'unquestionably, this ought to have impeded rather than promoted a capitalist trend.' He then considers counter-objections to this, such as Tawney's: these consist of arguing that the 'Christian casuistry of economic conduct', which *logically* should have impeded capitalism (i.e. if one considers what the statements in the text actually entail), in fact, in virtue of what they *meant* to the people concerned, 'braced the energies' and 'fortified the temper' of the capitalist spirit. In other words he convicts Tawney of claiming to know better than the texts what Puritanism really meant to its devotees. Samuelsson appears to have a great contempt for such implicit claims to access to hidden meanings: it is (p. 41) 'a somersault in the best Weberian style'. With irony he comments (p. 42, italics mine) that on the view he opposes, the capitalist spirit 'was the *true and genuine* Puritan spirit' (as opposed to the spirit actually found in the texts), and that thus 'Puritanism *in some other and more capitalist sense* . . . becomes the capitalistic spirit's principal source of power . . .'

I am not concerned, nor competent, to argue whether Samuelsson's employment, in this particular case, of his tacit principle that one must not re-interpret the assertions one actually finds, is valid. What is relevant here is that if such a principle is made explicit and generalized, it would make nonsense of most sociological studies of the relationship of belief and conduct. We shall find anthropologists driven to employ the very opposite principle, the insistence rather than refusal of contextual re-interpretation.

3. This is where Functionalism is relevant. The essence of Functionalism is perhaps the stress on context (rather than origin or overt motive) in the explanation of social behaviour. Formulated as an extreme doctrine, it asserts that each social institution is ideally suited to its context. The paradigm of explanation then becomes an account of just how a given institution does ideally fit its context, which means presumably just how it serves the survival and stability of the whole better than would any available alternative.

One of the charges made against this doctrine is that it is 'teleological', that it explains the present behaviour in terms of its consequences in the future, i.e. in terms of the manner in which those consequences *will* be desirable from the given society's viewpoint.

It seems to me that it is not difficult to answer this particular charge. All that is required is that each 'functional' explanation be as it were *read backwards*. The 'explanation' of institution X is not really the proper, causal explanation of *it*, but of the manner in which it contributes to the society as a whole. The 'real' explanation of X is provided when the functional accounts of the *other* institutions is given—of all of them, or of a relevant subset of those of them which contribute towards the maintenance of X—which jointly make up a 'real', causal explanation of X itself (just as the 'functional' account of X figures in *their* causal explanation). This of course implies that good, proper explanations can only be had when a whole society is seen as a unity, and that partial studies of institutions in isolation are incomplete, and only a step towards proper undertstanding. But such a stress on societies seen at unities is indeed a part of the 'Functionalist' syndrome of ideas.

But there cannot be many people today who hold Functionalism in its extreme form.[1] What needs to be said about that has been most brilliantly and succinctly said by Professor Lévi-Strauss:

> Dire qu'une société fonctionne est un truisme; mais dire que tout, dans une société, fonctionne est absurdité.[2]

The thesis of social adjustment is not really a theory: it is a promise of a theory, a promise that somewhere along the spectrum between an absurdity and a truism there is a point where truth without triviality is to be found. Until the precise point along that spectrum is located, it will not be a theory, and as far as I know no one has attempted to locate it, and it is difficult to see how one could. The corollary of the doctrine in its *extreme form*, the claim of perfect stability and self-maintenance of societies, is plainly false. The requirement that societies be seen as unities is unsatisfiable for most societies in the modern world, in view of their size, complexity and in view of the difficulties of delimiting 'societies'.

But whilst, for these reasons, 'strong' Functionalism is dead or moribund, moderate Functionalism, or Functionalism as a method

---

[1] But they do still exist. Consider Professor Ralph Piddington's essay, 'Malinowski's Theory of Needs', in *Man and Culture*, edited by Professor Raymond Firth, London, 1957, esp. p. 47.

[2] *Anthropologie Structurale*, Paris, 1958, p. 17.

rather than as a theory, is happily very much alive, Lévi-Strauss is perhaps right when he speaks of

> ... cette forme primaire du structuralisme qu' on appelle fonctionna-lisme.[1]

The exploration of social structure is one of the main preoccupations of sociology. It must require of the investigator of any one institution an awareness of its context, of the 'structure' within which that institution finds itself.

But if moderate Functionalism is justifiably alive, its application to the interpretation of concepts and doctrines is particularly relevant. It consists of the insistence on the fact that concepts and beliefs do not exist in isolation, in texts or in individual minds, but in the life of men and societies. The activities and institutions, in the context of which a word or phrase or set of phrases is used, must be known before that word or those phrases can be understood, before we can really speak of a *concept* or a *belief*.

4. The particular application of the functional, context-stressing method to concepts is nothing new. It can be found above all in the work of Emile Durkheim which is one of the fountainheads of Functionalism in general, in *Les Formes Élémentaires de la Vie Religieuse*. I think that less than justice is done to Durkheim when he is remembered as the author of a doctrine to the effect that primitive societies or societies in general really 'worship themselves'. The real essence of his doctrine in that remarkable work seems to me to lie elsewhere, in the view that concepts, as opposed to sensations, are only possible in a social context[2] (and *a fortiori* that they can only be understood when the social context is known), and that important, categorial concepts, on which all others depend, require ritual if they are to be sustained. It tends to be forgotten that Durkheim's main problem, as he saw it, was not to explain religion but to explain conceptual thought and above all the *necessity*, the compulsive nature of certain of our general concepts. This is a Kantian problem, and Durkheim claimed to have solved it in a way which resembled Kant's, but differed from it in various important ways.

Above all, it differed from it in two ways: the machinery, so to speak, which was responsible for the compulsive nature of our categorial concepts was collective and observable, rather than hidden in the

---

[1] op. cit., p. 357.
[2] *Much* later, L. Wittgenstein was credited with just this discovery.

backstage recesses of the individual mind; and secondly, it did not, like a Balliol man, function effortlessly, but needed for its effective working to keep in training, to be forever flexing its muscles and keeping them in trim—and just this was Durkheim's theory of ritual, which for him was the method by which the intelligibility and compulsiveness of crucial categories was maintained in the minds of members of a given society. Ritual and religion did publicly what the Kantian transcendental ego did only behind the impassable iron curtain of the noumenal. It was thus Durkheim who paved the way for modern anthropological fieldwork: it was his view that in observing (say) the rituals associated with a clan totem, we were privileged to observe the machinery which explains the conceptual, logical and moral compulsions of the members of *that* society, compulsions similar, for instance to our inability to think of the world outside time. Much later, a linguistic philospher commenting somewhere on transcendental beliefs, hinted that their source lay in language by saying that men needed a god of time as little as they needed a god of tenses. Durkheim's much more plausible point was precisely this in reverse: in order to have and understand tenses, we need first of all to have or to have had (something like) a god and a ritual of time . . .

Our contemporary invocations of the functional, social-context approach to the study and interpretation of concepts is in various ways very different from Durkheim's. Durkheim was not so much concerned to defend the concepts of primitive societies: in their setting, they did not need a defence, and in the setting of modern and changing societies he was not anxious to defend what was archaic, nor loath to suggest that some intellectual luggage might well be archaic. He was really concerned to explain the compulsiveness of what in practice did not seem to need any defence (and in so doing, he claimed he was solving the problem of knowledge whose solution had in his view evaded Kant and others, and to be solving it without falling into either empiricism or apriorism.) Whether he was successful I do not propose to discuss: for a variety of reasons it seems to me that he was not.[1]

[1] Somewhat to my surprise, Mr D. G. MacRae appears to think that he was: '. . . Durkheim *showed* . . . how time, space, causality and other fundamental categories . . . are in great measure social products . . . ' *Ideology and Society*, London, 1961, p. 83. (Italics mine.)

Much depends of course on how great a measure 'great measure' is. Durkheim was concerned to explain the compulsiveness of categories. He succeeded in showing, I think, how our power of *apprehending* them depended on society. He did not explain why, once they are in our possession, we cannot escape them.

By contrast, the modern user of the Functionalist approach to concepts is concerned to defend, rather than to explain a compulsion. In anthropology, he may be concerned to defend the objects of his particular study from the charge of absurdity or pre-logical thought; in philosophy he may be concerned with applying the crypto-Functionalist theory of language which is the basis of so much contemporary philosophy. And behind either of these motives, there is, more potent than either, the consideration springing from our general intellectual climate—the desire to assist or reinforce the tacit *concordat* which seems to have been reached between intellectual criticism and established concepts in the middle of the Twentieth century.

5. The situation, facing a social anthropologist who wishes to interpret a concept, assertion or doctrine in an alien culture, is basically simple. He is, say, faced with an assertion *S* in the local language. He has at his disposal the large or infinite set of possible sentences in his own language. His task is to locate the nearest equivalent or equivalents of *S* in his own language.

He may not be wholly happy about this situation, but he cannot avoid it. There is no third language which could mediate between the native language and his own, in which equivalances could be stated and which would avoid the pitfills arising from the fact that his own language has its own way of handling the world, which may not be those of the native language studied, and which consequently are liable to distort that which is being translated.

Naïvely, people sometimes think that *reality* itself could be this kind of mediator and 'third language': that equivalences between expressions in different languages could be established by locating just which objects in the world they referred to. (If the objects were identical, then so were the expressions . . .) For a variety of powerful reasons,

The distinction is important. Precisely the same is also true of Durkheim's (quite unwitting) follower and successor, Wittgenstein, who also supposed categories were validated by being parts of a 'form of life' and who, incidentally, like Durkheim also vacillated between supposing all concepts could be validated in this manner, and restricting this confirmation to categories.

I am quite prepared to believe that at the root of our ability to count, to relate things along a time series or spatially, is a social order which exemplifies and 'ritually' brings home to us the concepts involved. But I do not think this accounts either for their compulsiveness or for occasional lapses from it. There is something comic about this idea. Are we to say that Riemann and Lobachevsky were inadequately exposed to those rituals of Western society which make the Euclidean picture of space compulsive to its members?

this is of course no good. Language functions in a variety of ways other than 'referring to objects'. Many objects are simply not there, in any obvious physical sense, to be located: how could one, by this method, establish the equivalences, if they exist, between abstract or negative or hypothetical or religious expressions? Again, many 'objects' are in a sense created by the language, by the manner in which its terms carve up the world or experience. Thus the mediating third party is simply not to be found: either it turns out to be an elusive ghost ('reality'), or it is just one further language, with idiosyncrasies of its own which are as liable to distort in translation as did the original language of the investigator. Using it only multiplies the probability of distortion by adding to the number of conceptual middlemen, and in any case the procedure involves a vicious regress.

This situation is described, for instance, in a recent important study of primitive religion: '(The) unity and multiplicity of Divinity causes no difficulty in the context of Dinka language and life, but it is impossible entirely to avoid the logical and semantic problems which arise when Dinka statements bearing upon it are translated, together, into English,' in Godfrey Lienhardt, *Divinity and Experience: The Religion of the Dinka*.[1]

Or, as the same author puts it in the context of a general discussion of anthropology, in *The Institutions of Primitive Society*, by various authors:[2]

'The problem of describing to others how members of a remote tribe think then begins to appear *largely as one of translation*, of making the coherence primitive thought has . . . as clear as possible in our own.' (p. 97, italics mine.)

The situation facing the historical sociologist is not very different. Samuelsson says (op. cit., p. 36): 'Neither in St Paul nor in Baxter do the texts . . . form coherent chains of reasoning. . . . The source material, in both cases, consists of a few sentences, statements made on isolated occasions . . . often clearly contradictory and not infrequently framed with such oracular sophistry that it is impossible for the reader of a later age to determine with certainly the "intrinsic meaning" . . .'

The problem is analogous, though there are differences. One is that if the historical sociologist's material is disjointed and fragmentary, there is less he can do about it than the anthropologist confronting a

---

[1] Oxford 1961, p. 56.
[2] Oxford: Blackwell, 1954. Chapter VIII.

still continuing culture. Another difference is that this particular sociologist is not over-charitable in attributing coherence to the authors of his texts, whilst the anthropologist cited appears to make it a condition of a good translation that it conveys the coherence which he assumes is there to be found in primitive thought. Such charity, or lack of it, is a matter of fashion in various disciplines. Most anthropologists at present are, I think, charitable: in sociology the situation is not so clear, and there is no reason to think that Samuelsson is similarly typical.[1]

One main stream of contemporary philosophy is inclined towards similar charity towards the concepts of the philosopher's own society, Mr R. Wollheim, for instance, in *F. H. Bradley*,[2] observes '. . . there are those (philosophers) who think that . . . what we think is far truer, far profounder than we ordinarily take it to be . . .' and goes on, correctly, to cite as the contemporary origin of this charitable view the later Wittgenstein. But Wittgenstein is also the author of the insistence on seeing the meaning of utterances as their use, and on seeing language as a 'form of life': in anthropological terms, on interpreting them in the light of their function in the culture of which they are a part. This influential movement is of course liable to confirm anthropologists in their attitude, and at least one of them, in a brilliant essay,[3] has drawn attention to the parallelism. Time was when neither philosophers nor anthropologists were so charitable.

6. Thus the basic situation is simple, I am schematizing it below. Indigenous or textual sentence S faces a long or infinite column of all possible (say) English sentences. The investigator, with some misgivings, locates the nearest equivalent of S in the column. (See diag. I below.)

7. Having done this, the anthropologist simply cannot, whether he likes it or not, and however much he may strive to be *wertfrei*, prevent himself from noticing whether the equivalents found in his own language for S are sensible or silly, as assertions, One's first reaction to assertions in one's own language, inseparable from appreciating their

[1] For instance, Dr W. Stark, in *The Sociology of Knowledge*, London, 1958, recommends almost universal charity in this respect, with the help of arguments which differ both from Durkheim's and from those of Functionalists. See also 'Sociology of Faith', *Inquiry*, 1958. No. 4.

[2] Penguin Books, 1959, p. 67.

[3] E. R. Leach, in 'The Epistemological Background to Malinowski's Empiricism', in *Man and Culture*, ed. R. Firth, London, 1957, p. 119.

meaning, is to classify them in some way as Good or Bad. (I do not say 'true' or 'false', for this only arises with regard to some types of assertion. With regard to others, other dichotomies, such as 'meaning-ful' and 'absurd' or 'sensible' or 'silly' might apply. I deliberately use the 'Good' and 'Bad' so as to cover all such possible polar alternatives, whichever might best apply to the equivalent of S).

So in terms of our diagram, we have two boxes, G(ood) and B(ad); and having located the equivalents of S in his own language, the anthropologist willy-nilly goes on to note whether these equivalents

DIAGRAM I

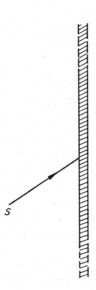

go into G or B. (He may of course think that he is doing this purely in his own private capacity, and not professionally as an anthropologist. No matter, he does do it.) So the schema becomes slightly more complex. Let us assume in this case that the anthropologist judges the equivalents of S to be silly, B(ad). The schema now is as in diagram 2.

8. But what diagram 2 (overleaf) describes is, as an account of contemporary interpretations, unrealistic. On the contrary, it describes

DIAGRAM 2

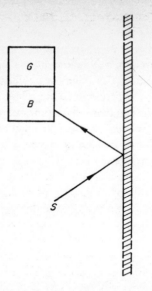

a state of affairs much more characteristic of an earlier period, of what may almost be called the pre-history of anthropology. To come out with an interpretation of the indigenous sentence which classifies it as *B*(ad), as false or irrational or absurd, or at any rate to do it often, is a sign of *ethnocentricity*. Ethnocentricity is a grave defect from the viewpoint of the standards of the anthropological community.

Like members of other tribes, anthropologists are socialized by means of legends. These legends of course need not be false: indeed the one I am about to describe has much truth in it. Nevertheless, it is their socializing, indoctrinating function rather than their historical accuracy which is relevant. The legend by means of which a new anthropologist is moulded runs something as follows: Once upon a time, the anthropological world was inhabited by a proto-population who were *ethnocentric*. They collected information about primitives mainly in order to poke fun at them, to illustrate the primitive's inferiority to themselves. The information collected, even if accurate (which it often wasn't) was worthless because it was torn out of context.

The pre-enlightenment anthropologist, struck by the frequency with which the interpretations resulted in assertions which were *B*(ad), and crediting this to the backwardness of the societies whose beliefs were being described, tended to explain this in terms of one of two theories: (a) Primitive Mentality theories, or (b) Jacob's Ladder (Evolutionist) theories of moral and intellectual growth. The former theory amounts to saying that savages get things wrong and confused so systematically, rather than being just occasionally in error, that one can characterize their thought as 'pre-logical'. The latter theory is somewhat more charitable and supposes that the savages are on the same ladder as we are, but so far behind that most of what he believes, whilst resulting from the application of the same logical principles as our own, is also an example of so unskilled an application of them that it is all too frequently wrong. Neither of these theories is much favoured at present.

For, one day the Age of Darkness came to an end. Modern anthropology begins with good, genuine, real modern fieldwork. The essence of such fieldwork is that it does see institutions, practices, beliefs etc. *in context*. At the same time, ethnocentrism is overcome. It is no longer the aim of studies to titillate a feeling of superiority by retailing piquant oddities. The two things, the seeing of institutions etc., in context, and the overcoming of ethnocentrism, are of course intimately connected. The schema which now applies is somewhat different:

DIAGRAM 3

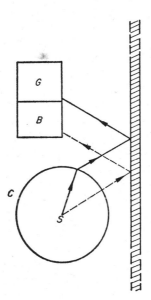

The circle C round the original indigenous assertion S stands for its social context. The contest so to speak refracts the line of interpretation: with the aid of context, one arrives at a different equivalent in English of the original sentence S. And, lo and behold, if one *then* asks oneself about the merit of the newly interpreted S, one finds oneself giving it a high mark of sensibleness, truth or whatnot. One ends at G(ood) rather than B(ad). The earlier, bad old practice is indicated on this diagram by a dotted line.

9. There are various motives and/or justifications for the new, contextual approach. One of them is simply that it contains a good deal of validity: one does indeed get incomparably better appreciation of a doctrine by seeing its setting and use. But there are other motives. One of them is the laudable desire to be tolerant, understanding and liberal, to refrain from an uncomprehending and presumptuous superiority in one's attitude to other (notably 'primitive') societies.

In the modern world, this can be an urgent concern and connected with the need to combat racialism. A notable example of this use of anthropological sophistication is Professor Lévi-Strauss' *Race and History*.[1] In a chapter entitled 'The Ethnocentric Attitude' he describes the widespread tendency to discount and despise members of other cultures as savages or barbarians, and speaks of it (p. 11) as 'this naïve attitude . . . deeply rooted in most men' and adds that 'this [i.e. his] booklet . . . in fact refutes it'. The main method he employs here to dissuade us from ethnocentricity is to point out that ethnocentrism characterizes above all just those whom one would describe as savages. 'This attitude of mind, which excludes as "savages" (or any people one may choose to regard as savages) from human kind, is precisely the attitude most strikingly characteristic of those same savages'. One may be worried by the fact that the second occurrence of the word *savages* in the preceding sentence does not occur in inverted commas: in other words, that Lévi-Strauss is attempting to dissuade us from speaking of 'savages' by warning us that *savages* do so. Does he not here presuppose their existence and a condemnation of them? The liberal is in great danger of falling into paradox: either he condemns the ethnocentrism of savages and thus his tolerance has an important limit, or he does not, and then he at least condones *their* intolerance . . .

The paradox emerges even more clearly in an aphoristic definition he offers a little later (p. 12) of the 'barbarian'. 'The barbarian is, first and foremost, the man who believes in barbarism'. What makes

[1] UNESCO, Paris, 1952.

one a savage, in other words, is the belief that some others *are* such.

Let us follow out this definition, taking it literally. A barbarian is he who believes that some others are barbarians. Notoriously, there are such people. They, therefore, are barbarians. *We* know they believe it. Hence, we believe they are barbarians. Ergo, we too are barbarians (by reapplication of the initial definition). And so is anyone who has noticed this fact and knows that *we* are, and so on. Lévi-Strauss' definition has the curious property that, by a kind of regression or contagion, it spreads barbarism like wildfire through the mere awareness of it . . .

This paradox follows logically from Lévi-Strauss' innocuous-seeming definition. But this is not merely a logical oddity, arising from some quirk or careless formulation. It reflects something far more funda-mental. It springs from a dilemma deep in the very foundations of the tolerant, understanding liberalism, of which sophisticated anthro-pology is a part, and it goes back at least to the thought of the En-lightenment which is the ancestor of such liberalism. The (unresolved) dilemma, which the thought of the Enlightenment faced, was between a relativistic-functionalist view of thought, and the absolutist claims of enlightened Reason. Viewing man as part of nature, as enlightened Reason requires, it wished to see his cognitive and evaluative activities as parts of nature too, and hence as varying, legitimately, from organism to organism and context to context. (This is the relativist-functional view). But at the same time in recommending life according to Reason and Nature, it wished at the very least to exempt this view itself (and, in practice, some others) from such a relativism.

This dilemma was never really resolved in as far as a naturalistic or third-person view of beliefs (individual or collective) leads us to relativism, whilst our thought at the same time make an exception in its own favour. We are here only concerned with the working out of this dilemma in anthropology. What characteristically happened in anthropology is rather like that pattern of alliances, in which one's neighbours are one's enemies, but one's neighbours-but-one are one's allies. Anthropologists were relativistic, tolerant, contextually-com-prehending vis-à-vis the savages who are after all some distance away, but absolutistic, intolerant vis-à-vis their immediate neighbours or predecessors, the members of our own society who do not share their comprehending outlook and are themselves 'ethnocentric' . . .

The anthropologists were roughly liberals in their own society and Tories on behalf of the society they were investigating: they 'understood' the tribesman but condemned the District Officer or the Missionary. A bitter and misinformed attack on this attitude occurs in A. J. Hanna's *European Rule in Africa*:[1] 'The rise of social anthropology did much to foster (the) attitude (of trying to perpetuate tribalism) . . . exploring with fascinated interest the subtle and complex ramifications of tribal structure, and disdaining to mention . . . murder, mutilation, torture, witch-hunting [sic], cattle-raiding, wife-raiding . . . A . . . psychological tendency led the anthropologist to become the champion not only of the tribe whose customs he studied, but of its customs themselves.'

It is interesting to note, however, that the pattern of alliances, as it were, has changed since the days of the liberals who were, in relativist spirit, tolerantly understanding of the intolerant absolutism of the distant tribesman, but less so of the absolutist beliefs in their own society. Nowadays, more sociological students of religion are themselves believers: in other words, contextual charity ends at home.

10. My main point about the tolerance-engendering contextual interpretation is that it calls for caution: that as a method it can be rather more wobbly that at first appears. Let us return to the diagram. What the last diagram expressed—the diagram schematizing context-respecting, enlightened investigation—can involve some self-deception. What really happens, at any rate sometimes, is this:

DIAGRAM 4

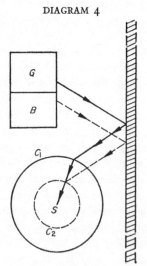

[1] London, 1961, p. 22.

This diagram differs from the preceding one partly in the direction of the arrows. What I mean is this: it is the *prior* determination that S, the indigenous affirmation, be interpreted favourably, which determines just how much context will be taken into consideration. The diagram shows how different ranges of context—C_1 or C_2—are brought in according to whether the starting point is charitable or not ... The context 'refracts' the line of interpretation: take a little more, or a little less, (as in the dotted lines), and a different interpretation of S in English will result. Or rather, the prior disposition concerning what kind of interpretation one wishes to find, determines the range of context brought in. (Apart from varying the range, there will also be different views of what the context is, either empirically, or in the way it is described and seen. A believing and an agnostic anthropologist may have differing views about what contexts there are to be seen). The dotted circle represents a different—in this case. smaller—range of context taken into consideration.

It may be that the sympathetic, positive interpretations of indigenous assertions are not the result of a sophisticated appreciation of context, but *the other way round*: that the manner in which the context is invoked, the amount and kind of context and the way the context itself is interpreted, depends on prior tacit determination concerning the kind of interpretation one wishes to find. ... After all, there is nothing in the nature of things or societies to dictate visibly just how much context is relevant to any given utterance, or how that context should be described.

Professor Raymond Firth has remarked in *Problem and Assumption in an Anthropological Study of Religion*:[1] 'From my own experience, I am impressed by the ease with which it is possible to add one's own personal dimension to the interpretation of an alien religious ideology, to raise the generalizations to a higher power than the empirical content of the material warrants'. My point is, really, that it is more than a matter of *ease*—it is a matter of necessity: for interpretation cannot be determinate without assumptions concerning the success or failure of the interpreted communication, and the criteria of such success are not manifest in the 'content of the material' itself. One has to work them out as best one can, and it will *not* do to take the short cut of reading them off the material by assuming that the material is always successful, i.e. that the statements investigated do satisfy and exemplify criteria of coherence, and hence that interpretation is not successful until this

[1] Huxley Memorial Lecture, 1959, p. 139.

coherence has been made manifest in the translation. The logical *assessment* of an assertion, and the identification of its nearest equivalent in our language, are intimately linked and inseparable.

11. But this formal argument may carry more conviction if illustrated by concrete examples. The first I shall take is Professor Evans-Pritchard's treatment of Nuer religion, notably in Chapter V, 'The Problem of Symbols', of *Nuer Religion*.[1] Evans-Pritchard's main theoretical concern in this book is to refute Lévy-Bruhl's thesis concerning 'pre-logical mentality'. Evans-Pritchard's method in the pursuit of this aim is to take Nuer assertions and doctrines which, on the face of it, would indeed provide excellent evidence for a doctrine of the 'pre-logical mentality' of primitives, and then to proceed with the help of contextual interpretation to show that in fact they do not.

Evans-Pritchard begins his discussion as follows (p. 123): 'Our problem . . . can be simply stated by the question: What meaning are we to attach to Nuer statements that such-and-such a thing is *kwoth*, spirit? The answer is not so simple'. For point is that the Nuer do make assertions which, prima facie, support a Lévy-Bruhl-type theory of 'primitive mentality', as Evans-Pritchard himself admits and stresses: 'It seems odd, if not absurd, to a European when he is told that a twin is a bird as though it were an obvious fact, for Nuer are not saying that a twin is like a bird but that he is a bird. There seems to be a complete contradiction in the statement: and it was precisely on statements of this kind recorded by observers of primitive peoples that Lévy-Bruhl based his theory of the pre-logical mentality of these peoples its chief characteristic being, in his view, that it permits such evident contradictions—that a thing can be what it is and at the same time something altogether different.' (p. 131) Or again, 'When a cucumber is used as a sacrificial victim Nuer speak of it as an ox. In doing so they are asserting something rather more than that it takes the place of an ox', (p. 128).

But this is not the only kind of apparently odd assertion in which the Nuer indulge. This kind of statement appears to be in conflict with the principle of identity or non-contradiction, or with common sense, or with manifest observable fact: human twins are *not* birds, and vice versa. But they *also* make assertions which are in conflict with good theology, or at any rate with the theology which, according to Evans-Pritchard, they really hold. '. . . Nuer religious thought . . . is pre-eminently dualistic'. '. . . there is . . . a duality between *kwoth*,

[1] Oxford, 1956.

Spirit, which is immaterial . . . and *cak*, creation, the material world known to the senses. Rain and lightning and pestilences and murrains belong to this created world . . .' (p. 124).

Nevertheless, Nuer do make assertions which appear to be in conflict with this theology as well. '. . . certain things are said, or may be said, "to be" God—rain, lightning, and various other natural . . . things . . .' (p. 123). 'They may say of rain or lightning or pestilence "*e kwoth*", "it is God" . . .' (p. 124).

What is the solution? How are the Nuer saved for both common-sense *and* for dualistic theology, when their assertions appear to convict them of self-contradiction *and* of a doctrine of the immanence of the Deity in the world?

I shall present the solution in Professor Evans-Pritchard's own words. Concerning the apparent contradiction in Nuer thought, arising from the identification of twins, and birds, it appears (p. 131) that 'no contradiction is involved in the statement, which, on the contrary, appears quite sensible and even true, to one who presents the idea to himself in the Nuer language and within their system of religious thought. . . . *They are not saying that a twin has a beak, feathers, and so forth. Nor in their everyday relations as twins do Nuers speak of them as birds or act towards them as though they were birds.*' (Italics mine).

One may ask here—but what, then, *would* count as pre-logical thought? Only, presumably, the behaviour of a totally demented person, suffering from permanent hallucinations, who *would* treat something which is perceptibly a human being as though it had all the physical attributes of a bird. But could Lévy-Bruhl conceivably have meant this when he was putting forward the doctrine of pre-logical mentality? He knew, and could hardly have helped knowing, that savages like everyone else are capable of distinguishing objects which are so unlike physically as a human being who happens to be a twin, and a bird. (In as far as there is nothing about the physical appearance of a human being who happens to be a twin—unless perhaps some socially significant markings, but Evans-Pritchard does not say that Nuer twins have something of this kind—to distinguish him from other human beings, the Nuer capacity to distinguish him from a bird follows from their very capacity to distinguish humans in general from birds, a capacity which can hardly be in doubt . . .) This being so, Lévy-Bruhl's thesis can hardly with fairness be interpreted as entailing that errors such as the confusion of human and bird bodies is genuinely committed by primitives. He could not have meant this: or rather, we may not attribute this doctrine to him if we extend to *him* too the courtesy or charity of contextual interpretation, which requires that we do not credit people with beliefs—whatever they *say*—which are plainly in conflict with what they can be assumed to know in the light of what they actually do. (E.g.—Nuer cannot believe twins to be birds as their conduct distinguishes between the two).

If it be adopted as a principle that people cannot mean what at some level (e.g. implicitly, through their conduct) they also know to be false or absurd, then this principle must be applicable to Lévy-Bruhl too. . . . The trouble with the principle is, of course, that it is *too* charitable: it absolves too many people of the charge of systematically illogical or false or self-deceptive thought.

It is worth considering just why the principle is so indiscriminately charitable. It insists, as Evans-Pritchard does when applying it, on interpreting assertions in the light of actual *conduct*. But no on-going viable system of conduct—and any society, and also any sane surviving man, exemplifies such a system—*can* be self-contradictory. Assertions, doctrines, can easily be illogical: conduct, and in particular the conduct of a *society* which is, by definition, a human group persisting over time, cannot easily be illogical. The object of anthropological inquiries are precisely human groups persisting over time. Their very persistence entails that they are reasonably viable: and this viability in turn ensures that a 'context' is available for the sympathetic interpretation which will make sense of the local doctrines and assertions, however odd they may seem on the surface. This hermeneutic principle tacitly employed by Evans-Pritchard, is too strong, for it ensures that no reasonably viable society can be said to be based on or to uphold absurd or 'pre-logical' doctrines. The trouble with such all-embracing logical charity is, for one thing, that it is unwittingly quite *a priori*: it may delude anthropologists into thinking that they have *found* that no society upholds absurd or self-contradictory beliefs, whilst in fact the principle employed has ensured in advance of any inquiry that nothing may count as pre-logical, inconsistent or categorially absurd though it may be. And this, apart from anything else, would blind one to at least one socially significant phenomenon: the social role of absurdity.

12. But before proceeding with this general consideration, one should also look at Evans-Pritchard's second re-interpretation of Nuer assertions. The first one was to save them for common sense or consistency from the charge of self-contradiction. The second was to save them from a dualist theology and from an immanentist one.

Again, it is best to present the case in Evans-Pritchard's own words. Referring to the fact that Nuer appear to speak of certain things—rain, lightning etc.—as being God (as quoted above), in contradiction of the dualist theology with which he credits them, Evans-Pritchard comments (pages 123 and 124):

'There is here an ambiguity, or an obscurity, to be elucidated, for Nuer are not now saying that God or Spirit is like this or that, but that this or that "is" God or Spirit'.

In interpreting this crucial sentence, a good deal depends on just what Evans-Pritchard meant by putting the final occurrence of the word *is* in inverted commas. He might simply have wished to accentuate it, by contrast to the expression *is like* in the preceding clause. But there are two good objections to this interpretation: had this been his intention, he might simply have italicized it, as is more customary, and secondly, he should have given the same treatment, whether inverted commas or italicization, to the contrasted expression *is like*. In fact, I interpret him as saying that the Nuer do not really say that these things are God, but merely that they 'are' God. They mean something other than what they say.

And indeed, we are told (p. 125), 'When Nuer say of rain or lightning that it is God they are making an elliptical statement. What is understood is not that the thing in itself is Spirit but that it is what we could call a medium or manifestation or sign of divine activity in relation to men and of significance for them'. And no doubt, elliptical statements are common in all languages. What is at issue are the procedures for filling in the gaps left by ellipsis.

It is important of course that the Nuer themselves being illiterate do not put any kind of inverted commas around their word for *is*, nor do they adopt any kind of phonetic equivalent of such a device. (Evans-Pritchard at no point suggests that they do). Hence the attribution of the inverted commas, of the non-literal meaning, is a matter of interpretation, not of direct observation of the utterance itself.

And what is the logic of this interpretation? How are the gaps filled? In part, the argument is based on the assumption that the Nuer *cannot* mean the assertion literally because (their notion of) Deity is such that this would make no sense. 'Indeed it is because Spirit is conceived of in itself, as the creator and the one, and quite apart from any of its material manifestations, that phenomena can be said to be sent by it or to be its instruments' (p. 125). But to argue thus is of course to assume precisely that they do have such a self-sufficient, substantial-Creator notion of Spirit as they are credited with, *and* that they follow out the implications consistently. Indeed one may doubt whether and in what sense the Nuer can be said to possess a notion of the One, self-sufficient substance and Creator, independent of these material manifestations, etc., difficult notions which, explicitly formulated in this way, seem to presuppose the context of scholastic philosphy. It is something like this that Schoolmen have done for God: can the same be meaningfully said of the Nuer God, the Nuer having no Schoolmen?

But the position is supported not only by this argument, but also by some good independent evidence. One argument is that '. . . Nuer readily expand such statements by adding that thunder, rain, and pestilence are all instruments . . . of God or that they are sent by . . . God . . .' (p. 125). This is indeed a good and independent piece of evidence. Another argument is from the irreversibility of the judgments which claim that those certain mundane manifestations 'are' God: God or Spirit cannot in Nuer be said to 'be' them. This does not seem to me to be so valid a point. It is of course difficult for one who speaks no Nuer to judge, but in English it is possible, in some contexts, to say that A is B without the statement being reversible, but at the same time implying that A is a part of B and in that sense identical with it (or rather with a part of it). To someone who inquires about my suburb, I may in some contexts say that Putney is London, (it is not Surrey): and I cannot say that London is Putney. It could be that for Nuer, rain etc., is in this sense (part of) the deity, and this would then indicate that the Nuer view of God is at least in part an immanent one, and not as severely transcendent as Evans-Pritchard seems to be arguing. ('. . . God not being an observable object, [the situation could scarcely arise] in which Nuer would require or desire to say about him that he is anything', p. 125). Again one may also wonder whether Nuer can be credited with so firm a theological position on a question which they can hardly have explicitly posed in such terms.

I do not wish to be misunderstood: I am *not* arguing that Evans-Pritchard's account of Nuer concepts is a bad one. (Nor am I anxious to revive a doctrine of pre-logical mentality *a la* Lévy-Bruhl). On the contrary, I have the greatest admiration for it. What I am anxious to argue is that contextual interpretation, which offers an account of what assertions 'really mean' in opposition to what they seem to mean in isolation, does not by itself clinch matters. I cannot arrive at determinate answers (concerning 'what they mean') without doing a number of things which may in fact prejudge the question: without delimiting just which context is to be taken into consideration, without crediting the people concerned with consistency (which is precisely what is *sub judice* when we discuss, as Evans-Pritchard does, Lévy-Bruhl's thesis), or without assumptions concerning what they can mean (which, again, is precisely what we do not know but are trying to find out). In fairness, one should add that Evans-Pritchard is aware of this, as just before he severely rebukes Lévy-Bruhl and others for their errors, he also remarks (p. 140): 'I can take the analysis no further: but if it is inconclusive it at least shows, if it is correct, how wide of the mark have been . . . (Lévy-Bruhl and some others)'.

13. To say all this is not to argue for a scepticism or agnosticism concerning what members of alien cultures and speakers of alien languages mean, still less to argue for an abstention from the contextual method of interpretation. (On the contrary, I shall argue for a fuller use of it, fuller in the sense of allowing for the possibility that what people mean is sometimes absurd).

In a sense, Evans-Pritchard's saving of the Nuer for a dualistic theology is a more difficult exercise than is his saving of them from a charge of pre-logical mentality. We know anyway, without fieldwork, that they could in conduct distinguish birds from men and bulls from cucumbers, and to argue from these premises to the absence of pre-logical thought does not perhaps really advance the question of whether pre-logical thought occurs. On the other hand nothing prior to field-work evidence could give us any reason for having views about whether Nuer theology was or was not dualistic.

14. It is interesting at this stage to contrast Evans-Pritchard's use of the method with that of another distinguished practitioner of it, Mr Edmund Leach.

We have seen how Evans-Pritchard takes Nuer statements which, on the face of it, violate common-sense and also others which go counter to a dualistic theology which separates a transcendent deity from the immanent world, and how, by holding these statements to be metaphorical or elliptical, he squares them with common sense and an acceptable theology. Mr Leach, in *Political Systems of Highland Burma*,[1] copes with other odd statements, made by Burmese Kachins.

Again, these statements are odd. It appears (p. 14) that a Kachin found killing a pig and asked what he is doing may reply that he is 'giving to the nats'. The oddity arises simply from the non-existence

[1] London, 1954.

of nats. On the face of it, we might accuse the Kachins, if not of 'pre-logical mentality', at any rate of populating the world with imaginary creatures in their own image. Indeed, this seems to be so, for Leach tells us (p. 173) that nats are 'magnified non-natural men', and that 'in the *nat* world, as in the human world, there are chiefs, aristocrats, commoners and slaves'.

Nevertheless, Leach does not, like Evans-Pritchard intend to give us a picture of what that supernatural world is like. (Evans-Pritchard gave us a picture of the Nuer vision of the supernatural which was sufficiently determinate to exclude some superficially plausible interpretations of some Nuer assertions). On the contrary, he tells us (p. 172) 'it is nonsensical to discuss the actions or qualities of supernatural beings except in terms of human action'. 'Myth . . . is not so much a justification for ritual as a description of it'. Or, (p. 13) 'Myth (and) . . . ritual . . . are one and the same'. '. . . myth regarded as a statement in words "says" the same thing as ritual regarded as a statement in action. To ask questions about the content of belief which are not contained in the content of ritual is nonsense.'[1] '. . . a very large part of anthropological literature on religion (is) a discussion of the content of belief and of the rationality or otherwise of that content. Most such arguments seem to me scholastic nonsense'.

Or again, (p. 14), when a Kachin is killing a pig and says he is giving to it the nats, 'it is nonsense to ask such questions as: "Do nats have legs? Do they eat flesh? Do they live in the sky?" ' (Given the fact that they are 'magnified non-natural men' and that they are 'chiefs, aristocrats, commoners and slaves', it seems odd that it should be nonsense to credit them with legs, a diet, and a habitat . . .)

Concerning his own procedure, Leach tells us (p. 14): '. . . I make frequent reference to Kachin mythology but I . . . make no attempt to find any logical coherence in the myths to which I refer. Myths for me are simply one way of describing certain types of human behaviour . . .' And, later, not only are myth and ritual one so that it makes no sense to ask non-contextual questions about the former, but also (p. 182) '. . . it becomes clear that the various nats of Kachin religious ideology are, in the last analysis, nothing more than ways of describing the formal relationships that exist between real persons and real groups in ordinary Kachin society'.

---

[1] If Mr Leach meant this quite literally, he should of course give us only the Kachin expressions itself plus a description of the ritual and of the society—and *not*, as in fact he does, *translations* of the ritual statements.

It is possible to discern what has happened. Leach's exegetic procedures have also saved the Kachins from being credited with meaning what they *appear* to be saying. Their assertions are reinterpreted in the light of the author's disregard for the supernatural, in the light of the doctrine that myths simply mean the ritual which they accompany and nothing else, and that the ritual in turn 'means', symbolizes, the society in which it occurs. The 'Social' theory of religion appears to have, in our society, the following function (amongst other, possible): to enable us to attribute meaning to assertions which might otherwise be found to lack it.

Again, I am not concerned, nor indeed inclined, to challenge Leach's specific interpretations of the Kachins; though one wishes that some enterprising teacher of anthropology would set his students the task of writing an essay on *kwoth* as it would be written by Leach, and another on *nats* as it would be written by Evans-Pritchard. The point with which I am concerned is to show how the range of context, and the manner in which the context is seen, necessarily affect the interpretation. Both Evans-Pritchard and Leach are charitable to their subjects, and neither allows them to be credited with nonsense: but in the case of Leach, the 'sense' with which they are credited is identified by means of an essentially *social* doctrine of religion, a doctrine which is also precisely that which Evans-Pritchard strives to refute with the help of *his* interpretations.

15. The crux of the matter is that when, in a sense rightly, the interpretation of people's assertions must be made in the light of what they do and the social setting they do it in, this requirement is profoundly ambiguous. Two quite different things may be intended (though those who postulate the requirement may have failed to be clear in their own minds about this). The distinction between these two things can best be brought out, at any rate to begin with, by means of a simplified imaginary social situation.

Assume that in the language of a given society, there is a word *boble* which is applied to characterize people. Research reveals that *bobleness* or *bobility* is attributed to people under *either* of the following conditions: (*a*) a person who antecedently displays certain characteristics in his conduct, say uprightness, courage and generosity, is called *boble*. (*b*) any person holding a certain office, or a certain social position, is also *ipso facto* described as *boble*. One is tempted to say that bobility (*a*) is a descriptive term whose operational definition consists of tests for the possession of certain attributes (and might consist of seeing how large a portion of his income he distributed as largesse, how he behaved in danger, etc.), whereas (b) is simply an ascription, depending on the will or whim of those in authority, or on the social situation, but not in any reasonably direct or identifiable way dependent on the characteristics of the person in question. But the point is: the society in question does not distinguish *two concepts*, boble (a) and boble (b). It only uses one word, boble *tout court*; and again its theories about bobility, expressed in proverbs, legends or even disquisitions of wise elders, only know bobility, one and indivisible. As a first and simplified approximation, the logic of bobility is not an unrecognizable model, perhaps, of some familiar concepts in our own languages.

But what is the observer to say about bobility-like, so to speak semi-operational concepts? Bobility is a conceptual device by which the privileged class of the society in question acquires some of the prestige of certain virtues respected in that society, without the inconvenience of needing to practice it, thanks to the fact that the same word is applied either to practitioners of those virtues or to occupiers of favoured positions. It is, at the same time, a manner of reinforcing the appeal of those virtues, by associating them, through the use of the same appellation, with prestige and power. But all this needs to be said, and to say it is to bring out the internal logical incoherence of the concept—an incoherence which, indeed, is socially functional.

What this shows, however, is that the over-charitable interpreter, determined to defend the concepts he is investigating from the charge of logical incoherence, is bound to misdescribe the social situation. To make sense of the concept is to make nonsense of the society. Thus the *uncharitable* may be 'contextualist' in the second, deeper and better sense.

It seems to me that anthropologists are curiously charitable to concepts. They are not unduly charitable to individuals. On the contrary, they are all too willing to describe how individuals 'manipulate' each other and the rules of the local game: indeed the word 'manipulation' has a certain vogue and is encountered with very great frequency. But why should concepts not be similarly open to manipulation? Why should it not be a part of their use that the ambiguity of words, the logically illicit transformation of one concept into another (like a spirit appearing in diverse forms) is exploited to the full by the users of what seems to be 'one' concept?

Excessive indulgence in contextual charity blinds us to what is best and what is worst in the life of societies. It blinds us to the possibility that social change may occur through the replacement of an inconsistent doctrine or ethic by a better one, or through a more consistent application of either. It equally blinds us to the possibility of, for instance, social control through the employment of absurd, ambiguous, inconsistent or unintelligible doctrines. I should not accept for one moment the contention that neither of these things ever occurs: but even if they never occurred it would be wrong to employ a method which excludes their possibility *a priori*.

16. It may be worth illustrating the point further with a real rather than schematized example, amongst central Moroccan Berbers, and I shall draw on my own fieldwork for this. Two concepts are relevant: *baraka* and *agurram* (pl. *igurramen*). *Baraka* is a word which can mean simply 'enough', but it also means plentitude, and above all blessedness manifested amongst other things in prosperity and the power to cause prosperity in others by supernatural means. An *agurram* is a possessor of *baraka*.[1] The concept *baraka* has been explored before, notably by Westermarck's *Ritual and Belief in Morocco*.[2] The concept of *agurram* has not to my knowledge previously been properly explored.

Igurramen are a minority in the wider tribal society of which they are a part. They are a fairly privileged and influential one, and they perform essential and important functions as mediators, arbitrators etc., amongst the feuding tribal population around them. They are selected from a range of potential *igurramen*, who are defined by descent—roughly speaking, to be one it is necessary that one's ancestors or at least some of them should have been *igurramen* too. The crucial question is—*how* are they selected?

The local belief is that they are selected by God. Moreover, God makes his choice manifest by endowing those whom he has selected with certain characteristics, including magical powers, and great generosity, prosperity, a consider-the-lilies attitude, pacifism, and so forth.

The reality of the situation is, however, that the *igurramen* are in fact selected by the surrounding ordinary tribesmen who use their services, by being called to perform those services and being preferred

[1] The term *baraka* is in use throughout North Africa by Arabs and Berbers, and also elsewhere. The term *agurram* is only known among Berbers, and not among all of these. It is used in central and southern Morocco, but not among the northern Berbers of the Rif mountains. It is also used by Algerian Berbers, but I do not know how extensively.

[2] London, 1926. Chapters II and III.

to the rival candidates for their performance. What appears to be *vox Dei* is in reality *vox populi*. Moreover, the matter of the blessed characteristics, the stigmata of *agurram*-hood is more complicated. It is essential that successful candidates to *agurram* status be *credited* with these characteristics, but it is equally essential, at any rate with regard to some of them, that they should not really possess them. For instance, an *agurram* who was extremely generous in a consider-the-lilies spirit would soon be empoverished and, as such, fail by another crucial test, that of prosperity.

There is here a crucial divergence between concept and reality, divergence which moreover is quite essential for the working of the social system. It is no use saying, as has been suggested to me by an advocate of the hermeneutic method which I am criticizing, that the notion of divine selection of *igurramen* is simply the local way of conceptualizing a popular election. This interpretation is excluded for a number of reasons. For one thing, the Berbers of central Morocco are perfectly familiar with *real* elections. In their traditional system, they also have, apart from the *igurramen*, lay tribal chiefs, (*amghar*, pl. *imgharen*) who are elected, annually, by tribal assembly. In these real elections the tribesmen do indeed hope for and request divine guidance, but they are quite clear that it is they themselves who do the electing. They distinguish clearly between this kind of genuine annual election, and the very long-drawn-out process (stretching over generations) by which *igurramen* are selected, in fact by the tribesmen, but ideally by God. But it would be presumptious and blasphemous for tribesmen to claim to appoint an *agurram*. Secondly, it is of the essence of the function of an *agurram* that he is given from the outside: he has to be a neutral who arbitrates and mediates between tribes. If he were chosen, like a chief or an ally, by the tribesmen, or rather if he were seen to be chosen by tribesmen (as in fact he is), for a litigant to submit to his verdict would be in effect to submit to those other tribesmen who had chosen the *agurram*. This, of course, would involve a loss of face and constitute a confession of weakness. Tribesmen sometimes do choose lay arbitrators: but they then know that they are doing and the point of invoking *igurramen* is the invoking of *independent* authority. Submission to a divinely chosen *agurram*, is a sign not of weakness but of piety. Not to submit to him is, and is explicitly claimed to be, *shameful*. (This illustrates a point which seems to me enormously important, namely that concepts generally contain *justifications* of practices, and hence that one misinterprets them grossly if one treats them simply as these practices, and their context, in another dress. The justifications are independent of the thing justified.)

It might be objected that my unwillingness to accept the indigenous account at its face value merely reflects my theological prejudices, i.e. my unwillingness to believe that the deity interferes in the political life of the central High Atlas. But this kind of objection does not have even a *prima facie* plausibility with regard to the other social mechanism mentioned. There is nothing in my conceptual spectacles to make me unwilling to conceive that some people might be generous and uncalculating, nor should I be unwilling to describe them in these terms if I found them to be so. It is just that fieldwork observation of *igurramen* and the social context in which they operate has convinced me that, whilst indeed *igurramen* must entertain lavishly and with an air of insouciance, they *must* also at least balance their income from donations from pilgrims with the outgoings from entertaining them, for a poor *agurram* is a no-good *agurram*. Here again, we are faced with a socially essential discrepancy between concept and reality. What is required is not disregard for social context, but, on the contrary, a fuller appreciation of it which is not wedded *a priori* to find good sense in the concepts.

One might sum up all this by saying that nothing is more false than the claim that, for a given assertion, *its use is its meaning*. On the contrary, its use may depend on its lack of meaning, its ambiguity, its possession of wholly different and incompatible meanings in different contexts, *and* on the fact that, at the same time, it as it were emits the impression of possessing a consistent meaning throughout —on retaining, for instance, the aura of a justification valid only in one context when used in quite another.

17. It is worth exploring this in connection with the other concept mentioned, *baraka*. I shall not say much about it, as the literature concerning it is already extensive (E. Westermarck's *Ritual and Belief in Morocco*).[1] Suffice it to say that the concept is a source of great joy to me, for it violates, simultaneously, no fewer than three of the major and most advertised categorial distinctions favoured by recent philosophers. It is an evaluative term, but it is used as though it were a descriptive one: possessors of *baraka* are treated as though they were possessors of an objective characteristics rather than recipients of high moral grades from their fellow men. And in as far as it is claimed to be an objective characteristic of people, manifest in their conduct, it could

[1] loc. cit.

only be a dispositional one—but it is treated as though it were the name of some *stuff*: apart from being transmitted genetically, it can also be transmitted by its possessor to another person by means of spitting into the mouth, etc. Thirdly, its attribution is really a case of the performative use of language, for people in fact become possessors of *baraka* by being treated as possessors of it—but, nevertheless, it is treated as though its possession were a matter wholly independent of the volition of those who attribute it. (This has already been explained in connection with the account of *agurram*, the possessor of *baraka*, and it has also been explained how this deception is essential for the working of the social system in question.)

In other words, the actual life of this concept goes dead against the celebrated work of recent philosophers. One may well speculate that the society in question could be undermined by acquainting its members with the works of Ryle, Ayer, Stevenson and J. L. Austin. The question is somewhat academic, for in its traditional form the society is virtually illiterate (that is, illiterate but for a small number of Muslim scribes whose range is severely circumscribed) and not amenable to the persuasion of external teachers, and by the time it has ceased to be illiterate and unreceptive, it shall have been disrupted anyway.

But this does illustrate a number of important points. I have already stressed that it is no use supposing that one can deal with this by claiming that the indigenous societies always live, as it were, in a conceptual dimension of their own, in which our categorial boundaries do not apply. On the contrary, we can sometimes only make sense of the society in question by seeing how the manipulation of concepts and the violation of categorial boundaries helps it to work. It is precisely the logical *in*consistency of *baraka* which enables it to be applied according to social need and to endow what is a social need with the appearance of external, given and indeed authoritative reality.

18. There are, both in philosophy and the wider intellectual climate of our time, considerable forces giving support to the kind of Functionalism which makes good sense of everything. In philosophy, it springs from the doctrine which identifies *meaning* with *use*, and there is already in existence at least one work by a philosopher about the social sciences in general[1]—which elaborates (and commends) the consequences of this doctrine. A proper discussion of the philosophic questions involved would of course take longer.

In the world at large, there is much incentive to paper over the

[1] P. Winch, op. cit.

incoherence, and inconveniences, of current ideologies by emulating this anthropological technique. How many ideologists treat their *own* beliefs with a technique similar to that employed by anthropologists for tribesmen! I for one do not feel that, in the realm of concepts and doctrines, we may say that *tout comprendre c'est tout pardonner*. On the contrary, in the social sciences at any rate, if we forgive too much we understand nothing. The attitude of *credo quia absurdum* is *also* a social phenomenon, and we miss its point and its social role if we water it down by interpretation to make it just one further form of non-absurdity, sensible simply in virtue of being viable.

19. One major charge against Functionalism in the past has been the allegation that it cannot deal with social change. With regard to Functionalism in general this charge has now little relevance, as it only applies to strong or extreme formulations of it, and these are held by few. But with regard to the Functionalist approach to interpretation of concepts, it applies very strongly. For it precludes us from making sense of those social changes which arise at least in part from the fact that people sometimes notice the incoherences of doctrines and concepts and proceed to reform the institutions justified by them. This may never happen *just* like that: it may be that it invariably is a discontented segment of society, a new rising class for instance, which exploits those incoherences. But even if this were so, and the discovery of incoherences were never more than a contributory rather than a sufficient cause, it still would not be legitimate for us to employ a method which inherently prevents any possible appreciation of this fact. When anthropologists were concerned primarily with stable societies (or societies held to be such), the mistake was perhaps excusable: but nowadays it is not.

In the end, it is illuminating to return to one of the sources of the functionalist approach, Durkheim. Durkheim is sometimes accused of overrating the cohesion-engendering function of belief. In the *Elementary Forms of Religious Life*, which is the object of these charges, he did also put forward, albeit briefly, a theory of social change.[1] This theory he sums up in one brief passage, and it is a theory plainly parallel to his theory of social cohesion.

Car une société (est) constituée . . . avant tout, par l'idée qu'elle se fait d'elle-même. Et sans doute, il arrive qu'elle hésite sur la manière dont elle doit se concevoir: elle se sent tiraillée en des sens diver-

---

[1] The work also contains some other suggestions on this subject, not so relevant to my argument here.

gents . . . ces conflits, quand ils éclatent, ont lieu non entre l'idéal et la réalité, mais entre idéaux différents . . . .[1]

This theory, the germ of which is contained in Durkheim, has been elaborated by Mr E. R. Leach's *Political Systems of Highland Burma.*[2] My main point here is that there was no need for Durkheim to look even that far for a theory of social change. He apparently thought that if the one set of ritually reinforced and inculcated concepts explained social stability, then it took the presence of *two sets* to account for social change. But ironically, such a refinement is not necessary. Some social change may be accounted for precisely because *one* set of ideas has been inculcated too well, or has come to have too great a hold over the loyalties and imaginations of the members of the society in question, or because one of its subgroups has chosen to exploit the imperfect application of those ideas, and to iron out the inconsistencies and incoherencies. Over-charitable exegesis would blind us to this.

Contextual interpretation is in some respects like the invocation of *ad hoc* additional hypotheses in science: it is inevitable, proper, often very valuable, and at the same time dangerous and liable to disastrous abuse. It is probably impossible in either case to draw up general rules for delimiting the legitimate and illegitimate uses of it. In science, the best safeguard may be a vivid sense of the possibility that the initial theory which is being saved may have been false after all; in sociological interpretation, an equally vivid sense of the possibility that the interpreted statement may contain absurdity.

20. There remains the issue in the wider society outside the social sciences, the question of the justifiability of 'Functionalist' whitewashing of concepts and doctrines. Professor Evans-Pritchard sternly rebukes Durkheim at the end of his book *Nuer Religion*, p. 313: 'It was Durkheim and not the savage who made society into a god.' Perhaps, but it is ironic that if the savage did not, modern man *does* seem to worship his own society through his religion.[3]

My plea against charity did not have as its aim the revival of a 'pre-logical primitive mentality' theory. On the contrary: I hope rather we shall be less charitable to ourselves. I agree entirely with Mr Leach's point in his contribution to 'Man and Culture', that when it comes to the general way in which concepts are embedded in use and

---

[1] *Les Formes Elémentaires de la Vie Religieuse*, 1925 édition, p. 604.
[2] London, 1959, esp. pp. 8–9.
[3] Cf. Will Herberg, *Catholic–Protestant–Jew*, 1955.

context, there is no difference between 'primitives' and us. There is no need to be too charitable to *either*.

My own view of Durkheim is that at the core of his thought there lies not the doctrine of worshipping one's own society, but the doctrine that concepts are essentially social and that religion is the way in which society endows us with them and imposes their hold over us. But, consistently or not, he did not combine this with a static view of society and intellectual life. It would be ironic if neo-Functionalist interpretation now became the means by which our own concepts were ossified amongst us.

3

Explaining Cargo Cults

I. C. JARVIE

I want to discuss several criticisms of cargo cult theories, criticisms which can also be used to allege the unsatisfactoriness of the situational logic solution. These criticisms say situational logic is no good: (*a*) because it explains these religious movements rationally and these movements in particular and even religion in general are not rational; (*b*) because it tries to explain all these cults together whereas each one is a unique phenomenon; (*c*) because it does this by assuming that the people in this situation are acting rationally, but they are not; (*d*) because it does this by assuming that what people believe or say they believe will explain what they do, but this is false.

Religion is not Rational

My theory of millenarian religion in general and therefore of cargo cult religion in particular is a rational one. I attribute reasonable aims to the actors in the situation and try to show that, within their frame of reference, their actions, if interpreted as trying to realize those aims, are perfectly rational. Against this way of approaching religion two attacks can be discovered in the literature: one that the religious reaction in this case is not a rational one, and the other that religion in general is not rational. The first is a theory put forward by Raymond Firth, the second a generalization of it by Dr Lucy Mair.

In anticipation of some difficulties up ahead I want at the inception of this discussion to make some preliminary distinctions connected with the idea of rationality. There seem to me to be at least three questions which the concept of rationality can be used to answer.

Originally published as Chapter 5 ('Methodological Discussion of The Theories') of *Revolution in Anthropology*, pp. 131–43. London: Routledge and Kegon Paul, 1964; (New Y9rk: Humanities Press).

(1) Is a given doctrine rational? (2) Is *belief in* a given doctrine rational? (3) Is a given action rational?

Our first question, (1), is a question about the rational status of some particular doctrine or belief, like the existence of God, or the succession of cause and effect. Normally rationality is attributed to those views which can be shown to be based on facts; or on science: which can, in other words, be justified. (It seems to me that this is a mistake and no doctrine can of itself be designated rational. I accept the view, so well argued by Popper and, following him, Bartley,[1] that no doctrine can be justified. I therefore do not think there is much sense in trying to talk of rational doctrines at all.

The second question, (2), concerns belief *in* a doctrine: is belief in God rational belief? There are a number of ideas all tangled up here. By a rationally held belief is very often simply meant something widely held, something which is, in fact, reasonable, or based on common sense, or on facts, or on modern science, or what not. This can be summed up in the term 'justification': belief in a doctrine is rational if that doctrine can be justified. (Since I have already stated that I do not believe any doctrine can be justified it follows I do not believe in rational belief. On the other hand, belief in any doctrine at all is not equally rational in every case. Bernard Shaw in his preface to *Androcles and the Lion* shows how belief in the Bible is not rational. He suggests asking a number of people whom one considers rational to say what parts of the Bible they believe in: he suggests the answers will vary in a random manner, i.e. be arbitrary, and therefore not rational. There is a strong school of modern philosophy, justly and severely criticized by Bartley, which believes that in fact the situation with all doctrines must be like this Bible case, because all positions are in the end irrational commitments, equally arbitrary and irrationally chosen. I would follow Popper's suggestion here that no doctrine can be justified or rationally believed in, but that we can adopt a more or less rational attitude to a position the more or less account we are prepared to take of the criticism of that doctrine.)

Finally, what about (3), rational action? Clearly the most common criterion for calling an action 'rational' is when the action is based upon rational belief. (Since I don't believe in rational belief I reject this criterion too.) Other criteria have been suggested, utilizing the

---

[1] W. W. Bartley III., 'Achilles, the Tortoise, and Explanation in Science and History', *British Journal of the Philosophy of Science* 13, pp. 15–33; idem *The Retreat to Commitment*, New York, 1962.

idea of the goal-directedness of an action, explicability of an action and of psychological reasonability of an action (i.e. action that is non-neurotic, or non-fanatic). (For my part I accept the idea of goal-directedness as the criterion of rationality.)

With the end of this short interpolation I return to my topic and discuss Firth's and Mair's idea of the irrationality of cargo cults.

Firth's reasons for believing the cargo cult religion to involve essentially 'other than rational elements' (see below) are two. First that the cults involve ethical demands, and second that they are, by native standards so to speak, non-rational. Both of Firth's arguments are to be found in his book *Elements of Social Organization*.[1] On p. 111, after some discussion of cargo cults, he suddenly says 'Such is the line of argument at the rational level. But other than rational elements enter into the situation.' I find some difficulty in understanding Firth's division of the discussion of the cults into that dealing with the rational elements and that dealing with the other than rational elements. There are two strands to his thinking from that place onwards, two kinds of things are discussed under this category of the 'other than rational elements'. The first of these things, the fact that ethical beliefs and demands are involved with the cult—as Firth puts it, ' "What we want is right" '—I shall deal with now.

We can have no reason for doubting Firth's contention that these demands are an inextricable part of the cults. What I do not accept is the idea that there is anything non-rational about these demands. It strikes me as being residual positivism to talk of ethics as 'other than rational'. We can accept some of the implications of Firth's distinction, even if we do not accept them all. We usually take ethical demands as a given part of the situation within which the actors act, rather than attempt to give a rational explanation of them. But because we do not (or cannot) give a rational explanation of ethical demands does not make them, say, psychologically non-rational, or incapable of being held open to criticism and thus not rational in those senses. By holding our ethical demands open to criticism and improvement we are being rational to some extent in ethics. Under this interpretation there is no essential rationality possessed *ipso facto* by certain doctrines like those of religion and ethics; what rationality there is consists mainly in the attitude towards rational discussion of the view in question.

I now want to examine how the beliefs are irrational within the

[1] London, 1961 (3rd ed.).

native frame of reference. First of all Firth points out that there is an 'incompatibility between wants and their means of satisfaction' (p. 113). Basically the natives simply lack the knowledge necessary in order to get what they want (European goods) and this *impasse* has 'turned [them] to fantasy' (p. 113). Why fantasy? Fantasy in *their* terms because here they are resorting to magic without scientific accompaniment. When the natives want crops they don't just chant: they chant *and they plant seeds*; they chant and they cast their fishing-nets; they pray and go out and hunt. That they indulge in magic does not mean they have no science; they fully realize that the two must go together. Perhaps this has been best put by Malinowski:

> If by science be understood a body of rules and conceptions, based on experience and derived from it by logical inference, embodied in material achievements and in a fixed form of tradition, . . . then there is no doubt that even the lowest savage communities have the beginnings of science, however rudimentary.[1]

Against my kind of view that cargo cult action is rational because based on a genuine doctrine, it is sometimes argued that cargo cult mythology is 'fantasy' even in native terms. The argument is that the natives have a store of knowledge of farming, fishing, what is good to eat, how to construct boats and houses and so on, and that this matter-of-fact knowledge somehow shows they are not the naïve magicians I make them out to be. Doubtless this argument is correct: they have a store of solid, technical knowledge. Further, Guiart has pointed out that some native magic is very recent. But he is not denying that some is also antediluvian. All this supports the case of those who would have us believe that it is not lack of technical knowledge but lack of means, techniques, and natural resources which make the natives so non-rational, so prone to 'fantasy'.

Against this I would argue that it is by no means clear that the Kanakas think in these categories—magic *versus* technique. According to my opponents the natives themselves consider their religion and magic as one—as we would say, irrational or fantastic—way of thinking about things; whereas they consider their practical, technical knowledge as another—as we would say, rational or sensible—way of thinking about things, I should imagine, on the face of it, that such a picture is highly unlikely. In reply it could be said that it is indeed

[1] B. Malinowski, *Magic Science and Religion*, Glencoe: Free Press 1948, p. 17, quoted in B. Barber, *Science and the Social Order*, Glencoe: Free Press, 1952, p. 56.

highly unlikely and that it is not what was meant at all. The distinction being made is between the traditional religion and its beliefs and the new and fantastic doctrines of the cargo. Now these are new and fantastic within native terms; within native terms, they are arbitrary and other-than-rational. Were he so inclined, then, such a person could well argue that it is the arbitrariness of the cargo myths, within the traditional world-view, that makes him suspect their rationality.

I think this would amount to a good case for attributing a degree of non-rationality to the cults. Still I think the position can be criticized. The first criticism would be that unless the theory were carefully applied it would make all innovation and change rationally suspect. A high price to pay for so viewing the cults. The decisive point would be whether the new myths embodied a coherent horizon of expecta- tions. If they did I think the cults would be rational; if not perhaps my opponent would be right. My second criticism is factual. Some authors do claim that similar cult-activity is part of the Melanesian cultural inheritance. This, if true, and if flexible enough to see the cargo cults as simply another variation on the tradition, would clinch the rationality of the cults on the criterion of arbitrariness.

I have asked two tricky questions: are all social changes non-rational, and, is the cult integrated into the previous background of myths and rituals of the people? One possible answer could be: only those social changes which are integrated into the background are rational The question is a simple empirical one: check whether they are integrated or not. This label of 'non-rational' is, then, more or less a confession that functionalism cannot handle social change; this we have known all along, the only new move is to disguise the failure under the label 'non-rational'. But why should anyone say that only integrated changes are rational? Answer: functionalists would say so because they are only interested in what is observable, in the ritual, not the belief; therefore social change to them is the changes that have taken place in what people do, and its rationality is the extent to which these changes are integrated.

Let us leave this digression which interprets the cults as non-rational because arbitrary and return to the problem of whether or not a person adopting the 'inadequate means' view provides us with a clear distinction between previous myths and their related technical know- ledge, and the new fatastic myths. The question, in fact, of the in- tegratedness of the cult. We would need more detail on the explanation patterns of the natives.

Just how do the natives explain their practical information, rules, and rules-of-thumb for gardening, fishing, building houses, and so on? Just how different are these accounts from their magical and religious doctrines? My guess is that, if pressed, they would give a 'fantasy' explanation of their technical knowledge. And even if they give recognizably scientific explanations of their techniques we still have to be shown that they see any rational/non-rational discontinuity between this and their magico-religious beliefs. One need not go to the South Seas or to Central Africa to find evidence against the view that people separate technology and magic. Our own society, in the Middle Ages and in isolated villages and suburbs now, manifests high technology with magical justifications for it, not to mention the mumbo-jumbo of the modern advertising industry.

The reason I suspect the natives will produce fantasy explanations of their technology is the theory I have developed out of Belshaw, that what is lacking is not technical knowledge (we admit they have a lot of that), but theoretical knowledge, *which explains the technical knowledge*. That is to say, native explanations of Europeans and of cargo are either fanciful and untestable, or concrete and already falsi-fied. Certainly, had the native the production techniques explained to him, and had he the necessary natural resources available, he could make the cargo goods without benefit of a western scientific and philosophical background. But wouldn't he then be like the Indian Ph.D. in physics who still believes in astrology? Is it not the whole animistic world-view, in which I include the natives' theoretical knowledge of the physical world and of the society of the white men, which marks them off from us? The cargo cult prophet Yali of the Garia (Lawrence, 1954), who had seen the manufacturing process at work in Australia, could still have an obscure connection with a cargo cult. It must be stressed that technical knowledge, i.e. predictions for practical use, are deducted from explanatory theories. It is quite possible to get the right results from the wrong theories, as readers of Mr Koestler on Kepler will know.[1] Native ignorance of the rationale of the white man's *mores* and of his cargoes is theoretical; they explain us animistically, which, when it says that cargo is made by the spirits, or that we are misappropriating cargoes intended for them, is false, but they have no way of finding this out independently. The difference between the native and the westerner is that faced with such evidence

[1] A. Koestler, *The Sleepwalkers*, London, 1959, pp. 326–8, where false hypothesis and mathematical mistake yield the right result.

we would revise our theories radically (or we ought to) while the native tends to invent *ad hoc* corrections to his explanations, as would bad scientists.

The foregoing is intended to combat the doctrine that the incompatibility of wants and their means of satisfaction turned the natives to irrational fantasy. My view is that the fantasies were entirely rational attempts, within the native framework, to explain the incompatibility. Now how is it that Firth, and many another anthropologist, advanced such a theory? I have a tentative theory which might answer this question: how anthropologists came to muddle up the rationality of the natives with their nonpossession of science. The theory is philosophical, so I apologize for it. First of all what the natives have is technology not science. This is not a verbal quibble but a vital distinction between rules-of-thumb and scientific theories; between 'knacks' which work and theories which are articulated and lay claim to truth. The natives' technique does not give them a claim to comparison with us, only their explanatory (magical, animistic) theories can be so compared. Secondly, social anthropologists have confused technique and science precisely on account of their slogan 'study the ritual, not the belief'. This slogan leads them to ignore the fact that the natives do not have on the one hand scientific theories of their technique and on the other hand magical ones of their magic, but that both the technology and the magic are explained magico-religiously. Thus Malinowski, speaking about this primitive science, and saying,

> detached from the craft, that is certainly true, it is only a means to an end, it is crude, rudimentary and inchoate, but with all that it is the matrix from which the higher developments have sprung. . . . [1]

utterly misses the point and the vital distinction between the two. Having agreed that the fantasies were rational, let me turn to whether the resort to fantasy was also rational. Firth in 1932 suggested that the native creates new illusions to counter disillusion and strain. He is more or less suggesting that the cult fantasies are a form of escapism from the reality of disillusionment. Now is this flight into fantasy non-rational or rational (psychological) behaviour? Are there good reasons for it or not? Let us take it for a moment that he means escapism is non-rational, there are no good reasons for it. To this it might be replied that it could equally well be a psychologically rational move. After all, if we interpret 'non-rational' as 'neurotic' then we can say

[1] B. Malinowski, op. cit.

that Freud provided rational accounts of the formation of neuroses. That is, he tried to show how people's resort to neuroses was, from their point of view, reasonable. But this attribution of neuroses to the cultists is not very plausible. First of all it is not clear what is being escaped from: is it the problem which has brought on the disillusionment, or is it perhaps the anxiety and strain brought on by the unsolved problem? Secondly, who is escaping from what? Can we even talk sensibly of the whole society experiencing disillusion and anxiety? I am not altogether convinced that we can. The question is whether we can explain the escapism rationally and, if we can, can we criticize Firth for not providing such an explanation? Such a rational explanation is provided, I think, by Cyril Belshaw on lines Firth employs elsewhere. Belshaw argues that within the native frame of reference cargo myths are not illusions but attempts to solve certain problems in native terms. The fact that their myth-explanations are in native terms does not warrant them the label non-rational; rather, the very fact that the natives use their belief to try to explain facts shows the natives to be rational about their beliefs. Rational activity is goal-directed. What is the goal of the myth-making activity? Its goal is, one may assume, to explain the Europeans, their wealth, native poverty, and so on, as Belshaw has shown, If this explanation is true the activity of resorting to fantasy is rational.

It is surprising from my viewpoint that Firth, who in another place stresses the resort to native means to achieve new ends, should have neglected the possibility of aruging in parallel that cargo myths are explanations, in native terms, of new problems. Why this oversight? Precisely because Firth, it seems to me, is assuming that we can judge the whole native magical frame of reference to be non-rational. My evidence is his very use of the word 'fantasy'. He is judging their *theories* to be fantastic. What Firth is judging non-rational is magico-religious explanation; the reason he is judging it non-rational is because it is magico-religious. But, I would say, the fact that we, with our western scientific knowledge, can see that the actions prescribed by these explanations will not bring about the promised ends tells no more about these natives than that their knowledge is inadequate—although that is a very tendentious way of putting it. What is it inadequate for? How do we know that it is inadequate? Only because it clashes with the 'rational' beliefs of modern science. But not only does the native not know of modern science, he might not believe it if he did. Would that be *ipso facto* non-rational if the native had never heard the arguments in favour of the scientific explanation? It would not; it would only be non-rational if, faced with all the arguments, *and able to appreciate their force*, the native still refused to accept that a western scientific explanation was any improvement on his own.

As far as I understand it Firth has tried to show that this magico-religious fantasy belief present in the cargo cults is 'other than rational'. I do not know whether he would say religion in general is other-than-rational, or fantasy. Many social anthropologists would. This is because there is a long tradition on the topic in social anthropology. Social anthropology has for a long time been intimately connected with the Rationalist movement. I mean the movement grouped around The Rationalist Association whose efforts perhaps culminated in Frazer's monumental *Golden Bough*—which explicitly sets out to discredit present-day religion as primitive and irrational. Believing as Rationalists do, that all religion is superstitious mumbo-jumbo, it is not surprising that when they come to study religion they prefer to concentrate on ritual rather than belief. At least ritual is an understandable, tangible thing, which is more than you can say for the superstitions behind rituals. This is one explanation, anyway, for anthropologists' persistent talk of 'ritual activity'. I can think of at least one other explanation of this oddity. By and large social anthropologists seem to have found religious beliefs terribly difficult and problematic to deal with, and for that reason they have sheered off them. Perhaps their position is defensible, for certainly the difficulties of the matter are immense. A casual glance at the volume *African Worlds* or at *Nuer Religion*, which are exceptional cases of attempts to study religious beliefs, will soon convince anyone of that. Nevertheless, I think the attitude some anthropologists adopt is highly arguable. Their attitude is not merely to avoid talk about religion if they can avoid it, but rather an over-readiness to talk only about its observable aspects, namely ritual. This is not leaving religion alone but giving an empiricist or even be-haviourist twist to religious studies. The move is justified on intellectual grounds by a theory of Radcliffe-Brown's that religion does not explain ritual. By this he means that if you ask why a man goes through the motions of prayer it is no answer to say he is worshipping God (since different people worship the same God in different ways). According to Radcliffe-Brown the motions of praying may have developed before the notion of worshipping God. It might either have been originally justified differently or it might be the case that the ritual action in itself is valued and the religious justification was *post hoc* or perhaps parallel and *ad hoc*. (Remember the transfer of pagan ritual to Christianity.) Thus anthropologists feel free to describe and discuss the actually existing, observable, ritual without having to bother much about the religious 'explanations' that are given of it. Indeed these, being origin explanations, are unacceptable to most social anthropologists. They accept a Durkheimian theory that ritual foregatherings are to be explained by their social or collective function of the reaffirmation of ties and community.

Before I go on, let me stress that this discussion of Rationalism extrapolates from Firth's arguments. It is not intended to attribute any beliefs to him. My extrapolation helps me to understand his position, by seeing it as a direct descendent of what might be called 'the Frazerian tradition' (of interpreting religion).

Consonant with this whole tradition comes the explicit argument of Dr Lucy Mair that religion as such is not rational.

Her thesis is most interesting and is based on a number of intriguing arguments. She believes religion to be non-rational in the sense that: (*a*) religious performances are recognizably different from other, non-mystical activities which are rational; (*b*) that religion prescribes means which the actors know cannot possibly achieve their ostensible ends. There is, I would say, still a third, somewhat more subtle, argument behind her position. We are trying to explain the actions of people more or less rationally. We all accept that rational actions is action directed to an end. Objectively speaking, however, we can say that some actions are more likely to realize their end than are others. Thus we might say that, given the knowledge and belief of the actor, he acts the more rationally the better suited, from an objective point of view, are his means to the realization of his aims. Clearly praying for rain is objectively much less likely to produce rain than is dropping dry ice into the clouds. Therefore, objectively, (*c*) science is more rational than religion.[1]

In arguing that religion is rational, whatever its protagonists or opponents may say, I am saying that the cults are rational too. The fact that some religious people agree that religious beliefs are irrational is a red herring. In the sense that religious beliefs are theoretical explanations of things and events in the world, they are as rational, I would say, as any other (say scientific) explanation, in one sense of

[1] Dr Mair states her view of religion in a review article of Peter Worsley's book [The Trumpet Shall Sound, London, McGibbon and Kee 1957] called 'The Pursuit of the Millernium in Melanesia', *British Journal of Sociology*, 9, 1958, pp. 175–82.

'rational'; in another sense science is more rational than magic, of course.[1] Dr Mair then brings up the argument that calling the cults irrational serves usefully to distinguish them from later 'non-mystical' movements. The force of this argument is difficult to see. These other movements are non-religious, while cargo cults are religious; this seems an adequate distinction. It is surely better than introducing the heavily value-loaded term 'irrational', with its over-tones of 'unreasonable' and even 'bad'. Perhaps a better use of 'rational' is to apply it to purposeful behaviour. The religious elements of cargo cults, in so far as they have the *purpose* of explaining something—of solving the problems created by conduct—seem to me to be rational.

Against this Dr Mair brings a final argument that the cults and, perhaps, religion, are irrational in the sense that they propose means which cannot possibly achieve their ostensible ends. This, I happen to believe, is true. But how can the *natives* or religious people know that the means are inappropriate to the achievement of the ends? The answer is they cannot; not, at least, without the kind of prior knowledge which Jarvie, Dr Mair, and the reader of *The British Journal of Sociology* have. I suggest that the only criterion by which we could find out if there was any relation between cult means and cult ends would be the success or failure of the cults. If successful (like modern science) then there is a relation, if not, not. How can we argue like this? The aim of Dr Mair's review is to show Worsley is in error. Were we to show (by Gallup poll) that her review had failed to do this would we then be allowed to call the review irrational? Of course not, Moreover, how do we know that all religion is unsuccessful, 'cannot possibly' achieve its ends? If some religious performance suddenly brought it off what would we do? Call it 'science' and rational? It would hardly be fair to use our (scientific) knowledge of the relations of means and ends as criteria for judging theirs irrational. Another argument, that the natives (and religious people) *do* know that the means cannot achieve the ends because they have technical knowledge of means-ends relationships in, e.g. fishing and farming, has been discussed earlier. In line with Firth, Dr Mair wants to see the cults and religion as 'irrational'; I resist this because I find the inference that is often drawn

[1] Namely in that the theories of empirical science are testable, tested and have survived tests. These *theories* are no more rational than magical ones, but some philosophers (Popper, Watkins, Bartley) have argued that they are more rationally held. If something like this is what Firth and Mair had in mind they have not made this clear, for they seem to go much further. In such case, my arguments can be read as directed against those further parts of their views only.

from it, namely, that religion and the cults are retreats into fantasy and escapism, has no explanatory power. I find it difficult not to believe that anthropologists' keenness to introduce the word 'irrational' is partly an attempt to label the cults 'unreasonable'; this, the contrary of my own view, is *ad hoc* psychologism.

What is really under discussion here is savage ignorance *versus* civilized knowledge. My position has been that savage ignorance is just as rational as civilized knowledge. Now this is a very curious position to be in. Can I be sincere? If I mean it then what possible ground can I have for believing in western civilized knowledge and not ignorance and magic?

If this is the worry at the back of the minds of the Rationalist anthropologists it must be admitted they have discovered a somewhat difficult point. Nevertheless, I still think my solution to this difficulty is more satisfactory than theirs. My solution is this. Magic and religion, to many people, are a part of common sense. As a part of common sense it is reasonable for them to hold it. If another part of their common sense is an uncritical attitude towards belief, an acceptance of the received or traditional ideas, then their belief in common sense is reinforced and doubly rational. In our society superstition and elementary popular science are all mixed up. But part of common sense in our society is the attitude of being critical towards traditional or received ideas. Once one becomes critical, and establishes standards of being critical, then I personally believe it is no longer reasonable to hold on to the more simple-minded magico-religious beliefs in prayers and spells. So I can provide a reason why I accept western science and not magic in, say, the matter of farming. At the same time I can insist that, within his common sense, or frame of reference, the savage is also being reasonable.

This sounds a trifle like relativism again. Having chastised relativism so much I must hastily disavow any tint of relativism. Within both savage and civilized frames of reference it is possible to appraise the system of belief of the other, but I think it can easily be shown that a critical attitude towards beliefs and ideas is better than an uncritical one. No relativism here then. Both we westerners and the savages have a degree of rationality in believing what we do. But our reasons for believing what we do are somewhat better than their reasons, at least by our standards of critical discussion. And our standards of critical discussion are better than no standards of critical discussion, and that latter is the situation of the savage.

4

Is Understanding Religion Compatible with Believing?

ALASDAIR MACINTYRE

Begin with an elementary puzzlement. In any discussion between sceptics and believers it is presupposed that, even for us to disagree, it is necessary to understand each other. Yet here at the outset the central problem arises. For usually (and the impulse to write 'always' is strong) two people could not be said to share a concept or to possess the same concept unless they agreed in at least some central applications of it. Two men may share a concept and yet disagree in some of the judgments they make in which they assert that objects fall under it. But two men who disagreed in *every* judgment which employed the concept—of them what could one say that they shared? For to possess a concept is to be able to use it correctly—although it does not preclude mishandling it sometimes. It follows that unless I can be said to share your judgments at least to some degree I cannot be said to share your concepts.

Yet sceptic and believer disagree *in toto* in their judgments on some religious matters; or so it seems. So how can they be in possession of the same concepts? If I am prepared to say *nothing* of what you will say about God or sin or salvation, how can my concepts of God, sin and salvation be the same as yours? And if they are not, how can we understand each other? There are parties to the discussion who would cut it short precisely at this point, both Protestants who believe that only saving grace can help us to understand the concepts of the Scriptures or the creeds, and sceptics who believe that religious utterances are flatly senseless. But each of these is presently convicted of paradox. For the Protestant will elsewhere deny what is entailed by his

This paper was originally published in John Hick (ed.), *Faith and the Philosophers*: London, Macmillan, 1964. I owe a great deal to conversations with Professor Ernest Gellner and Mr. Peter Winch, neither of whom will agree with the use I have made of what I have learned from them.

position, namely that nobody ever rejects Christianity (since anyone who thinks he has rejected it must have lacked saving grace and so did not understand Christianity and so in fact rejected something else); and the sceptic of this kind has to explain the meaning of religious utterances in order to reject them (that is, he never says—as he would have to if they were flatly senseless—'I can't understand a word of it'). So it seems that we do want to say that a common understanding of religious concepts by sceptics and by believers is both necessary and impossible. This dilemma constitutes my problem.

Someone might argue that this dilemma is an entirely artificial construction on the grounds that the concepts used in religion are concepts also used outside religion and that sceptics and believers agree in the non-religious judgments which make use of such concepts. Since I have said that it is far from necessary for two men who share a concept to agree in every judgment which they make in which they make use of the concept, there can be no objection to saying that sceptics and believers share the same concept and, *a fortiori*, no difficulty in mutual understanding. But this objection rests upon two mistakes. First of all it ignores those specifically religious concepts which have no counter part in nonreligious contexts; and the concepts I have already cited such as those of God, sin and salvation belong to this class. Secondly, when secular predicates such as 'powerful' and 'wise' are transferred to a religious application, they undergo a change. Certainly they are used analogically; but just this is the point. A new element is introduced with the analogical adaptation of the concept. The transition from 'powerful' to 'omnipotent' is not merely quantitative. For the notion of 'supreme in this or that class' cannot easily be transferred to a being who does not belong to a class (as God does not).[1] And thus a new concept has been manufactured. But if the understanding of this new concept can lead theologians to make one set of judgments and the understanding of what is apparently the same concept can lead sceptics to make quite another set of judgments, then how can it be the same concept which is in question? The dilemma stands. If by any chance examples were to be produced from religions which turned out to use no specifically religious concepts, and only to use secular predicates, without change of meaning, then certainly we should have no problems of meaning with them. And with them for that very reason I am not concerned.

An indirect way of approaching this dilemma as it arises for the

[1] *Summa Theologica*, Part I, Q. 3, Art. 5.

philosophy of religion would be to enquire whether the same dilemma arises in any other field; and at once it is clear that there is at least one field in which it *ought* to arise, namely the study of so-called primitive societies. For anthropologists and sociologists (I intend to use these terms interchangeably) claim to understand concepts which they do not share. They identify such concepts as *mana*, or *tabu*, without themselves using them—or so it seems. If we could discover what anthropological understanding consisted in therefore, we might be in a stronger position to restate the problem. And if, as I shall claim, we could also show that the variety of positions taken up by anthropologists reproduce a variety of positions already taken up in the philosophy of religion, the sense of relevance would be even stronger. I want to distinguish four different positions, each of which has defects.

(*a*) There is the now unfashionable view of Lévy-Bruhl that primitive thought is pre-logical. When Australian aborigines asserted that the sun is a white cockatoo[1] Lévy-Bruhl concluded that he was faced with a total indifference to inconsistency and contradiction. From the standpoint of rational discourse we can study primitive thought much as we study natural phenomena. It obeys laws as particles obey laws; but in speaking, primitives do not follow rules as we do. Therefore we cannot elucidate the rules that they use. In an important sense therefore, although we can describe what primitives say, we cannot grasp their concepts. For they do not possess concepts in the sense of recognizing that some uses of expression conform to and others break with rules for the use of such expressions. It is of course consistent with this view that we might by a kind of empathy imagine ourselves to be primitives and in this sense 'understand'; but we might equally understand by imaginative sympathy what it is to be a bear or a squirrel.

The counterpart in philosophy of religion to Lévy-Bruhl is the kind of position which wants to interpret religious language[2] as expressive of attitudes rather than as affirming or denying that anything is the case. On this view religious language simply does not function as *language*; for it is used either causally to evoke or aesthetically to express feelings or attitudes, and Carnap thinks that language can do these things in precisely the same way in which 'movements' can. We can thus study religious language, as in Lévy-Bruhl's writings, only as a natural phenomenon; we cannot grasp its concepts for they cannot,

[1] *Les Fonctions mentales dans les sociétés inférieures*, pp. 76 et. seq.

[2] Or metaphysical language—see R. Carnap, *Philosophy and Logical Syntax*, London: Kegan Paul, 1935.

on this view, be conceptual. The problem for writers like Lévy-Bruhl and Carnap is that they have to treat their own conclusions as palpably false in order to arrive at them. For unless Lévy-Bruhl had grasped that 'white cockatoo' and 'sun' were being used with apparently normal referential intentions, he could not have diagnosed the oddity of asserting that the sun is a white cockatoo; and unless Carnap had grasped the assertive form of religious or metaphysical statement, he would not have had to argue that this language is not assertive but expressive. That is, in Lévy-Bruhl and Carnap we find a tacit acknowledgement that primitive *language* and religious *language* are *language*. And that therefore something is there to be construed and not merely described or explained.

(*b*) At the opposite extreme from Lévy-Bruhl is the practice of Professor E. E. Evans-Pritchard in his book *Nuer Religion*, which is of course offered as an explicit refutation of Lévy-Bruhl. Like the Australian aborigines, the Sudanese Nuer appear to fly in the face of ordinary rules of consistency and contradiction. 'It seems odd, if not absurd, to a European when he is told that a twin is a bird as though it were an obvious fact, for Nuer are not saying that a twin is like a bird but that he is a bird.'[1] Evans-Pritchard begins from the Nuer concept of the divine, *kwoth*. The difficulties in the notion of *kwoth* spring from the fact that *kwoth* is asserted both to be sharply contrasted with the material creation and to be widely present in it. It is both one and many: and the many, as aspects of *kwoth*, are one with each other. In order to tease out the notion Evans-Pritchard has to allow full weight to the social context of practice in which the assertions about *kwoth* are used. By doing this he is able to show that the utterances of the Nuer are rule-governed, and on this rests his claim to have refuted Lévy-Bruhl. But Evans-Pritchard takes this to be the same as having made the utterances of the Nuer intelligible. Certainly he has shown us what the Nuer idea of intelligibility is. He has shown why the Nuer think their religion makes sense. But this is not to have shown that the Nuer are right. 'When a cucumber is used as a sacrificial victim Nuer speak of it as an ox. In doing so they are asserting something rather more than that it takes the place of an ox.'[2] When we have grasped the whole of Nuer practice have we grasped what more this could be? Or is there anything left over that we have not understood? Evans-Pritchard would have to answer this last question by 'No'. In doing so he brings

[1] E. E. Evans-Pritchard, *Nuer Religion*, Oxford: Clarendon Press, 1956, p. 131.
[2] Evans-Pritchard, op. cit. p. 128.

out the parallels between his position and the kind of Wittgensteinian-ism in philosophy of religion exemplified by Mr Peter Winch.[1]

Winch argues that 'intelligibility takes many and varied forms'; that there is no 'norm for intelligibility in general'.[2] He argues that 'criteria of logic are not a direct gift of God, but arise out of, and are only intelligible in the context of, ways of living or modes of social life as such. For instance, science is one such mode and religion is another; and each has criteria of intelligibility peculiar to itself. So within science or religion actions can be logical or illogical; in science, for example, it would be illogical to refuse to be bound by the results of a properly carried out experiment; in religion it would be illogical to suppose that one could pit one's own strength against God's; and so on. But we cannot sensibly say that either the practice of science itself or that of religion is either illogical or logical; both are non-logical.'[3] It follows from this that anything that counts as a 'way of living' or a 'mode of social life' can only be understood and criticized in its own terms. Winch indeed argues that so far as religion is concerned, a sociologist can only identify religious actions under their religious descriptions and if he answers any questions about them of the form 'Do these two acts belong to the same kind of activity?' the answer will have to be 'given according to criteria which are not taken from sociology, but from religion itself. But if the judgments of identity—and hence the generalizations—of the sociologist of religion rest on criteria taken from religion, then his relation to the performers of religious activity cannot be just that of observer to observed. It must rather be analogous to the participation of the natural scientist with fellow-workers in the activities of scientific investigation.'[4] That is, you can only understand it from the inside.

Winch therefore points to a theoretical justification for Evans-Pritchard's practice, and in so doing exposes its weakness. For there are not two alternatives: *either* embracing the metaphysical fiction of one over-all 'norm for intelligibility in general' *or* flying to total relativism. We can elicit the weakness of this position by considering the conceptual self-sufficiency claimed for 'ways of living' and 'modes of social life'. The examples given are 'religion' and 'science'. But at

[1] *The Idea of a Social Science and its Relation to Philosophy*, London: Routledge and Kegan Paul, 1958.
[2] Op. cit. p. 102.
[3] Op. cit. pp. 100–101.
[4] Op. cit. pp. 87–88.

any given date in any given society the criteria in current use by religious believers or by scientists will differ from what they are at other times and places.[1] Criteria have a history. This emerges strikingly if we ask how we are to think of magic on Winch's view. Is magic a 'mode of social life'? Or is it primitive religion? Or perhaps primitive science? For we do want to reject magic, and we want to reject it—in the terms which Winch has taken over for polemical purposes from Pareto—as illogical because it fails to come up to our criteria of rationality. An excellent case here is that of the witchcraft practised by the Azande.[2] The Azande believe that the performance of certain rites in due form affects their common welfare; this belief cannot in fact be refuted. For they also believe that if the rites are ineffective it is because someone present at them had evil thoughts. Since this is always possible, there is never a year when it is unavoidable for them to admit that the rites were duly performed, but that they did not thrive. Now the belief of the Azande is not unfalsifiable in principle (we know perfectly well what would falsify it—the conjunction of the rite, no evil thoughts and disasters). But in fact it cannot be falsified. Does this belief stand in need of rational criticism? And if so by what standards? It seems to me that one could only hold the belief of the Azande rationally *in the absence of* any practice of science and technology in which criteria of effectiveness, ineffectiveness and kindred notions had been built up. But to say this is to recognize the appropriateness of scientific criteria of judgment from our standpoint. The Azande do not intend their belief either as a piece of science or as a piece of non-science. They do not possess these categories. It is only *post eventum*, in the light of later and more sophisticated understanding that their belief and concepts can be classified and evaluated at all.

This suggests strongly that beliefs and concepts are not merely to be evaluated by the criteria implicit in the practice of those who hold and use them. This conviction is reinforced by other considerations. The criteria implicit in the practice of a society or of a mode of social life are not necessarily coherent; their application to problems set within that social mode does not always yield *one* clear and unambiguous answer. When this is the case people start questioning their own criteria.

[1] Consider Kepler using as a criterion in selecting from possible hypotheses what could be expected from a perfect God whose perfection included a preference for some types of geometrical figure as against others.

[2] E. E. Evans-Pritchard, *Witchcraft, Oracles and Magic Among the Azande*, Oxford University Press, 1937.

They try to criticize the standards of intelligibility and rationality which they have held hitherto. On Winch's view it is difficult to see what this could mean. This is to return to the point that criteria and concepts have a history; it is not just activities which have a history while the criteria which govern action are timeless.

What I am quarrelling with ultimately is the suggestion that agreement in following a rule is sufficient to guarantee making sense. We can discriminate different types of example here. There are the cases where the anthropologist, in order to interpret what people say, has to reconstruct imaginatively a possible past situation where expressions had a sense which they no longer bear. Consider theories about what taboo is. To call something taboo is to prohibit it, but it is not to say that it is prohibited. To say that something is taboo is to distinguish it from actions which are prohibited but are not taboo. We could say that it is to give a reason for a prohibition, except that it is unintelligible what reason can be intended. So some theorists have constructed[1] from the uses of taboo a sense which it might once have had and a possible history of how this sense was lost. One cannot take the sense from the use, for the use affords no sense, although the temptation to tell anthropologists that taboo is the name of a non-natural quality would be very strong for any Polynesian who had read G. E. Moore.

In the case of 'taboo' we can imagine lost sense for the expression. What about cases, however, where the sense is not lost, but is simply incoherent? According to Spencer and Gillen some aborigines carry about a stick or a stone which is treated *as if* it is or embodies the soul of the individual who carries it. If the stick or stone is lost, the individual anoints himself as the dead are anointed. Does the concept of 'carrying one's soul about with one' make sense? Of course we can re-describe what the aborigines are doing and transform it into sense, and perhaps Spencer and Gillen (and Durkheim who follows them) mis-describe what occurs. But if their reports are not erroneous, we confront a blank wall here, so far as meaning is concerned, although it is easy to give the rules for the use of the concept.

What follows from this is quite simply that there are cases where we cannot rest content with describing the user's criteria for an expression, but we can criticize what he does. Indeed, unless we could do this we could not separate the case where there are no problems of meaning, the case where now there is no clear sense to an expression, but where once there may well have been one (as with 'taboo') and

[1] See F. Steiner, *Taboo*, Harmondsworth: Penguin Books, 1968.

the case where there appears never to have been a clear and coherent sense available. What matters for our present purposes is that these examples suggest that sometimes to understand a concept involves not sharing it. In the case of 'taboo' we can only grasp what it is for something to be taboo if we extend our insight beyond the rules which govern the use of the expression to the point and purpose which these rules once had, but no longer have, and can no longer have in a different social context. We can only understand what it is to use a thoroughly incoherent concept, such as that of a soul in a stick, if we understand what has to be absent from the criteria of practice and of speech for this incoherence not to appear to the user of the concept. In other words we are beginning to notice requirements for the elucidation of concepts which are necessarily absent from the kind of account given by Evans-Pritchard or by Winch.

We have not only to give the rules for the use of the relevant expressions, but to show what the point could be of following such rules, and in bringing out this feature of the case one shows also whether the use of this concept is or is not a possible one for people who have the standards of intelligibility in speech and action which we have. But do we have to be thus self-centred in our application of criteria? Can we, as it might appear from this, only understand what makes sense to us already? Can we learn nothing from societies or modes of social life which we cannot understand within our present framework? Why dismiss what does not fit easily into that framework? Why not revise the framework? To find a clue to the answering of these questions let us examine yet a third doctrine of intelligibility in anthropology.

(c) Dr E. R. Leach[1] commits himself to a version of the philosophical theory that the meaning of an expression is nothing other than the way in which the expression is used. Myth is to be understood in terms of ritual, saying in terms of doing. To interpret any statement made by primitive people which appears unintelligible, ask what the people in question do. So Leach writes that 'myth regarded as a statement in words "says" the same thing as ritual regarded as a statement in action. To ask questions about the content of belief which are not contained in the content of ritual is nonsense.'[2] Leach, that is, adopts an opposite standpoint to Evans-Pritchard. Evans-Pritchard insists that the anthro-pologist has to allow the Nuer to make sense in the Nuer's own terms;

[1] *The Political Systems of Highland Burma*, London: Bell 1954.
[2] Op. cit.

Leach insists that his Burmese society must be made sense of in Leach's own terms. What is impressive here is that both Evans-Pritchard and Leach have written anthropological classics and this may be thought to be inconsistent with what I have just said. But the reason why we get insight both into Evans-Pritchard's *Nuer* and Leach's *Kachin* is that both are so explicit in presenting us both with their philosphical assumptions and with the field-material to which they apply those assumptions. Each furnishes us not merely with a finished inter-pretation but with a view of the task of interpretation while it is being carried out.

In Leach's case, although his attitude is the opposite of that of Evans-Pritchard, the results are oddly similar. In the case of the Nuer everything made sense, for the Nuer were judged on their own terms. In the case of the Kachin everything makes sense, for the rules of interpretation provide that every statement which appears not to make sense is to be translated into one that does. So Leach insists that metaphysical questions about the spirits in whom the Kachin believe (*nats*) are out of place. We cannot ask if *nats* eat or where they live for we are not to treat statements about *nats* as statements at all, but as ritual performances which can be performed properly or improperly, but which are scarcely true or false.

The counterpart to Leach in the philosophy of religion is perhaps Professor R. B. Braithwaite's reinterpretation of the meaning of religious utterances. Braithwaite sets out a classification of utterances derived from his philosphical empiricism and asks where religion can be fitted in.[1] The answer is that the room left for religion is in providing a specification and a backing for ways of life. I do not want to discuss Braithwaite's position in this paper. I only want to point out that Braithwaite's way of giving a sense to religious utterances distracts us from the question. What sense do these utterances have for those who make them? And because Braithwaite deprives us of this question, he makes it unintelligible that anyone should cease to believe, on the grounds that he can no longer find a sense in such utterances. So also it seems difficult to see what view Leach could take of a Kachin who was persuaded, for example by a Christian missionary, that his belief in *nats* was false and idolatrous.

It is therefore true that if the criteria of intelligibility with which we approach alien concepts are too narrow we may be liable not only

[1] 'An Empiricist's View of the Nature of Religious Belief', The Eddington Memorial Lecture, Cambridge University Press, 1955.

erroneously to dismiss them as senseless but even more misleadingly we may try to force them to a sense which they do not possess. It must seem at this point that my attempt to illuminate the original dilemma has merely led to the formulation of the second one. For it seems that we cannot approach alien concepts except in terms of our own criteria, and that yet to do this is to be in danger of distortion. But in fact if we are careful we shall be able to set out some of the necessary prerequisites for an adequate understanding of beliefs and concepts without this inconsistency.

Against Winch and Evans-Pritchard I have argued that to make a belief and the concepts which it embodies intelligible I cannot avoid invoking my own criteria, or rather the established criteria of my own society. Against Braithwaite and Leach I have argued that I cannot do this until I have already grasped the criteria governing belief and behaviour in the society which is the object of enquiry. And I only complete my task when I have filled in the social context so as to make the transition from one set of criteria to the other intelligible. These requirements can be set out more fully as follows:

(1) All interpretation has to begin with detecting the standards of intelligibility established in a society. As a matter of fact no one can avoid using clues drawn from their own society; and as a matter of exposition analogies from the anthropologist's society will often be helpful. But we have to begin with the society's implicit forms of self-description. Malinowski is contemptuous of the account which, so he says, a Trobriander would give of his own society; but Malinowski's own account of the Trobrianders is curiously like that which he puts in the mouth of his imagined Trobriand informant. And, had it not been, there would have been something radically wrong with it, since how a man describes himself is partially constitutive of what he is. It does not follow from this, as I have already suggested, that the descriptions used or the standards of intelligibility detected will always be internally coherent. And, if they are not, a key task will be to show how this incoherence does not appear as such to the members of the society or else does appear and is somehow made tolerable.

(2) But in detecting incoherence of this kind we have already invoked *our* standards. Since we cannot avoid doing this it is better to do it self-consciously. Otherwise we shall project on to our studies, as Frazer notoriously did, an image of our own social life. Moreover, if we are sufficiently sensitive we make it possible for us to partially escape from our own cultural limitations. For we shall have to ask not

just how we see the Trobrianders or the Nuer, but how they do or would see us. And perhaps what hitherto looked intelligible and obviously so will then appear opaque and question-begging.

(3) We can now pass on to the stage at which the difficult and important question can be put. How is it that what appears intelligible in one social context can appear not to make sense in another? What has to be underlined is that answers to this question are not necessarily all going to be of the same form.

There is the type of case where a concept works very well, so long as certain questions are not asked about it, and it may be that for a long time in a given society there is no occasion for raising such questions. The concept of the divine right of kings will undergo a strain which reveals internal incoherences only when rival claimants to sovereignty appear, for it contains no answer to the question, Which king has divine right? Then there is the type of case where incoherence and intelligibility are to some extent manifest to the users of the concept. But the use of the concept is so intimately bound up with forms of description which cannot be dispensed with if social and intellectual life is to continue that any device for putting up with the incoherence is more tolerable than dispensing with the concept. A third type of case is that in which the point of a concept or group of concepts lies in their bearing upon behaviour. But changed patterns of social behaviour deprive the concept of point. So that although there is no internal incoherence in the concept, the concept can no longer be embodied in life as it once was, and it is either put to new uses or it becomes redundant. An example of this would be the concept of honour detached from the institutions of chivalry. 'It is difficult', a British historian once wrote, 'to be chivalrous without a horse'. And the change in the importance of the horse in war can turn *Don Quixote* from a romance into a satire.

(d) I must seem to have come a very long way round. And it is therefore perhaps worth trying to meet the charge of irrelevance by saying what I hope the argument has achieved. I first posed the question: in what sense, if any, can sceptic and believer be said to share the same concepts, and so to understand one another? I then tried to show how the anthropologist might be said to grasp concepts which he does not share, in the sense that he does not make the same judgments employing them as do the people whom he studies. I now want to use my answer on this point to pose a new question which will begin the journey back to the original enquiry. This is still an anthropological question. Up to the seventeenth century we should in our society all have been believers and indeed there would be no question of our being anything else. We should not merely have believed that God existed and was revealed in Christ but we should have found it obvious and unquestionable that this was so. Since the seventeenth century, even for those who believe, the truth and in-telligibility of their beliefs is not obvious in the same sense. What accounts for the fact that what was once obvious is now not so? What accounts for the fact that nobody now believes in God in the way that mediaeval men did, simply because men are aware of alternatives? And more importantly still, what makes some of the alternatives appear as obvious to modern sceptics as belief in God did for pre-seventeenth-century Christians?

I pose this question as a background to another. If we can understand why one group of men in the past found Christian beliefs obviously true and intelligible and another group now find them opaque, and we can locate the difference between these two groups, perhaps we shall also be able to locate the difference between contemporary believers and contemporary sceptics. And if we do this we shall have solved our original problem. This brief excursus may make clear the relevance of my apparently rambling procedure. So it becomes urgent to attempt an answer, at least an outline, to the anthropological question. And the form of this answer will be to ask which of the different types of answer to the question How is it that what appears intelligible in one social context can appear not to make sense in another? is applicable in the case of the transition from mediaeval belief to modern scepticism.

It is obvious that the internal incoherences in Christian concepts did not go unnoticed in the Middle Ages. The antinomies of benevolent omnipotence and evil, or of divine predestination and human freedom, were never more clearly and acutely discussed. But it is not the case in general that mediaeval thinkers who were dissatisfied with the solutions offered to these antinomies differed in their attitude to belief in God or belief in Christ from thinkers who believed that they or others had offered satisfactory solutions. So the problem becomes: why do the same intellectual difficulties at one time appear as difficulties but no more, an incentive to enquiry but not a ground for disbelief, while at another time they appear as a final and sufficient ground for scepticism and for the abandonment of Christianity? The answers to this question are surely of the second and third types which I outlined in the last section. That is, the apparent incoherence of Christian concepts was taken to be tolerable (and treated as apparent and not real) because the concepts were part of a set of concepts which were indispensable to the forms of description used in social and intellectual life. It is the secularization of our forms of description, constituting part of the secularization of our life, that has left the contradictions high and dry. To take an obvious example, Christianity does not and never has depended upon the truth of an Aristotelian physics in which the physical system requires a Prime Mover, and consequently many sceptics as well as many believers have treated the destruction of the Aristotelian argument in its Thomist form as something very little germane to the question of whether or not Christianity is true. But in fact the replacement of a physics which requires a Prime Mover by a physics which does not secularizes a whole area of enquiry. It weakens the hold of the concept of God on our intellectual life by showing that in this area we can dispense with descriptions which have any connection with the concept.

Some Christian theologians such as Paul Tillich have welcomed this process of secularization, describing it in Tillich's terms as a transition from heteronomous to autonomous reason. But the counterpart to secularization is that the specific character of religion becomes clearer at the cost of diminishing its content. Primitive religion is part of the whole form of human life. Durkheim in *The Elementary Forms of the Religious Life* tried to show, and had at least some success in showing, that the most primitive modes of our categorical grasp of the world are inextricably embedded in religion. Thus it is even difficult to talk of 'religion' in this context, as though one could identify a separate and distinct element. But it is just this distinctiveness which can be identified in our culture. Religious apologists, not sceptics, stress the uniqueness of religious utterance. The slogan 'Every kind of utterance has its own kind of logic' finds a ready response from theologians.

The counterpart to this is an easy toleration for contradiction and incoherence, through the use of such concepts as 'the absurd' (Kierkegaard), 'paradox' (Barth) or 'mystery' (Marcel). We can in fact reach a point at which religion is made logically invulnerable. The attempt in the controversy over the falsification of religious assertions to show that if religion were irrefutable religious utterances would be deprived of sense failed for the same reason that attacks on Azande witchcraft would fail. Religious believers do know what would have to occur for their beliefs to be falsified—they can specify some occurrences with which the existence of omnipotent benevolence is incompatible ('utterly pointless evil' is one commonly used example). But just as the Azande can state what would falsify their assertions about witchcraft —but we could never know that such an occurrence had taken place— so the Christian will leave us in the same difficulty. For the after-life, that which we do not see, may always lend point to otherwise pointless evil, or absurd happenings. This line of argument is certainly open to attack; but the invocation of concepts such as 'mystery' or 'paradox' is always there in the background. Thus the logical invulnerability of Christianity seems to me a position that can be maintained.[1] But only at a cost. The cost is emptiness.

I have already produced reasons to explain why incoherences which only presented problems to an Occam could present insuperable obstacles to a T. H. Huxley or a Russell. But now I want to argue that the form of Christian apologetic on moral questions itself exhibits Christian concepts as irrelevant in the modern world in much the way in which the concepts of chivalry became irrelevant in the seventeenth century. For what Christian apologists try to show is that unless we live in a certain way certain ill consequences will follow (broken homes and delinquency, perhaps). But this turns Christianity into a testable nostrum. For we can always ask empirically: do particular religious practices in fact produce higher standards of behaviour? Again we return to the very simple point—are Christians in fact different from other people in our society, apart from their ritual practices? And if they are not what is the point of Christian belief, in so far as it issues an injunction? Now, whether Christians are different or not is an empirical question. Certainly empirical enquiry cannot tell us whether Christianity is true or not. But if Christian beliefs belong now to a social context in which their connection with behaviour has ceased to be clear (as it was clear in the Roman empire, say) the question of the truth of Christianity is put into a different perspective.

Christians here will perhaps want to point to the distinctively Christian forms of behaviour of the Confessional Church under Hitler, and this is certainly relevant. For the regressive primitivism of National Socialism with its idols provided a context sufficiently alike to that of early Christianity to make Christianity once more relevant. The Nazis desecularized society with a vengeance. But while to be asked

---

[1] As I myself did maintain it in 'The Logical Status of Religious Beliefs' in A. MacIntyre (Ed.) *Metaphysical Beliefs*, S.C.M. Press, 1957.

to choose for Christ has a clear meaning when the practical choices
are those of the Nazi society, does this injunction have a clear meaning
also in our society? And if it had would we not in fact find Christians
united on ways of behaving in a way that they are not?

From an historical point of view, of course, it is most unfair to
present Christianity as only the victim of secularization. Christianity,
especially Protestant Christianity, was itself a powerful secularizing
agent, destroying in the name of God any attempt to deify nature, and
so helping to rid the world of magic and making nature available for
scientific enquiry. The kind of negative theology which refuses to
identify any object with the divine (God is not this, not that) has its
final fruit in the kind of atheism which Simone Weil and Tillich both
see as a recognition of the fact that God cannot be identified with any
particular existing object. But what is left to Simone Weil or Tillich is
in fact a religious vocabulary without any remaining secular content.
Hegel's irreligion consists in his insight into the possibility of extracting
truth from its religious husks. Kierkegaard's answer to Hegel is the
assertion of a religion defined entirely in its own religious terms,
uncriticizable *ab externo*. Together Hegel and Kierkegaard reflect
accurately the status of religion in a secularized environment.

(*e*) For a sceptic to grasp the point of religious belief, therefore, he
has to supply a social context which is now lacking and abstract a
social context which is now present, and he has to do this for the
mediaeval Christian, just as the anthropologist has to do it for the
Azande or the aborigines. But in dialogue with contemporary Christians the sceptic is forced to recognize that they see a point in what
they say and do although they lack that context. And therefore either
he or they are making a mistake, and not a mistake over God, but a
mistake over criteria of intelligibility. What is at issue between sceptic
and Christian is the character of the difference between belief and
unbelief as well as the issue of belief itself. Thus the sceptic is committed to saying that he understands the Christian's use of concepts
in a way that the Christian himself does not, and presumably *vice versa*.
The discussion is therefore transferred to another level, and a Christian
refutation of this paper would have to provide an alternative account
of intelligibility. If I am right, understanding Christianity is incompatible with believing in it, not because Christianity is vulnerable to
sceptical objections, but because its peculiar invulnerability belongs
to it as a form of belief which has lost the social context which once
made it comprehensible. It is now too late to be mediaeval and it is

too empty and too easy to be Kierkegaardian. Thus sceptic and believer do not share a common grasp of the relevant concepts any more than anthropologist and Azande do. And if the believer wishes to he can always claim that we can only disagree with him because we do not understand him. But the implications of this defence of belief are more fatal to it than any attack could be.

5

Understanding a Primitive Society

PETER WINCH

This essay will pursue further some questions raised in my book, *The Idea of a Social Science*.[1] That book was a general discussion of what is involved in the understanding of human social life. I shall here be concerned more specifically with certain issues connected with social anthropology. In the first part I raise certain difficulties about Professor E. E. Evans-Pritchard's approach in his classic, *Witchcraft, Oracles and Magic among the Azande*.[2] In the second part, I attempt to refute some criticisms recently made by Mr Alasdair McIntyre of Evans-Pritchard and myself, to criticize in their turn MacIntyre's positive remarks, and to offer some further reflections of my own on the concept of learning from the study of a primitive society.

I. The Reality of Magic

Like many other primitive people, the African Azande hold beliefs that we cannot possibly share and engage in practices which it is peculiarly difficult for us to comprehend. They believe that certain of their members are witches, exercising a malignant occult influence on the lives of their fellows. They engage in rites to counteract witchcraft; they consult oracles and use magic medicines to protect themselves from harm.

An anthropologist studying such a people wishes to make those beliefs and practices intelligible to himself and his readers. This means presenting an account of them that will somehow satisfy the criteria of rationality demanded by the culture to which he and his readers belong:

This paper was first published in the *American Philosophical Quarterly* I, 1964, pp. 307–24.
[1] London and New York, 1958.
[2] Oxford, 1937.

a culture whose conception of rationality is deeply affected by the achievements and methods of the sciences, and one which treats such things as a belief in magic or the practice of consulting oracles as almost a paradigm of the irrational. The strains inherent in this situation are very likely to lead the anthropologist to adopt the following posture: *We* know that Zande beliefs in the influence of witchcraft, the efficacy of magic medicines, the role of oracles in revealing what is going on and what is going to happen, are mistaken, illusory. Scientific methods of investigation have shown conclusively that there are no relations of cause and effect such as are implied by these beliefs and practices. All we can do then is to show how such a system of mistaken beliefs and inefficacious practices can maintain itself in the face of objections that seem to us so obvious.[1]

Now although Evans-Pritchard goes a very great deal further than most of his predecessors in trying to present the sense of the institutions he is discussing as it presents itself to the Azande themselves, still, the last paragraph does, I believe, pretty fairly describe the attitude he himself took at the time of writing this book. There is more than one remark to the effect that 'obviously there are no witches'; and he writes of the difficulty he found, during his field work with the Azande, in shaking off the 'unreason' on which Zande life is based and returning to a clear view of how things really are. This attitude is not an unsophisticated one but is based on a philosophical position ably developed in a series of papers published in the 1930s in the unhappily rather inaccessible *Bulletin of the Faculty of Arts* of the University of Egypt. Arguing against Lévy-Bruhl, Evans-Pritchard here rejects the idea that the scientific understanding of causes and effects which leads us to reject magical ideas is evidence of any superior intelligence on our part. Our scientific approach, he points out, is as much a function of our culture as is the magical approach of the 'savage' a function of his:

> The fact that we attribute rain to meteorological causes alone while savages believe that Gods or ghosts or magic can influence the rainfall is no evidence that our brains function differently from their brains. It does not show that we 'think more logically' than savages, at least not if this expression suggests some kind of hereditary psychic

---

[1] At this point the anthropologist is very likely to start speaking of the 'social function' of the institution under examination. There are many important questions that should be raised about functional explanations and their relations to the issues discussed in this essay; but these questions cannot be pursued further here.

superiority. It is no sign of superior intelligence on my part that I attribute rain to physical causes. I did not come to this conclusion myself by observation and inference and have, in fact, little knowledge of the meteorological process that lead to rain, I merely accept what everybody else in my society accepts, namely that rain is due to natural causes. This particular idea formed part of my culture long before I was born into it and little more was required of me than sufficient linguistic ability to learn it. Likewise a savage who believes that under suitable natural and ritual conditions the rainfall can be influenced by use of appropriate magic is not on account of this belief to be considered of inferior intelligence. He did not build up this belief from his own observations and inferences but adopted it in the same way as he adopted the rest of his cultural heritage, namely, by being born into it. He and I are both thinking in patterns of thought provided for us by the societies in which we live.

It would be absurd to say that the savage is thinking mystically and that we are thinking scientifically about rainfall. In either case like mental processes are involved and, moreover, the content of thought is similarly derived. But we can say that the social content of our thought about rainfall is scientific, is in accord with objective facts, whereas the social content of savage thought about rainfall is unscientific since it is not in accord with reality and may also be mystical where it assumes the existence of supra-sensible forces.[1]

In a subsequent article on Pareto, Evans-Pritchard distinguishes between 'logical' and 'scientific'.

Scientific notions are those which accord with objective reality both with regard to the validity of their premises and to the inferences drawn from their propositions. . . . Logical notions are those in which according to the rules of thought inferences would be true were the premises true, the truth of the premises being irrelevant. . .

A pot has broken during firing. This is probably due to grit. Let us examine the pot and see if this is the cause. That is logical and scientific thought. Sickness is due to witchcraft. A man is sick. Let us consult the oracles to discover who is the witch responsible. That is logical and unscientific thought.[2]

I think that Evans-Pritchard is right in a great deal of what he says here, but wrong, and crucially wrong, in his attempt to characterize the scientific in terms of that which is 'in accord with objective reality'.

[1] E. E. Evans-Pritchard, 'Lévy-Bruhl's Theory of Primitive Mentality', *Bulletin of the Faculty of Arts*, University of Egypt, 1934.
[2] 'Science and Sentiment', *Bulletin of the Faculty of Arts*, ibid,. 1935.

Despite differences of emphasis and phraseology, Evans-Pritchard is in fact hereby put into the same metaphysical camp as Pareto: for both of them the conception of 'reality' must be regarded as intelligible and applicable *outside* the context of scientific reasoning itself, since it is that to which scientific notions do, and unscientific notions do not, have a relation. Evans-Pritchard, although he emphasizes that a member of scientific culture has a different conception of reality from that of a Zande believer in magic, wants to go beyond merely registering this fact and making the differences explicit, and to say, finally, that the scientific conception agrees with what reality actually is like, whereas the magical conception does not.

It would be easy, at this point, to say simply that the difficulty arises from the use of the unwieldy and misleadingly comprehensive expression 'agreement with reality'; and in a sense this is true. But we should not lose sight of the fact that the idea that men's ideas and beliefs must be checkable by reference to something independent—some reality— is an important one. To abandon it is to plunge straight into an extreme Protagorean relativism, with all the paradoxes that involves. On the other hand great care is certainly necessary in fixing the precise role that this conception of the independently real does play in men's thought. There are two related points that I should like to make about it at this stage.

In the first place we should notice that the check of the independently real is not peculiar to science. The trouble is that the fascination science has for us makes it easy for us to adopt its scientific form as a paradigm against which to measure the intellectual respectability of other modes of discourse. Consider what God says to Job out of the whirlwind: 'Who is this that darkeneth counsel by words without knowledge? . . . Where wast thou when I laid the foundations of the earth? declare, if thou hast understanding. Who hath laid the measures thereof, if thou knowest? or who hath stretched the line upon it. . . . Shall he that contendeth with the Almighty instruct him? he that reproveth God, let him answer it.' Job is taken to task for having gone astray by having lost sight of the reality of God; this does not, of course, mean that Job has made any sort of theoretical mistake, which could be put right, perhaps, by means of an experiment.[1] God's reality is certainly independent of what any man may care to think, but what that reality amounts

---

[1] Indeed, one way of expressing the point of the story of Job is to say that in it Job is shown as going astray by being induced to make the reality and goodness of God contingent on what happens.

to can only be seen from the religious tradition in which the concept of God is used, and this use is very unlike the use of scientific concepts, say of theoretical entities. The point is that it is *within* the religious use of language that the conception of God's reality has its place, though, I repeat, this does not mean that it is at the mercy of what anyone cares to say; if this were so, God would have no reality.

My second point follows from the first. Reality is not what gives language sense. What is real and what is unreal shows itself *in* the sense that language has. Further, both the distinction between the real and the unreal and the concept of agreement with reality themselves belong to our language. I will not say that they are concepts of the language like any other, since it is clear that they occupy a commanding, and in a sense a limiting, position there. We can imagine a language with no concept, of, say, wetness, but hardly one in which there is no way of distinguishing the real from the unreal. Nevertheless we could not in fact distinguish the real from the unreal without understanding the way this distinction operates in the language. If then we wish to understand the significance of these concepts, we must examine the use they actually do have—*in* the language.

Evans-Pritchard, on the contrary, is trying to work with a conception of reality which is *not* determined by its actual use in language. He wants something against which that use can itself be appraised. But this is not possible; and no more possible in the case of scientific discourse than it is in any other. We may ask whether a particular scientific hypothesis agrees with reality and test this by observation and experiment. Given the experimental methods, and the established use of the theoretical terms entering into the hypothesis, then the question whether it holds or not is settled by reference to something independent of what I, or anybody else, care to think. But the general nature of the data revealed by the experiment can only be specified in terms of criteria built into the methods of experiment employed and these, in turn, make sense only to someone who is conversant with the kind of scientific activity within which they are employed. A scientific illiterate, asked to describe the results of an experiment which he 'observes' in an advanced physics laboratory, could not do so in terms relevant to the hypothesis being tested; and it is really only in such terms that we can sensibly speak of the 'results of the experiment' at all. What Evans-Pritchard wants to be able to say is that the criteria applied in scientific experimentation constitute a true link between our ideas and an independent reality, whereas those characteristic of other systems of thought—in particular, magical methods of thought—do not. It is evident that the expressions 'true link' and 'independent reality' in the previous sentence cannot themselves be explained by reference to the scientific universe of discourse, as this would beg the question. We have then to ask how, by reference to what established universe of discourse, the use of those expressions *is* to be explained; and it is clear that Evans-Pritchard has not answered this question.

Two questions arise out of what I have been saying. First, is it in fact the case that a primitive system of magic, like that of the Azande, constitutes a coherent universe of discourse like science, in terms of which an intelligible conception of reality and clear ways of deciding what beliefs are and are not in agreement with this reality can be discerned! Second, what are we to make of the possibility of understanding primitive social institutions, like Zande magic, if the situation is as I have outlined? I do not claim to be able to give a satisfactory answer to the second question. It raises some very important and fundamental issues about the nature of human social life, which require conceptions different from, and harder to elucidate than, those I have hitherto introduced. I shall offer some tentative remarks about these issues in the second part of this essay. At present I shall address myself to the first question.

It ought to be remarked here that an affirmative answer to my first question would not commit me to accepting as rational all beliefs couched in magical concepts or all procedures practiced in the name of such beliefs. This is no more necessary than is the corresponding proposition that all procedures 'justified' in the name of science are immune from rational criticism. A remark of Collingwood's is apposite here:

> Savages are no more exempt from human folly than civilized men, and are no doubt equally liable to the error of thinking that they, or the persons they regard as their superiors, can do what in fact cannot be done. But this error is not the essence of magic; it is a perversion of magic. And we should be careful how we attribute it to the people we call savages, who will one day rise up and testify against us.[1]

It is important to distinguish a system of magical beliefs and practices like that of the Azande, which is one of the principal foundations of their whole social life and, on the other hand, magical beliefs that might be held, and magical rites that might be practised, by persons belonging

[1] R. G. Collingwood, *Principles of Art*, Oxford (Galaxy Books), 1958, p. 67.

to our own culture. These have to be understood rather differently. Evans-Pritchard is himself alluding to the difference in the following passage: 'When a Zande speaks of witchcraft he does not speak of it as we speak of the weird witchcraft of our own history. Witchcraft is to him a commonplace happening and he seldom passes a day without mentioning it. . . . To us witchcraft is something which haunted and disgusted our credulous forefathers. But the Zande expects to come across witchcraft at any time of the day or night. He would be just as surprised if he were not brought into daily contact with it as we would be if confronted by its appearance. To him there is nothing miraculous about it.'[1]

The difference is not merely one of degree of familiarity, however, although, perhaps, even this has more importance than might at first appear. Concepts of witchcraft and magic in our culture, at least since the advent of Christianity, have been parasitic on, and a perversion of other orthodox concepts, both religious and, increasingly, scientific. To take an obvious example, you could not understand what was involved in conducting a Black Mass, unless you were familiar with the conduct of a proper Mass and, therefore, with the whole complex of religious ideas from which the Mass draws its sense. Neither would you understand the relation between these without taking account of the fact that the Black practices are rejected as *irrational* (in the sense proper to religion) in the system of beliefs on which these practices are thus parasitic. Perhaps a similar relation holds between the contemporary practice of astrology and astronomy and technology. It is impossible to keep a discussion of the rationality of Black Magic or of astrology within the bounds of concepts peculiar to them; they have an essential reference to something outside themselves. The position is like that which Socrates, in Plato's *Gorgias*, showed to be true of the Sophists' conception of rhetoric: namely, that it is parasitic on rational discourse in such a way that its irrational character can be shown in terms of this dependence. Hence, when we speak of such practices as 'superstitious', 'illusory', 'irrational', we have the weight of our culture behind us; and this is not just a matter of being on the side of the big battalions, because those beliefs and practices belong to, and derive such sense as they seem to have, from that same culture. This enables us to show that the sense is only apparent, in terms which are culturally relevant.

It is evident that our relation to Zande magic is quite different. If

[1] *Witchcraft, Oracles and Magic among the Azande*, p. 64.

we wish to understand it, we must seek a foothold elsewhere. And while there may well be room for the use of such critical expressions as 'superstition' and 'irrationality', the kind of rationality with which such terms might be used to point a contrast remains to be elucidated. The remarks I shall make in Part II will have a more positive bearing on this issue. In the rest of this Part, I shall develop in more detail my criticisms of Evans-Pritchard's approach to the Azande.

Early in this book he defines certain categories in terms of which his descriptions of Zande customs are couched.

MYSTICAL NOTIONS . . . are patterns of thought that attribute to phenomena supra-sensible qualities which, or part of which, are not derived from observation or cannot be logically inferred from it, *and which they do not possess.*[1] COMMON-SENSE NOTIONS . . . attribute to phenomena only what men observe in them or what can logically be inferred from observation. So long as a notion does not assert something which has not been observed, it is not classed as mystical even though it is mistaken on account of incomplete observation. . . . SCIENTIFIC NOTIONS. Science has developed out of common sense but is far more methodical and has better techniques of observation and reasoning. Common sense uses experience and rules of thumb. Science uses experiment and rules of Logic. . . . *Our body of scientific knowledge and Logic are the sole arbiters of what are mystical, common sense, and scientific notions.* Their judgments are never absolute. RITUAL BEHAVIOUR. Any behaviour that is accounted for by mystical notions. *There is no objective nexus* between the behaviour and the event it is intended to cause. Such behaviour is usually intelligible to us only when we know the mystical notions associated with it. EMPIRICAL BEHAVIOUR. Any behaviour that is accounted for by common-sense notions.[2]

It will be seen from the phrases which I have italicized that Evans-Pritchard is doing more here than just defining certain terms for his own use. Certain metaphysical claims are embodied in the definitions: identical in substance with the claims embodied in Pareto's way of distinguishing between 'logical' and 'non-logical' conduct.[3] There is a very clear implication that those who use mystical notions and perform ritual behaviour are making some sort of mistake, detectable with the aid of science and logic. I shall now examine more closely

[1] The italics are mine throughout this quotation.
[2] Op. cit., p. 12.
[3] For further criticism of Pareto see Peter Winch, *The Idea of a Social Science*, pp. 95–111.

some of the institutions described by Evans–Pritchard to determine how far his claims are justified.

Witchcraft is a power possessed by certain individuals to harm other individuals by 'mystical' means. Its basis is an inherited organic condition, 'witchcraft-substance' and it does not involve any special magical ritual or medicine. It is constantly appealed to by Azande when they are afflicted by misfortune, not so as to exclude explanation in terms of natural causes, which Azande are perfectly able to offer themselves within the limits of their not inconsiderable natural knowledge, but so as to supplement such explanations. 'Witchcraft explains *why*[1] events are harmful to man and not *how*[1] they happen. A Zande perceives how they happen just as we do. He does not see a witch charge a man but an elephant. He does not see a witch push over the granary, but termites gnawing away its supports. He does not see a psychical flame igniting thatch, but an ordinary lighted bundle of straw. His perception of how events occur is as clear as our own.'[2]

The most important way of detecting the influence of witchcraft and of identifying witches is by the revelations of oracles, of which in turn the most important is the 'poison oracle'. This name, though convenient, is significantly misleading in so far as, according to Evans–Pritchard, Azande do not have our concept of a poison and do not think of, or behave towards, *benge*—the substance administered in the consultation of the oracle—as we do of and towards poisons. The gathering, preparation, and administering of *benge* is hedged with ritual and strict taboos. At an oracular consultation *benge* is administered to a fowl, while a question is asked in a form permitting a yes or no answer. The fowl's death or survival is specified beforehand as giving the answer 'yes' or 'no'. The answer is then checked by administering *benge* to another fowl and asking the question the other way round. 'Is Prince Ndoruma responsible for placing bad medicines in the roof of my hut? The fowl DIES giving the answer "Yes". . . . Did the oracle speak truly when it said that Ndoruma was responsible? The fowl SURVIVES giving the answer "Yes".' The poison oracle is all-pervasive in Zande life and all steps of any importance in a person's life are settled by reference to it.

A Zande would be utterly lost and bewildered without his oracle. The mainstay of his life would be lacking. It is rather as if an engineer, in our society, were to be asked to build a bridge without mathematical

[1] Evans–Pritchard's italics.
[2] Op. cit., p. 72.

calculation, or a military commander to mount an extensive co-ordinated attack without the use of clocks. These analogies are mine, but a reader may well think that they beg the question at issue. For, he may argue, the Zande practice of consulting the oracle, unlike my technological and military examples, is completely unintelligible and rests on an obvious illusion. I shall now consider this objection.

First I must emphasize that I have so far done little more than note the *fact*, conclusively established by Evans-Pritchard, that the Azande *do* in fact conduct their affairs to their own satisfaction in this way and are at a loss when forced to abandon the practice—when, for instance, they fall into the hands of European courts. It is worth remarking too that Evans-Pritchard himself ran his household in the same way during his field researches and says: 'I found this as satisfactory a way of running my home and affairs as any other I know of.'

Further, I would ask in my turn: *to whom* is the practice alleged to be unintelligible? Certainly it is difficult for us to understand what the Azande are about when they consult their oracles; but it might seem just as incredible to them that the engineer's motions with his slide rule could have any connection with the stability of his bridge. But this riposte of course misses the intention behind the objection, which was not directed to the question whether anyone in fact understands, or claims to understand, what is going on, but rather whether what is going on actually does make sense: i.e., in itself. And it may seem obvious that Zande beliefs in witchcraft and oracles cannot make any sense, however satisfied the Azande may be with them.

What criteria have we for saying that something does, or does not, make sense? A partial answer is that a set of beliefs and practices cannot make sense in so far as they involve contradictions. Now it appears that contradictions are bound to arise in at least two ways in the consultation of the oracle. On the one hand two oracular pronouncements may contradict each other; and on the other hand a self-consistent oracular pronouncement may be contradicted by future experience. I shall examine each of these apparent possibilities in turn.

Of course, it does happen often that the oracle first says 'yes' and then 'no' to the same question. This does not convince a Zande of the futility of the whole operation of consulting oracles: obviously, it cannot, since otherwise the practice could hardly have developed and maintained itself at all. Various explanations may be offered, whose possibility, it is important to notice, is built into the whole network of Zande beliefs and may, therefore, be regarded as belonging to the concept of an oracle. It may be said, for instance, that bad *benge* is being used; that the operator of the oracle is ritually unclean; that the oracle is being itself influenced by witchcraft or sorcery; or it may be that the oracle is showing that the question cannot be answered straightforwardly in its present form, as with 'Have you stopped beating your wife yet?' There are various ways in which the behaviour of the fowl under the influence of *benge* may be ingeniously interpreted by those wise in the ways of the poison oracle. We might compare this situation perhaps with the interpretation of dreams.

In the other type of case: where an internally consistent oracular revelation is apparently contradicted by subsequent experience, the situation may be dealt with in a similar way, by references to the influence of witchcraft, ritual uncleanliness, and so on. But there is another important consideration we must take into account here too. The chief function of oracles is to reveal the presence of 'mystical' forces—I use Evans-Pritchard's term without committing myself to his denial that such forces really exist. Now though there are indeed ways of determining whether or not mystical forces are operating, these ways do not correspond to what we understand by 'empirical' confirmation or refutation. This indeed is a tautology, since such differences in 'confirmatory' procedures are the main criteria for classifying something as a mystical force in the first place. Here we have one reason why the possibilities of 'refutation by experience' are very much fewer than might at first sight be supposed.

There is also another closely connected reason. The spirit in which oracles are consulted is very unlike that in which a scientist makes experiments. Oracular revelations are not treated as hypotheses and, since their sense derives from the way they are treated in their context, they therefore *are not* hypotheses. They are not a matter of intellectual interest but the main way in which Azande decide how they should act. If the oracle reveals that a proposed course of action is fraught with mystical dangers from witchcraft or sorcery, that course of action will not be carried out; and then the question of refutation or confirmation just does not arise. We might say that the revelation has the logical status of an unfulfilled hypothetical, were it not that the context in which this logical term is generally used may again suggest a mis-leadingly close analogy with scientific hypotheses.

I do not think that Evans-Pritchard would have disagreed with what I have said so far. Indeed, the following comment is on very similar lines:

Azande observe the action of the poison oracle as we observe it, but their observations are always subordinated to their beliefs and are incorporated into their beliefs and made to explain them and justify them. Let the reader consider any argument that would utterly demolish all Zande claims for the power of the oracle. If it were translated into Zande modes of thought it would serve to support their entire structure of belief. For their mystical notions are eminently coherent, being interrelated by a network of logical ties, and are so ordered that they never too crudely contradict sensory experience but, instead, experience seems to justify them. The Zande is immersed in a sea of mystical notions, and if he speaks about his poison oracle he must speak in a mystical idiom.[1]

To locate the point at which the important philosophical issue does arise, I shall offer a parody, composed by changing round one or two expressions in the foregoing quotation.

Europeans observe the action of the poison oracle just as Azande observe it, but their observations are always subordinated to their beliefs and are incorporated into their beliefs and made to explain them and justify them. Let a Zande consider any argument that would utterly refute all European scepticism about the power of the oracle. If it were translated into European modes of thought it would serve to support their entire structure of belief. For their scientific notions are eminently coherent, being interrelated by a network of logical ties, and are so ordered that they never too crudely contradict mystical experience but, instead, experience seems to justify them. The European is immersed in a sea of scientific notions, and if he speaks about the Zande poison oracle he must speak in a scientific idiom.

Perhaps this too would be acceptable to Evans-Pritchard. But it is clear from other remarks in the book to which I have alluded, that at the time of writing it he would have wished to add: and the European is right and the Zande wrong. This addition I regard as illegitimate and my reasons for so thinking take us to the heart of the matter.

It may be illuminating at this point to compare the disagreement between Evans-Pritchard and me to that between the Wittgenstein of the *Philosophical Investigations* and his earlier *alter ego* of the *Tractatus Logico-Philosophicus*. In the *Tractatus* Wittgenstein sought 'the general form of propositions': what made propositions possible. He said that this general form is: 'This is how things are'; the proposition was an

[1] Ibid., p. 319.

articulated model, consisting of elements standing in a definite relation
to each other. The proposition was true when there existed a corresponding arrangement of elements in reality. The proposition was
capable of saying something because of the identity of structure, of
logical form, in the proposition and in reality.

By the time Wittgenstein composed the *Investigations* he had come
to reject the whole idea that there must be a general form of propositions. He emphasized the indefinite number of different uses that
language may have and tried to show that these different uses neither
need, nor in fact do, all have something in common, in the sense
intended in the *Tractatus*. He also tried to show that what counts as
'agreement or disagreement with reality' takes on as many different
forms as there are different use of language and cannot, therefore, be
taken as given *prior* to the detailed investigation of the use that is in
question.

The *Tractatus* contains a remark strikingly like something that
Evans-Pritchard says.

> *The limits of my language mean the limits of my world.* Logic fills the
> world: the limits of the world are also its limits. We cannot therefore
> say in logic: This and this there is in the world, and that there is not.
>   For that would apparently presuppose that we exclude certain
> possibilities, and this cannot be the case since otherwise logic must
> get outside the limits of the world: that is, if it could consider these
> limits from the other side also.[1]

Evans-Pritchard discusses the phenomena of belief and scepticism, as
they appear in Zande life. There *is* certainly widespread scepticism
about certain things, for instance, about some of the powers claimed
by witchdoctors or about the efficacy of certain magic medicines. But,
he points out, such scepticism does not begin to overturn the mystical
way of thinking, since it is necessarily expressed in terms belonging to
that way of thinking.

> In this web of belief every strand depends on every other strand, and
> a Zande cannot get outside its meshes because this is the only world
> he knows. The web is not an external structure in which he is
> enclosed. It is the texture of his thought and he cannot think that
> his thought is wrong.[2]

Wittgenstein and Evans-Pritchard are concerned here with much

[1] Wittgenstein, *Tractatus Logico-Philosophicus*, 5. 6–5. 61.
[2] Evans-Pritchard, op. cit., p. 194.

the same problem, though the difference in the directions from which they approach it is important too. Wittgenstein, at the time of the *Tractatus*, spoke of 'language', as if all language is fundamentally of the same kind and must have the same kind of 'relation to reality'; but Evans-Pritchard is confronted by two languages which he recognizes as fundamentally different in kind, such that much of what may be expressed in the one has no possible counterpart in the other. One might, therefore, have expected this to lead to a position closer to that of the *Philosophical Investigations* than to that of the *Tractatus*. Evans-Pritchard is not content with elucidating the differences in the two concepts of reality involved; he wants to go further and say: our concept of reality is the correct one, the Azande are mistaken. But the difficulty is to see what 'correct' and 'mistaken' can mean in this context.

Let me return to the subject of contradictions. I have already noted that many contradictions we might expect to appear in fact do not in the context of Zande thought, where provision is made for avoiding them. But there are some situations of which this does not seem to be true, where what appear to us as obvious contradictions are left where they are, apparently unresolved. Perhaps this may be the foothold we are looking for, from which we can appraise the 'correctness' of the Zande system.[1]

Consider Zande notions about the inheritance of witchcraft. I have spoken so far only of the role of oracles in establishing whether or not someone is a witch. But there is a further and, as we might think, more 'direct' method of doing this, namely by post-mortem examination of a suspect's intestines for 'witchcraft-substance'. This may be arranged by his family after his death in an attempt to clear the family name of the imputation of witchcraft. Evans-Pritchard remarks: 'To our minds it appears evident that if a man is proven a witch the whole of his clan are *ipso facto* witches, since the Zande clan is a group of persons related biologically to one another through the male line. Azande see the sense of this argument but they do not accept its conclusions, and it would involve the whole notion of witchcraft in contradiction were they to do so.'[2] Contradiction would presumably arise because a few positive results of post-mortem examinations, scattered among all the clans, would very soon prove that everybody was a witch, and a few negative results, scattered among the same clans, would prove that

[1] I shall discuss this point in a more general way in Part II.
[2] Ibid., p. 24.

nobody was a witch. Though, in particular situations, individual
Azande may avoid personal implications arising out of the presence of
witchcraft-substance in deceased relatives, by imputations of bastardy
and similar devices, this would not be enough to save the generally
contradictory situation I have sketched. Evans-Pritchard comments:
'Azande do not perceive the contradiction as we perceive it because
they have no theoretical interest in the subject, and those situations in
which they express their belief in witchcraft do not force the problem
upon them.'[1]

It might now appear as though we had clear grounds for speaking
of the superior rationality of European over Zande thought, in so far as
the latter involves a contradiction which it makes no attempt to
remove and does not even recognize: one, however, which is recognizable as such in the context of European ways of thinking. But does
Zande thought on this matter really involve a contradiction? It appears
from Evans-Pritchard's account that Azande do not press their ways of
thinking about witches to a point at which they would be involved
in contradictions.

Someone may now want to say that the irrationality of the Azande
in relation to witchcraft shows itself in the fact that they do not press
their thought about it 'to its logical conclusion'. To appraise this point
we must consider whether the conclusion we are trying to force on
them is indeed a logical one; or perhaps better, whether someone who
does press this conclusion is being more rational than the Azande, who
do not. Some light is thrown on this question by Wittgenstein's
discussion of a game,

> such that whoever begins can always win by a particular simple
> trick. But this has not been realized—so it is a game. Now someone
> draws our attention to it—and it stops being a game.
>
> What turn can I give this, to make it clear to myself?—For I want
> to say: 'and it stops being a game'—not: 'and now we see that it
> wasn't a game.'
>
> That means, I want to say, it can also be taken like this: the other
> man did not *draw our attention* to anything; he taught us a different
> game in place of our own. But how can the new game have made
> the old one obsolete? We now see something different, and can no
> longer naïvely go on playing.
>
> On the one hand the game consisted in our actions (our play) on
> the board; and these actions I could perform as well now as before.

[1] Ibid., p. 25.

But on the other hand it was essential to the game that I blindly tried to win; and now I can no longer do that.[1]

There are obviously considerable analogies between Wittgenstein's example and the situation we are considering. But there is an equally important difference. Both Wittgenstein's games: the old one without the trick that enables the starter to win and the new one with the trick, are in an important sense on the same level. They are both *games*, in the form of a contest where the aim of a player is to beat his opponent by the exercise of skill. The new trick makes this situation impossible and this is why it makes the old game obsolete. To be sure, the situation could be saved in a way by introducing a new rule, forbidding the use by the starter of the trick which would ensure his victory. But our intellectual habits are such as to make us unhappy about the artificiality of such a device, rather as logicians have been unhappy about the introduction of a Theory of Types as a device for avoiding Russell's paradoxes. It is noteworthy in my last quotation from Evans-Pritchard however, that the Azande, when the possibility of this contradiction about the inheritance of witchcraft is pointed out to them, do *not* then come to regard their old beliefs about witchcraft as obsolete. 'They have no theoretical interest in the subject.' This suggests strongly that the context from which the suggestion about the contradiction is made, the context of our scientific culture, is not on the same level as the context in which the beliefs about witchcraft operate. Zande notions of witchcraft do not constitute a theoretical system in terms of which Azande try to gain a quasi-scientific understanding of the world.[2] This in its turn suggests that it is the European, obsessed with pressing Zande thought where it would not naturally go—to a contradiction— who is guilty of misunderstanding, not the Zande. The European is in fact committing a category-mistake.

Something else is also suggested by this discussion: the forms in which rationality expresses itself in the culture of a human society cannot be elucidated *simply* in terms of the logical coherence of the rules according to which activities are carried out in that society. For, as we have seen, there comes a point where we are not even in a

---

[1] L. Wittgenstein, *Remarks on the Foundations of Mathematics*, Pt. II, Para. 77. Wittgenstein's whole discussion of 'contradiction' in mathematics is directly relevant to the point I am discussing.

[2] Notice that I have *not* said that Azande conceptions of witchcraft have nothing to do with understanding the world at all. The point is that a different form of the concept of understanding is involved here.

position to determine what is and what is not coherent in such a context of rules, without raising questions about the point which following those rules has in the society. No doubt it was a realization of this fact which led Evans-Pritchard to appeal to a residual 'correspondence with reality' in distinguishing between 'mystical' and 'scientific' notions. The conception of reality is indeed indispensable to any understanding of the point of a way of life. But it is not a conception which can be explicated as Evans-Pritchard tries to explicate it, in terms of what science reveals to be the case; for a form of the conception of reality must already be presupposed before we can make any sense of the expression 'what science reveals to be the case'.

II. Our Standards and Theirs

In Part I, I attempted, by analysing a particular case, to criticize by implication a particular view of how we can understand a primitive institution. In this Part I shall have two aims. First, I shall examine in a more formal way a general philosophical argument, which attempts to show that the approach I have been criticizing is in principle the right one. This argument has been advanced by Mr Alasdair MacIntyre in two places: (a) in a paper entitled *Is Understanding Religion Compatible with Believing?* read to the Sesquicentennial Seminar of the Princeton Theological Seminar in 1962.[1] (b) In a contribution to *Philosophy, Politics and Society (Second Series)*,[2] entitled *A Mistake about Causality in Social Science*. Next, I shall make some slightly more positive suggestions about how to overcome the difficulty from which I started: how to make intelligible in our terms institutions belonging to a primitive culture, whose standards of rationality and intelligibility are apparently quite at odds with our own.

The relation between MacIntyre, Evans-Pritchard, and myself is a complicated one. MacIntyre takes Evans-Pritchard's later book, *Nuer Religion*, as an application of a point of view like mine in *The Idea of a Social Science*; he regards it as an object lesson in the absurd results to which such a position leads, when applied in practice. My own criticisms of Evans-Pritchard, on the other hand, have come from precisely the opposite direction. I have tried to show that Evans-Pritchard did not at the time of writing *The Azande* agree with me *enough*; that he

[1] Published along with other papers in *Faith and the Philosophers*, ed. John Hick. See above pp. 62–77.

[2] Edited by Peter Laslett and W. G. Runciman, Oxford: Blackwell, 1962.

did not take seriously enough the idea that the concepts used by primitive peoples can only be interpreted in the context of the way of life of those peoples. Thus I have in effect argued that Evans-Pritchard's account of the Azande is unsatisfactory precisely to the extent that he agrees with MacIntyre and not me.

The best point at which to start considering MacIntyre's position is that at which he agrees with me—in emphasizing the importance of possibilities of *description* for the concept of human action. An agent's action 'is identified fundamentally as what it is by the description under which he deems it to fall'. Since, further, descriptions must be intelligible to other people, an action 'must fall under some description which is socially recognizable as the description of an action'.[1] 'To identify the limits of social action in a given period', therefore, 'is to identify the stock of descriptions current in that age'.[2] MacIntyre correctly points out that descriptions do not exist in isolation, but occur 'as constituents of beliefs, speculations and projects'. As these in turn 'are continually criticized, modified, rejected, or improved, the stock of descriptions changes. The changes in human action are thus intimately linked to the thread of rational criticism in human history.'

This notion of rational criticism, MacIntyre points out, requires the notion of choice between alternatives, to explain which 'is a matter of making clear what the agent's criterion was and why he made use of this criterion rather than another and to explain why the use of this criterion appears rational to those who invoke it'.[3] Hence 'in explaining the rules and conventions to which action in a given social order conform [sic] we cannot omit reference to the rationality or otherwise of those rules and conventions'. Further, 'the beginning of an explanation of why certain criteria are taken to be rational in some societies is that they *are* rational. And since this has to enter into our explanation we cannot explain social behaviour independently of our own norms of rationality.'

I turn now to criticism of this argument. Consider first MacIntyre's account of changes in an existing 'stock' of available descriptions of actions. How does a candidate for inclusion *qualify* for admission to the stock? Unless there are limits, all MacIntyre's talk about possibilities of description circumscribing possibilities of action becomes nugatory, for there would be nothing to stop anybody inventing some arbitrary

[1] Ibid., p. 58.
[2] Ibid., p. 60.
[3] Ibid., p. 61.

verbal expression, applying to it some arbitrary bodily movement, and thus adding that expression to the stock of available descriptions. But of course the new description must be an *intelligible* one. Certainly, its intelligibility cannot be decided by whether or not it belongs to an *existing* stock of descriptions, since this would rule out precisely what is being discussed: the addition of *new* descriptions to the stock. 'What can intelligibly be said' is not equivalent to 'what has been intelligibly said', or it would never be possible to say anything new. *Mutatis mutandis* it would never be possible to *do* anything new. Nevertheless the intelligibility of anything new said or done does depend in a certain way on what already has been said or done and understood. The crux of this problem lies in how we are to understand that 'in a certain way'.

In *Is Understanding Religion Compatible with Believing?* MacIntyre asserts that the development through criticism of the standards of intelligibility current in a society is ruled out by my earlier account (in *The Idea of a Social Science*) of the origin in social institutions themselves of such standards. I shall not now repeat my earlier argument, but simply point out that I did, in various passages,[1] emphasize the *open* character of the 'rules' which I spoke of in connection with social institutions: i.e. the fact that in changing social situations, reasoned decisions have to be made about what is to count as 'going on in the same way'. MacIntyre's failure to come to terms with this point creates difficulties for him precisely analogous to those which he mistakenly attributes to my account.

It is a corollary of his argument up to this point, as well as being intrinsically evident, that a new description of action must be intelligible to the members of the society in which it is introduced. On my view the point is that what determines this is the further development of rules and principles already implicit in the previous ways of acting and talking. To be emphasized are not the actual members of any 'stock' of descriptions; but the *grammar* which they express. It is through this that we understand their structure and sense, their mutual relations, and the sense of new ways of talking and acting that may be introduced. These new ways of talking and acting may very well at the same time involve modifications in the grammar, but we can only speak thus if the new grammar is (to its users) intelligibly related to the old.

But what of the intelligibility of such changes to observers from another society with a different culture and different standards of intelligibility? MacIntyre urges that such observers must make clear

[1] Pp. 57–65; 91–94; 121–23.

'what the agent's criterion was and why he made use of this criterion rather than another and why the use of this criterion appears rational to those who invoke it'. Since what is at issue is the precise relation between the concepts of rationality current in these different societies it is obviously of first importance to be clear about *whose* concept of rationality is being alluded to in this quotation. It seems that it must be that which is current in the society in which the criterion is invoked. Something can appear rational to someone only in terms of *his* understanding of what is and is not rational. If *our* concept of rationality is a different one from his, then it makes no sense to say that anything either does or does not appear rational to *him* in *our* sense.

When MacIntyre goes on to say that the observer 'cannot omit reference to the rationality or otherwise of those rules and conventions' followed by the alien agent, whose concept of rationality is now in question: ours or the agent's? Since the observer must be understood now as addressing himself to members of his own society, it seems that the reference must here be to the concept of rationality current in the observer's society. Thus there is a *non sequitur* in the movement from the first to the second of the passages just quoted.

MacIntyre's thought here and in what immediately follows, seems to be this. The explanation of why, in Society *S*, certain actions are taken to be rational, has got to be an explanation for *us*; so it must be in terms of concepts intelligible to us. If then, in the explanation, we say that in fact those criteria *are* rational, we must be using the word '*rational*' in *our* sense. For this explanation would require that we had previously carried out an independent investigation into the actual rationality or otherwise of those criteria, and we could do this only in terms of an understood concept of rationality—*our* understood concept of rationality. The explanation would run: members of Society *S* have seen to be the case something that we know to be the case. If 'what is seen to be the case' is common to us and them, it must be referred to under the same concept for each of us.

But obviously this explanation is not open to us. For we start from the position that standards of rationality in different societies do not always coincide; from the possibility, therefore, that the standards of rationality current in *S* are different from our own. So we cannot assume that it will make sense to speak of members of *S* as discovering something which we have also discovered; such discovery presupposes initial conceptual agreement.

Part of the trouble lies in MacIntyre's use of the expression, 'the rationality of criteria', which he does not explain. In the present context to speak thus is to cloak the real problem, since what we are concerned with are differences in *criteria of rationality*. MacIntyre seems to be saying that certain standards are taken as criteria of rationality because they *are* criteria of rationality. But whose?

There are similar confusions in MacIntyre's other paper: *Is Understanding Religion Compatible with Believing?*[1] There he argues that when we detect an internal incoherence in the standards of intelligibility current in an lien society and try to show why this does not appear, or is made tolerable to that society's members, 'we have already invoked our standards'. In what sense is this true? In so far as *we* 'detect' and 'show' something, obviously we do so in a sense intelligible to us; so we are limited by what *counts* (for us) as 'detecting', 'showing' something. Further, it may well be that the interest in showing and detecting such things is peculiar to our society—that we are doing something in which members of the studied society exhibit no interest, because the institutions in which such an interest could develop are lacking. Perhaps too the pursuit of that interest in our society has led to the development of techniques of inquiry and modes of argument which again are not to be found in the life of the studied society. But it cannot be guaranteed in advance that the methods and techniques we have used in the past— e.g., in elucidating the logical structure of arguments in our own language and culture—are going to be equally fruitful in this new context. They will perhaps need to be extended and modified. No doubt, if they are to have a logical relation to our previous forms of investigation, the new techniques will have to be recognizably continuous with previously used ones. But they must also so extend our conception of intelligibility as to make it possible for us to see what intelligibility amounts to in the life of the society we are investigating.

The task MacIntyre says we must undertake is to make intelligible (*a*) (to us) why it is that members of S think that certain of their practices are intelligible (*b*) (to them), when in fact they are not. I have introduced differentiating letters into my two uses of 'intelligible', to mark the complexity that MacIntyre's way of stating the position does not bring out: the fact that we are dealing with two different senses of the word 'intelligible'. The relation between these is precisely the question at issue. MacIntyre's task is not like that of making intelligible a natural phenomenon, where we are limited only by what counts as intelligibility for us. We must somehow bring S's conception of

[1] See above, pp. 62–77.

intelligibility (*b*) into (intelligible!) relation with our own conception of intelligibility (*a*). That is, we have to create a new unity for the concept of intelligibility, having a certain relation to our old one and perhaps requiring a considerable realignment of our categories. We are not seeking a state in which things will appear to us just as they do to members of *S*, and perhaps such a state is unattainable anyway. But we *are* seeking a way of looking at things which goes beyond our previous way in that it has in some way taken account of and incorporated the other way that members of *S* have of looking at things. Seriously to study another way of life is necessarily to seek to extend our own—not simply to bring the other way within the already existing boundaries of our own, because the point about the latter in their present form, is that they *ex hypothesi* exclude that other.

There is a dimension to the notions of rationality and intelligibility which may make it easier to grasp the possibility of such an extension. I do not think that MacIntyre takes sufficient account of this dimension and, indeed, the way he talks about 'norms of rationality' obscures it. Rationality is not *just* a concept *in* a language like any other; it is this too, for, like any other concept it must be circumscribed by an established use: a use, that is, established in the language. But I think it is not a concept which a language may, as a matter of fact, have and equally well may not have, as is, for instance, the concept of politeness. It is a concept necessary to the existence of any language: to say of a society that it has a language[1] is also to say that it has a concept of rationality. There need not perhaps be any *word* functioning in its language as 'rational' does in ours, but at least there must be features of its members' use of languages analogous to those features of *our* use of language which are connected with our use of the word 'rational'. Where there is language it must make a difference what is said and this is only possible where the saying of one thing rules out, on pain of failure to communicate, the saying of something else. So in one sense MacIntyre is right in saying that we have already invoked our concept of rationality in saying of a collection of people that they constitute a society with a language: in the sense, namely, that we imply formal analogies between their behaviour and that behaviour in our society which we refer to in distinguishing between rationality and irrationality. This, however, is so far to say nothing about what in particular constitutes rational behaviour in that society; that would require more particular knowledge about the norms they appeal to in living their

---

[1] I shall not discuss here what justifies us in saying *this* in the first place.

lives. In other words, it is not so much a matter of invoking 'our own norms of rationality' as of invoking our notion of rationality in speaking of their behaviour in terms of 'conformity to norms'. But how precisely this notion is to be applied to them will depend on our reading of their conformity to norms—what counts for them as conformity and what does not.

Earlier I criticized MacIntyre's conception of a 'stock of available descriptions'. Similar criticisms apply to his talk about 'our norms of rationality', if these norms are taken as forming some finite set. Certainly we learn to think, speak, and act rationally *through* being trained to adhere to particular norms. But having learned to speak, etc., rationally does not *consist* in having been trained to follow those norms; to suppose that would be to overlook the importance of the phrase 'and so on' in any description of what someone who follows norms does. We must, if you like, be open to new possibilities of what could be invoked and accepted under the rubric of 'rationality'— possibilities which are perhaps suggested and limited by what we have hitherto so accepted, but not uniquely determined thereby.

This point can be applied to the possibilities of our grasping forms of rationality different from ours in an alien culture. First, as I have indicated, these possibilities are limited by certain formal requirements centering round the demand for consistency. But these formal requirements tell us nothing about what in particular is to *count* as consistency, just as the rules of the propositional calculus limit, but do not themselves determine what are to be proper values of p, q, etc. We can only determine this by investigating the wider context of the life in which the activities in question are carried on. This investigation will, take us beyond merely specifying the rules governing the carrying out of those activities. For, as MacIntyre quite rightly says, to note that certain rules are followed is so far to say nothing about the *point* of the rules; it is not even to decide whether or not they have a point at all.

MacIntyre's recipe for deciding this is that 'in bringing out this feature of the case one shows also whether the use of this concept is or is not a possible one for people who have the standards of intelligibility in speech and action which we have'.[1] It is important to notice that his argument, contrary to what he supposes, does not in fact show that our *own* standards of rationality occupy a peculiarly central position. The appearance to the contrary is an optical illusion engendered by the fact that MacIntyre's case has been advanced in the English language

---

[1] *Is Understanding Religion Compatible with Believing?* Above, p. 69.

and in the context of 20th century European culture. But a formally similar argument could be advanced in *any* language containing concepts playing a similar role in that language to those of 'intelligibility' and 'rationality' in ours. This shows that, so far from overcoming relativism, as he claims, MacIntyre himself falls into an extreme form of it. He disguises this from himself by committing the very error of which, wrongly as I have tried to show, he accuses me: the error of overlooking the fact that 'criteria and concepts have a history'. While he emphasizes this point when he is dealing with the concepts and criteria governing action in particular social contexts, he forgets it when he comes to talk of the *criticism* of such criteria. Do not the criteria appealed to in the criticism of existing institutions equally have a history? And in whose society do they have that history? MacIntyre's implicit answer is that it is in ours; but if we are to speak of difficulties and incoherencies appearing and being detected in the way certain practices have hitherto been carried on in a society, surely this can only be understood in connection with problems arising *in* the carrying on of the activity. Outside that context we could not begin to grasp what was problematical.

Let me return to the Azande and consider something which Mac-Intyre says about them, intended to support the position I am criticizing

> The Azande believe that the performance of certain rites in due form affects their common welfare; this belief cannot in fact be refuted. For they also believe that if the rites are ineffective it is because someone present at them had evil thoughts. Since this is always possible, there is never a year when it is unavoidable for them to admit that the rites were duly performed, but they did not thrive. Now the belief of the Azande is not unfalsifiable in principle (we know perfectly well what would falsify it—the conjunction of the rite, no evil thoughts and disasters). But in fact it cannot be falsified. Does this belief stand in need of rational criticism? And if so by what standards? It seems to me that one could not hold the belief of the Azande rational *in the absence of* any practice of science and technology in which criteria of effectiveness, ineffectiveness and kindred notions had been built up. But to say this is to recognize the appropriateness of scientific criteria of judgment from our standpoint. The Azande do not intend their belief either as a piece of science or as a piece of non-science. They do not possess these categories. It is only *post eventum*, in the light of later and more sophisticated understanding that their belief and concepts can be classified and evaluated at all.[1]

[1] Ibid. Above, p. 67.

Now in one sense classification and evaluation of Zande beliefs and concepts does require 'a more sophisticated understanding' than is found in Zande culture; for the sort of classification and evaluation that are here in question are sophisticated philosophical activities. But this is not to say that Zande forms of life are to be classified and evaluated in the way MacIntyre asserts: in terms of certain specific forms of life to be found in our culture, according as they do or do not measure up to what is required within these. MacIntyre confuses the sophistication of the interest in classification with the sophistication of the concepts employed in our classificatory work. It is of interest to us to understand how Zande magic is related to science; the concepts of such a comparison is a very sophisticated one; but this does not mean that we have to see the unsophisticated Zande practice in the light of more sophisticated practices in our own culture, like science—as perhaps a more primitive form of it. MacIntyre criticizes, justly, Sir James Frazer for having imposed the image of his own culture on more primitive ones; but that is exactly what MacIntyre himself is doing here. It is extremely difficult for a sophisticated member of a sophisticated society to grasp a very simple and primitive form of life: in a way he must jettison his sophistication, a process which is itself perhaps the ultimate in sophistication. Or, rather, the distinction between sophistication and simplicity becomes unhelpful at this point.

It may be true, as MacIntyre says, that the Azande do not have the categories of science and non-science. But Evans-Pritchard's account shows that they do have a fairly clear working distinction between the technical and the magical. It is neither here nor there that individual Azande may sometimes confuse the categories, for such confusions may take place in any culture. A much more important fact to emphasize is that *we* do not initially have a category that looks at all like the Zande category of magic. Since it is we who want to understand the Zande category, it appears that the onus is on us to extend our understanding so as to make room for the Zande category, rather than to insist on seeing it in terms of our own ready-made distinction between science and non-science. Certainly the sort of understanding we seek requires that we see the Zande category in relation to our own already understood categories. But this neither means that it is right to 'evaluate' magic in terms of criteria belonging to those other categories; nor does it give any clue as to *which* of our existing categories of thought will provide the best point of reference from which we can understand the point of the Zande practices.

MacIntyre has no difficulty in showing that *if* the rites which the Azande perform in connection with their harvests are 'classified and evaluated' by reference to the criteria and standards of science or technology, then they are subject to serious criticism. He thinks that the Zande 'belief' is a sort of *hypothesis* like, e.g., an Englishman's belief that all the heavy rain we have been having is due to atomic explosions.[1] MacIntyre believes that he is applying as it were a neutral concept of '*A* affecting *B*', equally applicable to Zande magic and western science. In fact, however, he is applying the concept with which *he* is familiar, one which draws its significance from its use in scientific and technological contexts. There is no reason to suppose that the Zande magical concept of '*A* affecting *B*' has anything like the same significance. On the contrary, since the Azande do, in the course of their practical affairs, apply something very like our technical concept— though perhaps in a more primitive form—and since their attitude to and thought about their magical rites are quite different from those concerning their technological measures, there is every reason to think that their concept of magical 'influence' is quite different. This may be easier to accept if it is remembered that, even in our own culture, the concept of causal influence is by no means monolithic: when we speak, for example, of 'what made Jones get married', we are not saying the same kind of thing as when we speak of 'what made the aeroplane crash'; I do not mean simply that the events of which we speak are different in kind but that the relation between the events is different also. It should not then be difficult to accept that in a society with quite different institutions and ways of life from our own, there may be concepts of 'causal influence' which behave even more differently.

But I do not want to say that we are quite powerless to find ways of thinking in our own society that will help us to see the Zande institution in a clearer light. I only think that the direction in which we should look is quite different from what MacIntyre suggests. Clearly the nature of Zande life is such that it is of very great importance to them that their crops should thrive. Clearly too they take all kinds of practical 'technological' steps, within their capabilities, to ensure that they *do* thrive. But that is no reason to see their magical rites as a further, misguided such step. A man's sense of the importance of something to

---

[1] In what follows I have been helped indirectly, but greatly, by some unpublished notes made by Wittgenstein on Frazer, which Mr Rush Rhees was kind enough to show me; and also by various scattered remarks on folklore in *The Notebooks* of Simone Weil, London, 1963.

him shows itself in all sorts of ways: not merely in precautions to safeguard that thing. He may want to come to terms with its importance to him in quite a different way: to contemplate it, to gain some sense of his life in relation to it. He may wish thereby, in a certain sense, to *free* himself from dependence on it. I do not mean by making sure that it does not let him down, because the point is that, *whatever* he does, he may still be let down. The important thing is that he should understand *that* and come to terms with it. Of course, merely to understand that is not to come to terms with it, though perhaps it is a necessary condition for so doing, for a man may equally well be transfixed and terrorized by the contemplation of such a possibility. He must see that he can still go on even if he is let down by what is vitally important to him; and he must so order his life that he still *can* go on in such circumstances. I stress once again that I do not mean this in the sense of becoming 'technologically independent', because from the present point of view technological independence is yet another form of dependence. Technology destroys some dependencies but always creates new ones, which may be fiercer—because harder to understand—than the old. This should be particularly apparent to *us*.[1]

In Judaeo-Christian cultures the conception of 'If it be Thy Will', as developed in the story of Job, is clearly central to the matter I am discussing. Because this conception is central to Christian prayers of supplication, they may be regarded from one point of view as freeing the believer from dependence on what he is supplicating for.[2] Prayers cannot play this role if they are regarded as a means of influencing the outcome for in that case the one who prays is still dependent on the outcome. He frees himself from this by acknowledging his complete dependence on God; and this is totally unlike any dependence on the outcome precisely because God is eternal and the outcome contingent.

I do not say that Zande magical rites are at all like Christian prayers of supplication in the positive attitude to contingencies which they express. What I do suggest is that they are alike in that they do, or may, express an attitude to contingencies; one, that is, which involves recognition that one's life is subject to contingencies, rather than an

[1] The point is beautifully developed by Simone Weil in her essay on 'The Analysis of Oppression' in *Oppression and Liberty*, London, Routledge and Kegan Paul, 1958.
[2] I have been helped to see this point by D. Z. Phillips, *The Concept of Prayer*, London and New York, 1965.

attempt to control these. To characterize this attitude more specifically one should note how Zande rites emphasize the importance of certain fundamental features of their life which MacIntyre ignores. MacIntyre concentrates implicitly on the relation of the rites to consumption, but of course they are also fundamental to social relations and this seems to be emphasized in Zande notions of witchcraft. We have a drama of resentments, evil-doing, revenge, expiation, in which there are ways of dealing (symbolically) with misfortunes and their disruptive effect on a man's relations with his fellows, with ways in which life can go on despite such disruptions.

How is my treatment of this example related to the general criticisms I was making of MacIntyre's account of what it is for us to see the *point* of the rules and conventions followed in an alien form of life? MacIntyre speaks as though our own rules and conventions are somehow a paradigm of what it is for rules and conventions to have a point, so that the only problem that arises is in accounting for the point of the rules and conventions in some other society. But in fact, of course, the problem is the same in relation to our own society as it is in relation to any other; no more than anyone else's are *our* rules and conventions immune from the danger of being or becoming pointless. So an account of this matter cannot be given simply in terms of any set of rules and conventions at all: our own or anyone else's; it requires us to consider the relation of a set of rules and conventions to something else. In my discussion of Zande magical rites just now what I tried to relate the magical rites to was a sense of the significance of human life. This notion is, I think, indispensable to any account of what is involved in understanding and learning from an alien culture; I must now try to say more about it.

In a discussion of Wittgenstein's philosophical use of language games[1] Mr Rush Rhees points out that to try to account for the meaningfulness of language solely in terms of isolated language games is to omit the important fact that ways of speaking are not insulated from each other in mutually exclusive systems of rules. What can be said in one context by the use of a certain expression depends for its sense on the uses of that expression in other contexts (different language games). Language games are played by men who have lives to live—lives involving a wide variety of different interests, which have all kinds of different bearings on each other. Because of this, what a man says or

---

[1] Rush Rhees, 'Wittgenstein's Builders', *Proceedings of the Aristotelian Society*, vol. 20, 1960, pp. 171–86.

does may make a difference not merely to the performance of the
activity upon which he is at present engaged, but to his *life* and to the
lives of other people. Whether a man sees point in what he is doing
will then depend on whether he is able to see any unity in his multifarious interests, activities, and relations with other men; what sort of
sense he sees in his life will depend on the nature of this unity. The
ability to see this sort of sense in life depends not merely on the individual concerned, though this is not so say it does not depend on him
at all; it depends also on the possibilities for making such sense which
the culture in which he lives does, or does not, provide.

What we may learn by studying other cultures are not merely
possibilities of different ways of doing things, other techniques. More
importantly we may learn different possibilities of making sense of
human life, different ideas about the possible importance that the
carrying out of certain activities may take on for a man, trying to
contemplate the sense of his life as a whole. This dimension of the
matter is precisely what MacIntyre misses in his treatment of Zande
magic; he can see in it only a (misguided) technique for producing
consumer goods. But a Zande's crops are not just potential objects of
consumption: the life he lives, his relations with his fellows, his chances
for acting decently or doing evil, may all spring from his relation to his
crops. Magical rites constitute a form of expression in which these
possibilities and dangers may be contemplated and reflected on—and
perhaps also thereby transformed and deepened. The difficulty we find
in understanding this is not merely its remoteness from science, but an
aspect of the general difficulty we find, illustrated by MacIntyre's
procedure, of thinking about such matters at all except in terms of
'efficiency of production'—production, that is, for consumption. This
again is a symptom of what Marx called the 'alienation' characteristic
of man in industrial society, though Marx's own confusions about the
relations between production and consumption are further symptoms
of that same alienation. Our blindness to the point of primitive modes
of life is a corollary of the pointlessness of much of our own life.

I have now explicitly linked my discussion of the 'point' of a system
of conventions with conceptions of good and evil. My aim is not to
engage in moralizing, but to suggest that the concept of *learning from*
which is involved in the study of other cultures is closely linked with
the concept of *wisdom*. We are confronted not just with different
techniques, but with new possibilities of good and evil, in relation to
which men may come to terms with life. An investigation into this

dimension of a society may indeed require a quite detailed inquiry into alternative techniques (e.g., of production), but an inquiry conducted for the light it throws on those possibilities of good and evil. A very good example of the kind of thing I mean is Simone Weil's analysis of the techniques of modern factory production in *Oppression and Liberty*, which is not a contribution to business management, but part of an inquiry into the peculiar form which the evil of oppression takes in our culture.

In saying this, however, I may seem merely to have lifted to a new level the difficulty raised by MacIntyre of how to relate our own conceptions of rationality to those of other societies. Here the difficulty concerns the relation between our own conceptions of good and evil and those of other societies. A full investigation would thus require a discussion of ethical relativism at this point. I have tried to show some of the limitations of relativism in an earlier paper.[1] I shall close the present essay with some remarks which are supplementary to that.

I wish to point out that the very conception of human life involves certain fundamental notions—which I shall call 'limiting notions'—which have an obvious ethical dimension, and which indeed in a sense determine the 'ethical space', within which the possibilities of good and evil in human life can be exercised. The notions which I shall discuss very briefly here correspond closely to those which Vico made the foundation of his idea of natural law, on which he thought the possibility of understanding human history rested: birth, death, sexual relations. Their significance here is that they are inescapably involved in the life of all known human societies in a way which gives us a clue where to look, if we are puzzled about the point of an alien system of institutions. The specific forms which these concepts take, the particular institutions in which they are expressed, vary very considerably from one society to another; but their central position within a society's institutions is and must be a constant factor. In trying to understand the life of an alien society, then, it will be of the utmost importance to be clear about the way in which these notions enter into it. The actual practice of social anthropologists bears this out, although I do not know how many of them would attach the same kind of importance to them as I do.

I speak of a 'limit' here because these notions, along no doubt with others, give shape to what we understand by 'human life'; and because

[1] Peter Winch, 'Nature and Convention', *Proceedings of the Aristotelian Society*, vol. 20, 1960, pp. 231–52.

a concern with questions posed in terms of them seems to me constitutive of what we understand by the 'morality' of a society. In saying this, I am of course, disagreeing with those moral philosophers who have made attitudes of approval and disapproval, or something similar, fundamental in ethics, and who have held that the *objects* of such attitudes were conceptually irrelevant to the conception of morality. On that view, there might be a society where the sorts of attitude taken up in *our* society to questions about relations between the sexes were reserved, say, for questions about the length people wear their hair, and *vice versa*. This seems to me incoherent. In the first place, there would be a confusion in *calling* a concern of that sort a 'moral' concern, however passionately felt. The story of Samson in the Old Testament confirms rather than refutes this point, for the interdict on the cutting of Samson's hair is, of course, connected there with much else: and pre-eminently, it should be noted, with questions about sexual relations. But secondly, if that is thought to be merely verbal quibbling, I will say that it does not seem to me a merely conventional matter that T. S. Eliot's trinity of 'birth, copulation and death' happen to be such deep objects of human concern. I do not mean that they are made such by fundamental psychological and sociological forces, though that is no doubt true. But I want to say further that the very notion of human life is limited by these conceptions.

Unlike beasts, men do not merely live but also have a conception of life. This is not something that is simply added to their life; rather, it changes the very sense which the word 'life' has, when applied to men. It is no longer equivalent to 'animate existence'. When we are speaking of the life of man, we can ask questions about what is the right way to live, what things are most important in life, whether life has any significance, and if so what.

To have a conception of life is also to have a conception of death. But just as the 'life' that is here in question is not the same as animate existence, so the 'death' that is here in question is not the same as the end of animate existence. My conception of the death of an animal is of an event that will take place in the world; perhaps I shall observe it —and my life will go on. But when I speak of 'my death', I am not speaking of a future event in my life;[1] I am not even speaking of an event in anyone else's life. I am speaking of the cessation of my world. That is also a cessation of my ability to do good or evil. It is not just that *as a matter of fact* I shall no longer be able to do good or evil after

[1] Cf. Wittgenstein, *Tractatus Logico-Philosophicus*, 6.431–6.4311.

I am dead; the point is that my very *concept* of what it is to be able to do good or evil is deeply bound up with my concept of my life as ending in death. If ethics is a concern with the right way to live, then clearly the nature of this concern must be deeply affected by the concept of life as ending in death. One's attitude to one's life is at the same time an attitude to one's death.

This point is very well illustrated in an anthropological datum which MacIntyre confesses himself unable to make any sense of.

> According to Spencer and Gillen some aborigines carry about a stick or stone which is treated *as if* it is or embodies the soul of the individual who carries it. If the stick or stone is lost, the individual anoints himself as the dead are anointed. Does the concept of 'carrying one's soul about with one' make sense? Of course we can re-describe what the aborigines are doing and transform it into sense, and perhaps Spencer and Gillen (and Durkheim who follows them) misdescribe what occurs. But if their reports are not erroneous, we confront a blank wall here, so far as meaning is concerned, although it is easy to give the rules for the use of the concept.[1]

MacIntyre does not say why he regards the concept of carrying one's soul about with one in a stick 'throughly incoherent'. He is presumably influenced by the fact that it would be hard to make sense of an action like this if performed by a twentieth-century Englishman or American; and by the fact that the soul is not a material object like a piece of paper and cannot, therefore, be carried about in a stick as a piece of paper might be. But it does not seem to me as hard to see sense in the practice, even from the little we are told about it here. Consider that a lover in our society may carry about a picture or lock of hair of the beloved; that this may symbolize for him his relation to the beloved and may, indeed, change the relation in all sorts of ways: for example, strengthening it or perverting it. Suppose that when the lover loses the locket he feels guilty and asks his beloved for her forgiveness: there might be a parallel here to the aboriginal's practice of anointing himself when he 'loses his soul'. And is there necessarily anything irrational about either of these practices? Why should the lover not regard his carelessness in losing the locket as a sort of betrayal of the beloved? Remember how husbands and wives may feel about the loss of a wedding ring. The aborigine is clearly expressing a concern with his life as a whole in this practice; the anointing shows the close connection between such a concern and contemplation of death. Perhaps it is

[1] *Is Understanding Religion Compatible with Believing?* Above, p. 68

precisely this practice which makes such a concern possible for him, as religious sacraments make certain sorts of concern possible. The point is that a concern with one's life as a whole, involving as it does the limiting conception of one's death, if it is to be expressed *within* a person's life, can necessarily only be expressed quasi-sacramentally. The form of the concern shows itself in the form of the sacrament.

The sense in which I spoke also of sex as a 'limiting concept' again has to do with the concept of a human life. The life of a man is a man's life and the life of a woman is a woman's life: the masculinity or the femininity are not just *components* in the life, they are its *mode*. Adapting Wittgenstein's remark about death, I might say that my masculinity is not an experience in the world, but my way of experiencing the world. Now the concepts of masculinity and femininity obviously require each other. A man is a man in relation to women; and a woman is a woman in relation to men.[1] Thus the form taken by man's relation to women is of quite fundamental importance for the significance he can attach to his own life. The vulgar identification of morality with sexual morality certainly *is* vulgar; but it is a vulgarization of an important truth.

The limiting character of the concept of birth is obviously related to the points I have sketched regarding death and sex. On the one hand, my birth is no more an event in my life than is my death; and through my birth ethical limits are set for my life quite independently of my will: I am, from the outset, in specific relations to other people, from which obligations spring which cannot but be ethically fundamental.[2] On the other hand, the concept of birth is fundamentally linked to that of relations between the sexes. This remains true, however much or little may be known in a society about the contribution of males and females to procreation; for it remains true that man is born of woman, not of man. This, then, adds a new dimension to the ethical institutions in which relations between the sexes are expressed.

I have tried to do no more, in these last brief remarks, than to focus attention in a certain direction. I have wanted to indicate that forms of these limiting concepts will necessarily be an important feature of any

[1] These relations, however, are not simple converses. See Georg Simmel, 'Das Relative und das Absolute im Geschlechter-Problem' in *Philosophische Kultur*, Leipzig, 1911.
[2] For this reason, among others, I think A. I. Melden is wrong to say that present-child obligations and rights have nothing directly to do with physical genealogy. Cf. Melden, *Rights and Right Conduct*. Oxford: Blackwell, 1959.

human society and that conceptions of good and evil in human life will necessarily be connected with such concepts. In any attempt to understand the life of another society, therefore, an investigation of the forms taken by such concepts—their role in the life of the society—must always take a central place and provide a basis on which understanding may be built.

Now since the world of nations has been made by men, let us see in what institutions men agree and always have agreed. For these institutions will be able to give us the universal and eternal principles (such as every science must have) on which all nations were founded and still preserve themselves.

We observe that all nations, barbarous as well as civilized, though separately founded because remote from each other in time and space, keep these three human customs: all have some religion, all contract solemn marriages, all bury their dead. And in no nation, however savage and crude, are any human actions performed with more elaborate ceremonies and more sacred solemnity than the rites of religion, marriage and burial. For by the axiom that 'uniform ideas, born among peoples unknown to each other, must have a common ground of truth', it must have been dictated to all nations that from these institutions humanity began among them all, and therefore they must be most devoutly guarded by them all, so that the world should not again become a bestial wilderness. For this reason we have taken these three eternal and universal customs as the first principles of this Science.[1]

[1] Giambattista Vico, *The New Science*, paras. 332–333.

6

The Idea of a Social Science

ALASDAIR MACINTYRE

My aim in this paper is to express dissent from the position taken in Mr Peter Winch's book whose title is also the title of this paper.[1] Winch's book has been the subject of a good deal of misunderstanding and he has been accused on the one hand of reviving familiar and long-refuted views[2] and on the other of holding views so eccentric in relation to social science as it actually is that they could not possibly have any practical effect on the conduct of that science.[3] In fact, however, Winch articulates a position which is at least partly implicit in a good deal of work already done, notably in anthropology, and he does so in an entirely original way. He writes in a genre recognizable to both sociologists and philosophers. Talcott Parsons and Alain Touraine have both found it necessary to preface their sociological work by discussions of norms and actions and have arrived at rather different conclusions from those of Winch; the importance of his work is therefore undeniable.

'Wittgenstein says somewhere that when one gets into philosophical difficulties over the use of some of the concepts of our language, we

Originally published in Aristotelian Society Supplement, XLI, 1967.

[1] All otherwise unidentified page references are to *The Idea of a Social Science*. I have in this paper focused attention upon Winch's arguments in such a way that, although it will be obvious that I am either indebted to or at odds with various other philosophers, I have not usually made this explicit. But I ought to acknowledge that in arguing with Winch I shall also be arguing with myself, and that the arguments of Section II of this paper entail the falsity of some assertions in Section II of 'A Mistake About Causality in the Social Sciences' (in Peter Laslett and W. G. Runciman (eds.), *Philosophy, Politics and Society* II, Oxford: Blackwell, 1963.

[2] See, for example, Richard Rudner, *The Philosphy of Social Sciences*, London: Prentice-Hall, 1966, pp. 81–3.

[3] See A. R. Louch's review in *Inquiry*, 1963, p. 273.

are like savages confronted with something from an alien culture. I am simply indicating a corollary of this: that sociologists who mis-interpret an alien culture are like philosophers getting into difficulty over the use of their own concepts.' This passage (p. 114) epitomizes a central part of Winch's thesis with its splendid successive characteriza-tions of the figure baffled by an alien culture; a savage at one moment, he has become a sociologist at the next. And this is surely no slip of the pen. According to Winch the successful sociologist has simply learnt all that the ideal native informant could tell him; sociological know-ledge is the kind of knowledge possessed in implicit and partial form by the members of a society rendered explicit and complete (p. 88). It is not at first entirely clear just how far Winch is at odds in this contention with, for example, Malinowski, who insisted[1] that the native Trobriander's account of Trobriand society must be inadequate, that the sociologists' account of institutions is a construction not available to the untutored awareness of the native informant. For Winch of course is willing to allow into the sociologist's account concepts 'which are not taken from the forms of activity which he is investigating; but which are taken rather from the context of his own investigation', although he adds that 'these technical concepts will imply a prior understanding of those other concepts which belong to the activities under investigation.' Perhaps this might seem sufficient to remove the apparent disagreement of Winch and Malinowski, until we remember the conclusion of Malinowski's critique of the native informant's view. The sociologist who relies upon that view, he says, 'obtains at best that lifeless body of laws, regulations, morals and conventionalities which *ought* to be obeyed, but in reality are often only evaded. For in actual life rules are never entirely conformed to, and it remains, as the most difficult but indispensable part of the ethnographers' work, to ascertain the extent and mechanism of the deviations' (op. cit., pp. 428–9). This makes two points clear.

First, Malinowski makes a distinction between the rules acknow-ledged in a given society and the actual behaviour of individuals in that society, whereas Winch proclaims the proper object of sociological study to be that behaviour precisely as rule-governed. The second is that in the study of behaviour Malinowski is willing to use notions such as that of mechanism which are clearly causal; whereas Winch warns us against comparing sociological understanding with under-standing in terms of 'Statistics and causal laws' and says of the notion of

[1] *The Sexual Life of Savages*, pp. 425–9.

function, so important to Malinowski, that it 'is a quasi-causal notion, which it is perilous to apply to social institutions' (p. 116).

It does appear therefore that although Winch and Malinowski agree in seeing the ideal native informant's account of his own social life as incomplete by comparison with the ideal sociologist's account, they do disagree about the nature of that incompleteness and about how it is to be remedied. My purpose in this paper will be to defend Malinowski's point of view on these matters against Winch's, but this purpose can only be understood if one reservation is immediately added. It is that in defending Malinowski's views on these points I must not be taken to be endorsing Malinowski's general theoretical position. I have in fact quoted Malinowski on these matters, but I might have quoted many other social scientists. For on these matters Malinowski speaks with the *consensus*.

II

A regularity or uniformity is the constant recurrence of the same kind of event on the same kind of occasion; hence statements of uniformities presuppose judgments of identity. But . . . criteria of identity are necessarily relative to some rule: with the corollary that two events which count as qualitively similar from the point of view of one rule would count as different from the point of view of another. So to investigate the type of regularity studied in a given enquiry is to examine the nature of the rule according to which judgments of identity are made in that enquiry. Such judgments are intelligible only relatively to a given mode of human behaviour, governed by its own rules (p. 83-4).

This passage is the starting point for Winch's argument that J. S. Mill was mistaken in supposing that to understand a social institution is to formulate empirical generalizations about regularities in human behaviour, generalizations which are causal and explanatory in precisely the same sense that generalizations in the natural sciences are. For the natural scientist makes the relevant judgments of identity according to *his* rules, that is the rules incorporated in the practice of his science; whereas the social scientist must make his judgments of identity in accordance with the rules governing the behaviour of those whom he studies. *Their* rules, not *his*, define the object of his study. 'So it is quite mistaken in principle to compare the activity of a student of a form of social behaviour with that of, say, an engineer studying the working of a machine. If we are going to compare the social student to an engineer, we shall do better to compare him to an apprentice engineer who is studying what engineering—that is, the activity of engineering—is all about' (p. 88).

What the type of understanding which Winch is commending consists in is made clearer in two other passages. He says that although prediction is possible in the social sciences, it 'is quite different from predictions in the natural sciences, where a falsified prediction always implies some sort of mistake on the part of the predictor: false or inadequate data, faulty calculation, or defective theory' (pp. 91-2). This is because 'since understanding something involves understanding its contradictory, someone who, with understanding, performs X must be capable of envisaging the possibility of doing not-X' (p. 91). Where someone is following a rule, we cannot predict how he will interpret what is involved in following that rule in radically new circumstances; where decisions have to be made, the outcome 'cannot be *definitely* predicted', for otherwise 'we should not call them decisions.'

These points about prediction, if correct, reinforce Winch's arguments about the difference between the natural sciences and the social sciences. For they amount to a denial of that symmetry between explanation and prediction which holds in the natural sciences.[1] But when we consider what Winch says here about decision, it is useful to take into account at the same time what he says about motives and reasons. Winch treats these as similar in this respect: that they are made intelligible by reference to the rules governing the form of social life in which the agent participates. So Winch points out that 'one can act "from considerations" only where there are accepted standards of what is appropriate to appeal to' (p. 82) and argues against Ryle that the 'law-like proposition' in terms of which someone's reasons must be understood concerns not the agent's disposition 'but the accepted standards of reasonable behaviour current in his society' (p. 81).

From all this one can set out Winch's view of understanding and explanations in the social sciences in terms of a two-stage model. An action is *first* made intelligible as the outcome of motives, reasons, and decisions; and is then made *further* intelligible by those motives, reasons and decisions being set in the context of the rules of a given form of social life. These rules logically determine the range of reasons and

---

[1] It has been argued often enough that this symmetry does not hold in the natural sciences; Professor Adolf Grünbaum's arguments in Chapter IX of the *Philosophy of Space and Time* seem a more than adequate rebuttal of these positions.

motives open to a given set of agents and hence also the range of decisions open to them. Thus Winch's contrast between explanation in terms of causal generalizations and explanations in terms of rules turns out to rest upon a version of the contrast between explanations in terms of causes and explanations in terms of reasons. This latter contrast must therefore be explored, and the most useful way of doing this will be to understand better what it is to act for a reason.

Many analyses of what it is to act for a reason have written into them an incompatibility between acting for a reason and behaving from a cause, just because they begin from the apparently simple and uncomplicated case where the action is actually performed, where the agent had one and only one reason for performing it and where no doubt could arise for the agent as to why he had done what he had done. By concentrating attention upon this type of example a basis is laid for making central to the analyses a contrast between the agent's knowledge of his own reasons for acting and his and others' knowledge of causes of his behaviour. For clearly in such a case the agent's claim that he did X for reason Y does not seem to stand in need of any warrant from a generalization founded upon observation; while equally clearly any claim that one particular event or state of affairs was the cause of another does stand in need of such a warrant. But this may be misleading. Consider two somewhat more complex cases than that outlined above. The first is that of a man who has several quite different reasons for performing a given action. He performs the action; how can he as agent know whether it was the conjoining of all the different reasons that was sufficient for him to perform the action or whether just one of the reasons was by itself alone sufficient or whether the action was over-determined in the sense that there were two or more reasons, each of which would by itself alone have been sufficient? The problem arises partly because to know that one or other of these possibilities was indeed the case entails knowing the truth of certain unfulfilled conditionals.

A second case worth considering is that of two agents, each with the same reasons for performing a given action; one does not in fact perform it, the other does. Neither agent had what seemed to him a good reason or indeed had any reason for not performing the action in question. Here we can ask what made these reasons or some sub-set of them productive of action in the one case, but not in the other? In both these types of case we need to distinguish between the agent's having a reason for performing an action (not just in the sense of there being a reason for him to perform the action, but in the stronger sense of his being aware that he has such a reason) and the agent's being actually moved to action by his having such a reason. The importance of this point can be brought out by reconsidering a very familiar example, that of post-hypnotic suggestion.

Under the influence of post-hypnotic suggestion a subject will not only perform the action required by the hypnotist, but will offer apparently good reasons for performing it, while quite unaware of the true cause of the performance. So someone enjoined to walk out of the room might on being asked why he was doing this, reply with all sincerity that he had felt in need of fresh air or decided to catch a train. In this type of case we would certainly not accept the agent's testimony as to the connection between reason and action, unless we are convinced of the untruth of the counter-factual, 'He would have walked out of the room, if no reason for doing so had occurred to him', and the truth of the counter-factual. 'He would not have walked out of the room, if he had not possessed some such reason for so doing'. The question of the truth or otherwise of the first of these is a matter of the ex-perimentally established facts about post-hypnotic suggestion, and these facts are certainly expressed as causal generalizations. To establish the truth of the relevant generalization would entail establishing the un-truth of the second counter-factual. But since to establish the truth of such causal generalizations entails consequences concerning the truth or untruth of generalizations about reasons, the question inevitably arises as to whether *the possession of a given reason* may not be the cause of an action in precisely the same sense in which hypnotic suggestion may be the cause of an action. The chief objection to this view has been that the relation of reason to action is internal and conceptual, not external and contingent, and cannot therefore be a causal relationship; but although nothing could count as a reason unless it stood in an internal relation-ship to an action, *the agent's possessing a reason* may be a state of affairs identifiable independently of the event which is *the agent's performance of the action*. Thus it does seem as if the possession of a reason by an agent is an item of a suitable type to figure as a cause, or an effect. But if this is so then to ask whether it was the agent's reason that roused him to act is to ask a causal question, the true answer to which depends upon what causal generalizations we have been able to establish. This puts in a different light the question of the agent's authority as to what roused him to act; for it follows from what has been said that this authority is at best *prima facie*. Far more of course needs to be said on this and related topics; but perhaps the argument so far entitles us to treat with scepticism Winch's claim that understanding in terms of rule-following and causal explanations have mutually exclusive subject-matters.

This has obvious implications for social science, and I wish to suggest some of these in order to provide direction for the rest of my argument. Clearly if the citing of reasons by an agent, with the concomitant appeal to rules, is not necessarily the citing of those reasons which are causally effective, a distinction may be made between those rules which agents in a given society sincerely profess to follow and to which their actions may in fact conform, but which do not in fact direct their actions, and those rules which, whether they profess to follow them or not, do in fact guide their acts by providing them with reasons and motives for acting in one way rather than another. The making of this distinction is essential to the notions of *ideology* and of *false consciousness*, notions which are extremely important to some non-Marxist as well as to Marxist social scientists.

But to allow that these notions could have application is to find one-self at odds with Winch's argument at yet another point. For it seems quite clear that the concept of ideology can find application in a society where the concept is not available to the members of the society, and furthermore that the application of this concept implies that criteria beyond those available in the society may be invoked to judge its rationality; and as such it would fall under Winch's ban as a concept unsuitable for social science. Hence there is a connexion between Winch's view that social science is not appropriately concerned with causal generalizations and his view that only the concepts possessed by the members of a given society (or concepts logically tied to those concepts in some way) are to be used in the study of that society. Furthermore it is important to note that Winch's views on those matters necessarily make his account of rules and their place in social behaviour defective.

III

The examples which Winch gives of rule-following behaviour are very multifarious: games, political thinking, musical composition, the monastic way of life, an anarchist's way of life, are all cited. His only example of non-rule-governed behaviour is 'the pointless behaviour of a beserk lunatic' (p. 53), and he asserts roundly 'that all behaviour which is meaningful (therefore all specifically human behaviour) is *ipso facto* rule-governed.' Winch allows for different kinds of rules (p. 52); what he does not consider is whether the concept of a rule is perhaps being used so widely that quite different senses of *rule-governed* are being confused, let alone whether his account of meaningful behaviour can be plausibly applied to some actions at all.

If I go for a walk, or smoke a cigarette, are my actions rule-governed in the sense in which my actions in playing chess are rule-governed? Winch says that 'the test of whether a man's actions are the application of a rule is . . . whether it makes sense to distinguish between a right and a wrong way of doing things in connection with what he does.' What is the wrong way of going for a walk? And, if there is no wrong way, is my action in any sense rule-governed? To ask these questions is to begin to bring out the difference between those activities which form part of a coherent mode of behaviour and those which do not. It is to begin to see that although many actions must be rule-governed in the sense that the concept of some particular kinds of action may involve reference to a rule, the concept of an action as such does not involve such a reference. But even if we restrict our attention to activities which form part of some coherent larger whole, it is clear that rules may govern activity in quite different ways. This is easily seen if we consider the variety of uses to which social scientists have put the concept of a role and role-concepts.

Role-concepts are at first sight peculiarly well-fitted to find a place in the type of analysis of which Winch would approve. S. F. Nadel wrote that 'the role concept is not an invention of anthropologists or sociologists but is employed by the very people they study,' and added that 'it is the existence of names describing classes of people which make us think of roles.' It would therefore be significant for Winch's thesis if it were the case that role-concepts had to be understood in relation to causes, if they were to discharge their analytic and explanatory function.

Consider first a use of the notion of role where causal questions do not arise. In a society such as ours there are a variety of roles which an individual may assume or not as he wills. Some occupational roles provide examples. To live out such a role is to make one's behaviour conform to certain norms. To speak of one's behaviour being governed by the norms is to use a sense of 'governed' close to that according to which the behaviour of a chess-player is governed by the rules of chess. We are not disposed to say that the rules of chess or the norms which define the role of a head-waiter constrain the individual who conforms to them. The observation of the rules constitutes the behaviour as what it is; it is not a causal agency.

Contrast with this type of example the enquiry carried on by Erving Goffmann in his book *Asylums*.[1] One of Goffman's concerns was to pose a question about mental patients: how far are the characteristic patterns of behaviour which they exhibit determined, not by the nature of the mental disorders from which they suffer, but by the nature of the institutions to which they have been consigned? Goffmann concludes that the behaviour of patients is determined to a considerable degree by institutional arrangements which provide a severely limited set of possible roles both for patients and for the doctors and orderlies with whom they have to deal. Thus the behaviour of individual patients of a given type might be explained as the effect of the role-arrangements open to a person of this type. In case it is thought that the role-structure of mental hospitals only has a causal effect upon the patients because they are *patients* (and the implication might be that they are not therefore rational agents but approach the condition of the exception Winch allows for, that of the beserk lunatic) it is worth noting that Goffmann's study of mental hospitals is part of a study of what he calls 'total institutions'. These include monasteries and armed services as well as mental hospitals. A successful terminus to his enquiry would therefore be the formulation of generalizations about the effects upon agents of different types of character of the role-structure of such different types of institution.

If Winch were correct and rule-governed behaviour was not to be understood as causal behaviour, then the contrast could not be drawn between those cases in which the relation of social structure to individuals may be correctly characterized in terms of control or constraint and those in which it may not. Winch's inability to make this contrast adequately in terms of his conceptual scheme is the counterpart to Durkheim's inability to make it adequately in terms of his; and the resemblance of Winch's failure to Durkheim's is illuminating in that Winch's position is roughly speaking that of Durkheim turned upside-down. Durkheim in a passage cited by Winch insisted first 'that social life should be explained, not by the notions of those who participate in it, but by more profound causes which are unperceived by consciousness' and secondly 'that these causes are to be sought mainly in the

[1] New York: Doubleday Anchor Books, 1961; Harmondsworth: Penguin Books, 1968.

manner according to which the associated individuals are grouped'.[1] That is, Durkheim supposes, just as Winch does, that an investigation of social reality which uses the concept available to the members of the society which is being studied and an investigation of social reality which utilizes concepts not so available and invokes causal explanations of which the agents themselves are not aware are mutually exclusive alternatives. But Durkheim supposes, as Winch does not, that the latter alternative is the one to be preferred. Yet his acceptance of the same dichotomy involves him in the same inability to understand the different ways in which social structure may be related to individual action.

Durkheim's concept of *anomie* is the concept of a state in which the constraints and controls exercised by social structure have been loosed and the bonds which delimit and contain individual desire have therefore been at least partially removed. The picture embodied in the Durkheimian concept is thus one according to which the essential function of norms in social life is to restrain and inhibit psychological drives. For Durkheim, rules are an external imposition upon a human nature which can be defined independently of them; for Winch, they are the guide-lines of behaviour which, did it not conform to them, could scarcely be human. What is equally odd in both is the way in which rules or norms are characterized as though they were all of a kind. Durkheim is unable to recognize social structure apart from the notions of constraint and control by the structure; Winch's concept of society has no room for these notions.

Just as Winch does not allow for the variety of relationships in which an agent may stand to a rule to which his behaviour conforms, so he does not allow also for the variety of types of deviance from rules which behaviour may exhibit. I quoted Malinowski earlier on the important gap between the rules professed in a society and the behaviour actually exhibited. On this Winch might well comment that his concern is with human behaviour as rule-following, not only with mere professions of rule-following, except in so far as professing to follow rules is itself a human and (for him) *ipso facto* a rule-following activity. Moreover he explicitly allows that 'since understanding something involves understanding its contradictory, someone who, with understanding, performs X must be capable of envisaging the possibility of doing not-X.' He makes this remark in the context of his discussion of predictability; and what he does not allow for in this discussion is that in

[1] Review of A. Labriola's *Essays on Historical Materialism*.

fact the behaviour of agents may exhibit regularities of a Humean kind and be predictable just as natural events are predictable, even although it can also be characterized and in some cases must also be characterized in terms of following and deviating from certain rules. That this is so makes it possible to speak not only, as Malinowski does in the passage quoted earlier, of mechanisms of deviation, but also of mechanisms of conformity. Of course those who deviate from the accepted rules may have a variety of reasons for so doing, and in so far as they share the same reasons their behaviour will exhibit rule-following regularities. But it may well be that agents have a variety of reasons for their deviance, and yet deviate uniformly in certain circumstances, this uniformity being independent of their reasons. Whether in a particular case this is so or not seems to me to be an empirical question and one which it would be well not to attempt to settle *a priori*.

I can put my general point as follows. We can in a given society discover a variety of systematic regularities. There are the systems of rules which agents professedly follow; there are the systems of rules which they actually follow; there are causal regularities exhibited in the correlation of statuses and forms of behaviour, and of one form of behaviour and another, which are not rule-governed at all; there are regularities which are in themselves neither causal nor rule-governed, although dependent for their existence perhaps on regularities of both types, such as the cyclical patterns of development exhibited in some societies; and there are the inter-relationships which exist between all these. Winch concentrates on some of these at the expense of the others. In doing so he is perhaps influenced by a peculiarly British tradition in social anthropology and by a focus of attention in recent philosophy.

The anthropological tradition is that centred on the work of Professor E. E. Evans-Pritchard, work which exemplifies the rewards to be gained from understanding a people first of all in their own terms. Winch[1] rightly treats Evans-Pritchard's writing as a paradigm case of a social scientist knowing his own business; but neglects the existence of alternative paradigms. Edmund Leach, for example,[2] has remarked how ecological factors do not in fact genuinely figure in the explanatory framework of Evans-Pritchard's *The Nuer*. Now it is clear that such factors may affect the form of social life either in ways of which the agents are conscious (by posing problems to which they have to formulate solutions) or in ways of which they are unaware. This elemen-

---

[1] In *Understanding a Primitive Society*, above pp. 78–111.
[2] In his *Pul Eliya, a village in Ceylon*, Cambridge, 1961.

tary distinction is perhaps not given its full weight in a recent discussion by Walter Goldschmidt[1] in which the very problems discussed by Winch are faced from the standpoint of an anthropologist especially concerned with ecological factors. Goldschmidt offers the example of the high correlation between agnatic segmentary kinship systems and nomadic pastoralism as a form of economy. He argues that nomadic pastoralism, to be a viable form of economy, has to satisfy requirements which are met most usually by segmentary lineages, but 'Age-sets can perform some of the same functions—especially those associated with the military—with equal effectiveness . . .'. Goldschmidt's claim is at least superficially ambiguous. He might be read (at least by a critic determined to be captious) as asserting that first there are economic forms, these pose problems of which the agents become aware and seg- mentary or age-set patterns are constructed as solutions by the agents. Or he might be read (more profitably, I imagine) as moving towards a theory in which social patterns (including kinship patterns) represent adaptations (of which the agents themselves are not aware) to the en- vironment, and to the level of technology prevailing. It would then in principle be possible to formulate causal laws governing such adaptations, and work like Leach's on Pul Eliya or Goldschmidt's on East Africa could be placed in a more general explanatory framework. This type of project is at the opposite extreme from Evans-Pritchard's concern with conceptual particularity.

Secondly, on Winch's account the social sciences characterize what they characterize by using action-descriptions. In his stress upon these Winch follows much recent philosophical writing. It is on what people *do*, and not what they *are* or *suffer* that he dwells. But social scientists are concerned with the causes and effects of *being unemployed*, *having kin-relations of a particular kind*, *rates of population change*, and a myriad of conditions of individuals and societies the descriptions of which have a logical character other than that of action descriptions. None of this appears in Winch's account.

IV

The positive value of Winch's book is partly as a corrective to the Durkheimian position which he rightly castigates. But it is more than a corrective because what Winch characterizes as the whole task of the social sciences is in fact their true starting-point. Unless we begin by a

[1] In *Comparative Functionalism*, California and Cambridge, 1966, pp. 122–4.

characterization of a society in its own terms, we shall be unable to identify the matter that requires explanation. Attention to intentions, motives and reasons must precede attention to causes; description in terms of the agent's concepts and beliefs must precede description in terms of our concepts and beliefs. The force of this contention can be brought out by considering and expanding what Winch says about Durkheim's *Suicide*.[1] Winch invites us to notice the connexion between Durkheim's conclusion that the true explanation of suicide is in terms of factors outside the consciousness of the agents themselves such that the reasons of the agents themselves are effectively irrelevant and his initial decision to give the term 'suicide' a meaning quite other than that which it had for those agents. What is he inviting us to notice?

A number of points, I suspect, of which one is a central insight, the others in error. The insight is that Durkheim's particular procedure of giving to 'suicide' a meaning of his own *entails* the irrelevance of the agents' reasons in the explanation of suicide. Durkheim does in fact bring forward independent arguments designed to show that reasons are either irrelevant or inaccessible, and very bad arguments they are. But even if he had not believed himself to have grounds drawn from these arguments, he would have been unable to take reasons into account, given his decision about meaning. For Durkeim arbitrarily equates the concept of *suicide* with that of *doing anything that the agent knows will bring about his own death* and thus classifies as suicide both the intended self-destruction of the Prussian or English officer who shoots himself to save the regiment the disgrace of a court-martial and the death of such an officer in battle who has courageously headed a charge in such a way that he knows that he will not survive. (I choose these two examples because they both belong to the same catagory in Durkheim's classification.) Thus he ignores the distinction between *doing X intending that Y shall result and doing X knowing that Y will result*. Now clearly of these two are to be assimilated, the roles of deliberation and the relevance of the agent's reasons will disappear from view. For clearly in the former case the character of Y must be central to the reasons the agent has for doing X, but in the latter case the agent may well be doing X either in spite of the character of Y, or not caring one way or the other about the character of Y, or again finding the character of Y desirable, but not desirable enough for him for it to constitute a reason or a motive for doing X. Thus the nature of the reasons *must* differ in the two cases and if the two cases are to have the

[1] Winch, op. cit., p. 110.

same explanation the agent's reasons can scarcely figure in that explanation. That is, Durkheim is forced by his initial semantic decision to the conclusion that the agent's reasons are in cases of what agents in the society which he studies would have called suicide (which are included as a sub-class of what he calls suicide) *never* causally effective.

But there are two further conclusions which might be thought to, but do not in fact follow. It does not follow that all such decisions to bring actions under descriptions other than those used by the agents themselves are bound to lead to the same *a priori* obliteration of the explanatory role of reasons; for this obliteration was in Durkheim's case, as I have just shown, a consequence of certain special features of this treatment of the concept of suicide, and not a consequence of any general feature of the procedure of inventing new descriptive terms in social sciences. Secondly, from the fact that explanation in terms of reasons ought not to be excluded by any initial decision of the social scientist, it does not follow that such explanation is incompatible with causal explanation. Here my argument in the second section of this paper bears on what Winch says about Weber. Winch says that Weber was confused because he did not realize that 'a context of humanly followed rules . . . cannot be combined with a context of causal laws' without creating logical difficulties, and he is referring specifically to Weber's contention that the manipulation of machinery and the manipulation of his employees by a manufacturer may be understood in the same way, so far as the logic of the explanation is concerned. So Weber wrote, 'that in the one case "events of consciousness" do enter into the causal chain and in the other case do not, makes "logically" not the slightest difference'. I also have an objection to Weber's argument, but it is in effect that Weber's position is too close to Winch's. For Weber supposes that in order to introduce causal explanation he must abandon description of the social situation in terms of actions, roles and the like. So he proposes speaking not of the workers being paid, but of their being handed pieces of metal. In so doing Weber concedes Winch's point that descriptions in terms of actions, reasons, and all that falls under his term 'events of consciousness' cannot figure in causal explanations without a conceptual mistake being committed. But in this surely he is wrong.

Compare two situations: first, one in which managers minimize shop-floor trade union activity in a factory by concentrating opportunities of extra over-time and of earning bonuses in those parts of the factory where such activity shows signs of flourishing; and then one in which managers similarly minimize trade union activity by a process of continual transfers between one part of the factory and another or between different factories. In both cases it may be possible to explain the low level of trade union activity causally by reference to the manager's policies; but in the former case the reasons which the workers have for pursuing over-time and bonuses can find a place in the explanation without it losing its causal character and in both cases a necessary condition of the managers' actions being causally effective may well be that the workers in question remain ignorant of the policy behind the actions. The causal character of the explanations can be brought out by considering how generalizations might be formulated in which certain behaviour of the managers can supply either the necessary or the sufficient condition or both for the behaviour of the workers. But in such a formulation one important fact will emerge, namely, that true causal explanations cannot be formulated—where actions are concerned—unless intentions, motives and reasons are taken into account. That is, it is not only the case as I have argued in the second section of this paper that a true explanation in terms of reasons must entail some account of the causal background, it is also true that a causal account of action will require a corresponding account of the intentions, motives and reasons involved. It is this latter point that Durkheim misses and Winch stresses. In the light of this it is worth returning to one aspect of the explanation of suicide.

In modern cities more than one study has shown a correlation between the suicide rate for different parts of the city and the proportion of the population living in isolated single-room apartment existence. What are the conditions which must be satisfied if such a correlation is to begin to play a part in explaining why suicide is committed? First it must be shown that at least a certain proportion of the individuals who commit suicide live in such isolated conditions; otherwise (unless, for example, it was the landlord of such apartments who committed suicide) we should find the correlation of explanatory assistance only in so far as it pointed us towards a common explanation of the two rates. But suppose that we do find that it is the individuals who live in such isolated conditions who are more likely to commit suicide. We still have to ask whether it is the pressure on the emotions of the isolation itself, or whether it is the insolubility of certain other problems in conditions of isolation which leads to suicide. Unless such questions about motives and reasons are answered, the casual generalization 'Isolated living of a certain kind tends to lead to acts of suicide' is no so much an explanation in itself as an additional fact to be explained, even although it is a perfectly sound generalization, and even although to learn its truth might be to learn how the suicide rate could be increased or decreased in large cities by changing our local authority housing policy.

Now we cannot raise the questions about motives and reasons, the answers to which would explain why isolation has the effect which it has, unless we first of all understand the acts of suicide in terms of the intentions of the agents and therefore in terms of their own action-descriptions. Thus Winch's starting-point proves to be the correct one, provided it is a starting-point. We could not even formulate our initial causal generalization about isolation and suicide, in such a way that the necessary question about motives and reasons could be raised later, unless the expression 'suicide' and kindred expressions which figured in our causal generalizations possessed the same meaning as they did for the agents who committed the acts. We can understand very clearly why Winch's starting-point must be substantially correct if we remember how he compares sociological understanding with under-standing a language (p. 115). The crude notion that one can first learn a language and then secondly and separately go on to understand the social life of those who speak it, can only flourish where the languages studied as those of peoples whose social life is so largely the same as our own so that we do not notice the understanding of social life embodied in our grasp of the language; but attempts to learn the alien language of an alien culture soon dispose of it. Yet the understanding that we thus acquire, although a necessary preliminary, is only a preliminary. It would be equally harmful if Winch's attempt to make of this preliminary the substance of social science were to convince or if a proper understanding of the need to go further were not to allow for the truth in his arguments.

V

These dangers are likely to be especially inhibiting in the present state of certain parts of social science. Two important essays by anthro-pologists, Leach's *Rethinking Anthropology*[1] and Goldschmidt's *Comparative Functionalism*[2] focus upon problems to which adherence to Winch's conclusions would preclude any solution. At the outset I

[1] London, 1966.
[2] Op. cit.

contrasted Winch with Malinowski, but this was in respects in which
most contemporary social scientists would take the standpoint quoted
from Malinowski for granted. We owe also to Malinowski, however,
the tradition of what Goldschmidt calls 'the detailed internal analysis
of individual cultures' with the further comparison of institutional
arrangements in different societies resting on such analysis. This
tradition has been criticized by both Leach and Goldschmidt; the
latter believes that because institutions are defined by each culture in
its own terms, it is not at the level of institutions that cross-cultural
analyses will be fruitful. The former has recommended us to search
for recurrent topological patterns in, for example, kinship arrangements, with the same aim of breaking free from institutional ethnocentrism. I think that both Leach and Goldschmidt are going to prove
to be seminal writers on this point and it is clear that their arguments
are incompatible with Winch's. It would therefore be an important
lacuna in this paper if I did not open up directly the question of the
bearing of Winch's arguments on this topic.

Winch argues, consistently with his rejection of any place for
causal laws in social science, that comparison between different cases
is not dependent on any grasp of theoretical generalizations (pp.
134–6), and he sets limits to any possible comparison by his insistence
that each set of activities must be understood solely in its own terms.
In so doing he must necessarily reject for example all those various
theories which insist that religions of quite different kinds express
unacknowledged needs of the same kind. (No such theory needs to be
committed to the view that religions are and do no more than this.)
Indeed in his discussion of Pareto (pp. 104–11) he appears to make such
a rejection explicit by the generality of the grounds on which he rejects
Pareto's comparison of Christian baptism with pagan rites. I hold no
brief for the theory of residues and derivations. But when Winch
insists that each religious rite must be understood in its own terms to
the exclusion of any generalization about religion, or that each social
system must be so understood to the exclusion of any generalization
about status and prestige, he must be pressed to make his grounds
precise. In his later discussion of Evans-Pritchard, one aspect of
Winch's views becomes clear, namely, the implication of his remark
that 'criteria of logic are not a direct gift of God, but arise out of, and
are only intelligible in the context of, ways of living or modes of social
life' (p. 100). Winch's one substantial point of difference with Evans-
Pritchard in his treatment of witchcraft among the Azande is that he

thinks it impossible to ask whether the Zande beliefs about witches are true.[1] We can ask from within the Zande system of beliefs if there are witches and will receive the answer 'Yes'. We can ask from within the system of beliefs of modern science if there are witches and will receive the answer 'No'. But we cannot ask which system of beliefs is the superior in respect of rationality and truth; for this would be to invoke criteria which can be understood independently of any particular way of life, and on Winch's view there are no such criteria.

This represents a far more extreme view of the difficulties of cultural comparison than Goldschmidt, for example, advances. Both its extreme character and its error can be understood by considering two arguments against it. The first is to the effect that on Winch's view certain actual historical transitions are made unintelligible; I refer to those transitions from one system of beliefs to another which are necessarily characterized by raising questions of the kind that Winch rejects. In seventeenth century Scotland, for example, the question could not but be raised, 'But are there witches?' If Winch asks, from within what way of social life, under what system of belief was this question asked, the only answer is that it was asked by men who confronted alternative systems and were able to draw out of what confronted them independent criteria of judgment. Many Africans today are in the same situation.

This type of argument is of course necessarily inconclusive; any historical counter-example to Winch's thesis will be open to questions of interpretation that will make it less than decisive. But there is another important argument. Consider the statement made by some Zande theorist or by King James VI and I, 'There are witches', and the statement made by some modern sceptic, 'There are no witches.' Unless one of these statements denies what the other asserts, the negation of the sentence expressing the former could not be a correct translation of the sentence expressing the latter. Thus if we could not deny from our own standpoint and in our own language what the Azande or King James assert in theirs, we should be unable to translate their expression into our language. Cultural idiosyncrasy would have entailed linguistic idiosyncrasy and cross-cultural comparison would have been rendered logically impossible. But of course translation is not impossible.

Yet if we treat seriously, not what I take to be Winch's mistaken thesis that we cannot go beyond a society's own self-description, but

[1] Above, pp. 79 ff.

what I take to be his true thesis that we must not do this except and until we have grasped the criteria embodied in that self-description, then we shall have to conclude that the contingently different conceptual schemes and institutional arrangements of different societies make translation difficult to the point at which attempts at cross-cultural generalization too often becomes little more than a construction of lists. Goldschmidt and Leach have both pointed out how the building up of typologies and classificatory schemes becomes empty and purposeless unless we have a theory which gives point and criteria to our classificatory activities. Both have also pointed out how if we compare for example marital institutions in different cultures, our definition of 'marriage' will either be drawn from one culture in terms of whose concepts other cultures will be described or rather misdescribed, or else will be so neutral, bare and empty as to be valueless.[1] That is, the understanding of a people in terms of their own concepts and beliefs does in fact tend to preclude understanding them in any other terms. To this extent Winch is vindicated. But an opposite moral to his can be drawn. We may conclude not that we ought not to generalize, but that such generalization must move at another level. Goldschmidt argues for the recommendation: Don't ask what an institution means for the agents themselves, ask what necessary needs and purposes it serves. He argues for this not because he looks for functionalist explanations of a Malinowskian kind, but because he believes that different institutions, embodying different conceptual schemes, may be illuminatingly seen as serving the same social necessities. To carry the argument further would be to raise questions that are not and cannot be raised within the framework of Winch's book. It is because I believe writers such as Goldschmidt are correct in saying that one must transcend such a framework that I believe also that Winch's book deserves close critical attention.

[1] See Kathleen Gough, 'The Nayars and the definition of marriage' in P. B. Hammond (ed.), *Cultural and Social Anthropology*, London, New York: Collier-Macmillan, 1964; E. R. Leach, 'Polyandry, inheritance and the definition of marriage with particular reference to Sinhalese customary law', in *Rethinking Anthropology*, op. cit.; and Goldschmidt, op. cit., pp. 17–26.

7

African Traditional Thought and Western Science

ROBIN HORTON

FROM TRADITION TO SCIENCE

Social anthropologists have often failed to understand traditional religious thought for two main reasons. First, many of them have been unfamiliar with the theoretical thinking of their own culture. This has deprived them of a vital key to understanding. For certain aspects of such thinking are the counterparts of those very features of traditional thought which they have tended to find most puzzling. Secondly, even those familiar with theoretical thinking in their own culture have failed to recognize its African equivalents, simply because they have been blinded by a difference of idiom. Like Consul Hutchinson wandering among the Bubis of Fernando Po, they have taken a language very remote from their own to be no language at all.

My approach is also guided by the conviction that an exhaustive exploration of features common to modern Western and traditional African thought should come before the enumeration of differences. By taking things in this order, we shall be less likely to mistake differences of idiom for differences of substance, and more likely to end up identifying those features which really do distinguish one kind of thought from the other.

Not surprisingly, perhaps, this approach has frequently been misunderstood. Several critics have objected that it tends to blur the undeniable distinction between traditional and scientific thinking; that indeed it presents traditional thinking as a species of science.[1] In order to clear up such misunderstandings, I propose to devote the second part of this paper to enumerating what I take to be the salient differences

This paper first appeared in a rather longer form in *Africa* XXXVII, Nos. 1 and 2 (January and April, 1967), pp. 50–71 and 155–87.

[1] See, for instance, John Beattie, 'Ritual and Social Change', *Journal of the Royal Anthropological Institute*, 1966, vol. I, No. 1.

between traditional and scientific thinking and to suggesting a tentative explanation of these differences.

In consonance with this programme, I shall start by setting out a number of general propositions on the nature and functions of theoretical thinking. These propositions are derived, in the first instance, from my own training in Biology, Chemistry, and Philosophy of Science. But, as I shall show, they are highly relevant to traditional African religious thinking. Indeed, they make sense of just those features of such thinking that anthropologists have often found most incomprehensible.

1. *The quest for explanatory theory is basically the quest for unity underlying apparent diversity; for simplicity underlying apparent complexity; for order underlying apparent disorder; for regularity underlying apparent anomaly*

Typically, this quest involves the elaboration of a scheme of entities or forces operating 'behind' or 'within' the world of common-sense observations. These entities must be of a limited number of kinds and their behaviour must be governed by a limited number of general principles. Such a theoretical scheme is linked to the world of everyday experience by statements identifying happenings within it with happenings in the everyday world. In the language of Philosophy of Science, such identification statements are known as Correspondence Rules. Explanations of observed happenings are generated from statements about the behaviour of entities in the theoretical scheme, plus Correspondence-Rule statements. In the sciences, well-known explanatory theories of this kind include the kinetic theory of gases, the planetary-atom theory of matter, the wave theory of light, and the cell theory of living organisms.

One of the perennial philosophical puzzles posed by explanations in terms of such theories derives from the Correspondence-Rule statements. In what sense can we really say that an increase of pressure in a gas 'is' an increase in the velocity of a myriad tiny particles moving in an otherwise empty space? How can we say that a thing is at once itself and something quite different? A great variety of solutions has been proposed to this puzzle. The modern positivists have taken the view that it is the things of common sense that are real, while the 'things' of theory are mere fictions useful in ordering the world of common sense. Locke, Planck, and others have taken the line that it is the 'things' of theory that are real, while the things of the everyday world are mere appearances. Perhaps the most up-to-date line is that there are good reasons for conceding the reality both of common-sense things and of theoretical entities. Taking this line implies an admission that the 'is' of Correspondence-Rule statements is neither the 'is' of identity nor the 'is' of class-membership. Rather, it stands for a unity-in-duality uniquely characteristic of the relation between the world of common sense and the world of theory.

What has all this got to do with the gods and spirits of traditional African religious thinking? Not very much, it may appear at first glance. Indeed, some modern writers deny that traditional religious thinking is in any serious sense theoretical thinking. In support of their denial they contrast the simplicity, regularity, and elegance of the theoretical schemas of the sciences with the unruly complexity and caprice of the world of gods and spirits.[1]

But this antithesis does not really accord with modern field-work data. It is true that, in a very superficial sense, African cosmologies tend towards proliferation. From the point of view of sheer number, the spirits of some cosmologies are virtually countless. But in this superficial sense we can point to the same tendency in Western cosmology, which for every common-sense unitary object gives us a myriad molecules. If, however, we recognize that the aim of theory is the demonstration of a limited number of *kinds* of entity or process underlying the diversity of experience, then the picture becomes very different. Indeed, one of the lessons of such recent studies of African cosmologies as Middleton's *Lugbara Religion*, Lienhardt's *Divinity and Experience*, Fortes's *Oedipus and Job*, and my own articles on Kalabari, is precisely that the gods of a given culture do form a scheme which interprets the vast diversity of everyday experience in terms of the action of a relatively few *kinds* of forces. Thus in Middleton's book, we see how all the various oppositions and conflicts in Lugbara experience are interpreted as so many manifestations of the single underlying opposition between ancestors and *adro* spirits. Again, in my own work, I have shown how nearly everything that happens in Kalabari life can be interpreted in terms of a scheme which postulates three basic *kinds* of forces: ancestors, heroes, and water-spirits.

The same body of modern work gives the lie to the old stereotype of the gods as capricious and irregular in their behaviour. For it shows that each category of beings has its appointed functions in relation to the

[1] See Beattie, op. cit.

world of observable happenings. The gods may sometimes appear capricious to the unreflective ordinary man. But for the religious expert charged with the diagnosis of spiritual agencies at work behind observed events, a basic modicum of regularity in their behaviour is the major premiss on which his work depends. Like atoms, molecules, and waves, then, the gods serve to introduce unity into diversity, simplicity into complexity, order into disorder, regularity into anomaly.

Once we have grasped that this is their intellectual function, many of the puzzles formerly posed by 'mystical thinking' disappear. Take the exasperated, wondering puzzlements of Lévy-Bruhl over his 'primitive mentality'. How could primitives believe that a visible, tangible object was at once its solid self and the manifestation of an immaterial being? How could a man literally see a spirit in a stone? These puzzles, raised so vividly by Lévy-Bruhl, have never been satisfactorily solved by anthropologists. 'Mystical thinking' has remained uncomfortably, indigestibly *sui generis*. And yet these questions of Lévy-Bruhl's have a very familiar ring in the context of European philosophy. Indeed, if we substitute atoms and molecules for gods and spirits, these turn out to be the very questions posed by modern scientific theory in the minds of Berkeley, Locke, Quine, and a whole host of European philosophers from Newton's time onwards.

Why is it that anthropologists have been unable to see this? One reason is that many of them move only in the common-sense world of Western culture, and are unfamiliar with its various theoretical worlds. But perhaps familarity with Western theoretical thinking is not by itself enough. For a thoroughly unfamiliar idiom can still blind a man to a familiar form of thought. Because it prevents one from taking anything for granted, an unfamiliar idiom can help to show up all sorts of puzzles and problems inherent in an intellectual process which normally seems puzzle-free. But this very unfamiliarity can equally prevent us from seeing that the puzzles and problems are ones which crop up on our own doorstep. Thus it took a 'mystical' theorist like Bishop Berkeley to see the problems posed by the materialistic theories of Newton and his successors; but he was never able to see that the same problems were raised by his own theoretical framework. Again, it takes materialistically inclined modern social anthropologists to see the problems posed by the 'mystical' theories of traditional Africa; but, for the same reasons, such people can hardly be brought to see these very problems arising within their own theoretical framework.

2. Theory places things in a causal context wider than that provided by common sense

When we say that theory displays the order and regularity underlying apparent disorder and irregularity, one of the things we mean is that it provides a causal context for apparently 'wild' events. Putting things in a causal context is, of course, one of the jobs of common sense. But although it does this job well at a certain level, it seems to have limitations. Thus the principal tool of common sense is induction or 'putting two and two together', the process of inference so beloved of the positivist philosophers. But a man can only 'put two and two together' if he is looking in the right direction. And common sense furnishes him with a pair of horse-blinkers which severely limits the directions in which he can look. Thus common-sense thought looks for the antecedents of any happening amongst events adjacent in space and time: it abhors action at a distance. Again, common sense looks for the antecedents of a happening amongst events that are in some way commensurable with it. Common sense is at the root of the hard-dying dictum 'like cause, like effect'. Gross incommensurability defeats it.

Now one of the essential functions of theory is to help the mind transcend these limitations. And one of the most obvious achievements of modern scientific theory is its revelation of a whole array of causal connexions which are quite staggering to the eye of common sense. Think for instance of the connexion between two lumps of a rather ordinary looking metal, rushing towards each other with a certain acceleration, and a vast explosion capable of destroying thousands of people. Or think again of the connexion between small, innocuous water-snails and the disease of bilharziasis which can render whole populations lazy and inept.

Once again, we may ask what relevance all this has to traditional African religious thinking. And once again the stock answer may be 'precious little'. For a widely current view of such thinking still asserts that it is more interested in the supernatural causes of things than it is in their natural causes. This is a misinterpretation closely connected with the one we discussed in the previous section. Perhaps the best way to get rid of it is to consider the commonest case of the search for causes in traditional Africa—the diagnosis of disease. Through the length and breadth of the African continent, sick or afflicted people go to consult diviners as to the causes of their troubles. Usually, the answer they receive involves a god or other spiritual agency, and the remedy prescribed involves the propitiation or calling-off of this being.

But this is very seldom the whole story. For the diviner who diagnoses the intervention of a spiritual agency is also expected to give some acceptable account of what moved the agency in question to intervene. And this account very commonly involves reference to some event in the world of visible, tangible happenings. Thus if a diviner diagnoses the action of witchcraft influence or lethal medicine spirits, it is usual for him to add something about the human hatreds, jealousies, and misdeeds, that have brought such agencies into play. Or, if he diagnoses the wrath of an ancestor, it is usual for him to point to the human breach of kinship morality which has called down this wrath.

The situation here is not very different from that in which a puzzled American layman, seeing a large mushroom cloud on the horizon, consults a friend who happens to be a physicist. On the one hand, the physicist may refer him to theoretical entities. 'Why this cloud?' 'Well, a massive fusion of hydrogen nuclei has just taken place.' Pushed further, however, the physicist is likely to refer to the assemblage and dropping of a bomb containing certain special substances. Substitute 'disease' for 'mushroom cloud', 'spirit anger' for 'massive fusion of hydrogen nuclei', and 'breach of kinship morality' for 'assemblage and dropping of a bomb', and we are back again with the diviner. In both cases reference to theoretical entities is used to link events in the visible, tangible world (natural effects) to their antecedents in the same world (natural causes).

To say of the traditional African thinker that he is interested in supernatural rather than natural causes makes little more sense, therefore, than to say of the physicist that he is interested in nuclear rather than natural causes. Both are making the same use of theory to transcend the limited vision of natural causes provided by common sense.

Granted this common preoccupation with natural causes, the fact remains that the causal link between disturbed social relations and disease or misfortune, so frequently postulated by traditional religious thought, is one which seems somewhat strange and alien to many Western medical scientists. Following the normal practice of historians of Western ideas, we can approach the problem of trying to understand this strange causal notion from two angles. First of all, we can inquire what influence a particular theoretical idiom has in moulding this and similar traditional notions. Secondly, we can inquire whether the range of experience available to members of traditional societies has influenced causal notions by throwing particular conjunctions of events into special prominence.

Theory, as I have said, places events in a wider causal context than that provided by common sense. But once a particular theoretical idiom has been adopted, it tends to direct people's attention towards certain kinds of causal linkage and away from others. Now most traditional African cultures have adopted a personal idiom as the basis of their attempt to understand the world. And once one has adopted such an idiom, it is a natural step to suppose that personal beings underpin, amongst other things, the life and strength of social groups. Now it is in the nature of a personal being who has his designs thwarted to visit retribution on those who thwart him. Where the designs involve maintaining the strength and unity of a social group, members of the group who disturb this unity are thwarters, and hence are ripe for punishment. Disease and misfortune are the punishment. Once a personal idiom has been adopted, then, those who use it become heavily predisposed towards seeing a nexus between social disturbance and individual affliction.

Are these traditional notions of cause merely artefacts of the prevailing theoretical idiom, fantasies with no basis in reality? Or are they responses to features of people's experience which in some sense are 'really there'? My own feeling is that, although these notions are ones to which people are pre-disposed by the prevailing theoretical idiom, they also register certain important features of the objective situation.

Let us remind ourselves at this point that modern medical men, though long blinded to such things by the fantastic success of the germ theory of disease, are once more beginning to toy with the idea that disturbances in a person's social life can in fact contribute to a whole series of sicknesses, ranging from those commonly thought of as mental to many more commonly thought of as bodily. In making this rediscovery, however, the medical men have tended to associate it with the so-called 'pressures of modern living'. They have tended to imagine traditional societies as psychological paradises in which disease-producing mental stresses are at a minimum.

If life in modern industrial society contains sources of mental stress adequate to causing or exacerbating a wide range of sicknesses, so too does life in traditional village communities. Hence the need to approach traditional religious theories of the social causation of sickness with respect. Such respect and readiness to learn is, I suggest, particularly appropriate with regard to what is commonly known as mental disease. I say this because the grand theories of Western psychiatry have a notoriously insecure empirical base and are probably culture-bound to a high degree.

Even of those diseases in which the key factor is definitely an infecting micro-organism, I suggest, traditional religious theory has something to say which is worth listening to.

Over much of traditional Africa, let me repeat, we are dealing with small-scale, relatively self-contained communities. These are the sort of social units that, as my friend Dr Oruwariye puts it, 'have achieved equilibrium with their diseases'. A given population and a given set of diseases have been co-existing over many generations. Natural selection has played a considerable part in developing human resistance to diseases such as malaria, typhoid, small-pox, dysentery, etc. In addition, those who survive the very high peri-natal mortality have probably acquired an extra resistance by the very fact of having lived through one of these diseases just after birth. In such circumstances, an adult who catches one of these (for Europeans) killer diseases has good chances both of life and of death. In the absence of antimalarials or antibiotics, what happens to him will depend very largely on other factors that add to or subtract from his considerable natural resistance. In these circumstances the traditional healer's efforts to cope with the situation by ferreting out and attempting to remedy stress-producing disturbances in the patient's social field is probably very relevant. Such efforts may seem to have a ludicrously marginal importance to a hospital doctor wielding a nivaquine bottle and treating a non-resistant European malaria patient. But they may be crucial where there is no nivaquine bottle and a considerable natural resistance to malaria.

After reflecting on these things the modern doctor may well take some of these traditional causal notions seriously enough to put them to the test. If the difficulties of testing can be overcome, and if the notions pass the test, he will end up by taking them over into his own body of beliefs. At the same time, however, he will be likely to reject the theoretical framework that enabled the traditional mind to form these notions in the first place.

This is fair enough; for although, as I have shown, the gods and spirits do perform an important theoretical job in pointing to certain interesting forms of causal connexion, they are probably not very useful as the basis of a wider view of the world. Nevertheless, there do seem to be few cases in which the theoretical framework of which they are the basis may have something to contribute to the theoretical framework of modern medicine. To take an example, there are several points at which Western psycho-analytic theory, with its apparatus of personalized mental entities, resembles traditional West African religious theory. More specifically, as I have suggested elsewhere,[1] there are striking resemblances between psycho-analytic ideas about the individual mind as a congeries of warring entities, and West African ideas, about the body as a meeting place of multiple souls. In both systems of belief, one personal entity is identified with the stream of consciousness, whilst the others operate as an 'unconscious', sometimes co-operating with consciousness and sometimes at war with it. Now the more flexible psycho-analysts have long suspected that Freud's allocation of particular desires and fears to particular agencies of the mind may well be appropriate to certain cultures only. Thus his allocation of a great load of sexual desires and fears to the unconscious may well have been appropriate to the Viennese sub-culture he so largely dealt with, but it may not be appropriate to many other cultures. A study of West African soul theories, and of their allocation of particular desires and emotions to particular agencies of the mind, may well help the psycho-analyst to reformulate his theories in terms more appropriate to the local scene.

Modern Western medical scientists have long been distracted from noting the causal connexion between social disturbance and disease by the success of the germ theory. It would seem, indeed, that a conjunction of the germ theory, of the discovery of potent antibiotics and immunization techniques, and of conditions militating against the build-up of natural resistance to many killer infections, for long made it very difficult for scientists to see the importance of this connexion. Conversely, perhaps, a conjunction of no germ theory, no potent antibiotics, no immunization techniques, with conditions favouring the build-up of considerable natural resistance to killer infections, served to throw this same causal connexion into relief in the mind of the traditional healer. If one were asked to choose between germ theory innocent of psychosomatic insight and traditional psychosomatic theory innocent of ideas about infection, one would almost certainly choose the germ theory. For in terms of quantitative results it is clearly the more vital to human well-being. But it is salutary to remember that not all the profits are on one side.

From what has been said in this section, it should be clear that one commonly accepted way of contrasting traditional religious thought

[1] Robin Horton, 'Destiny and the Unconscious in West Africa', *Africa* XXXI, 2, 1961, pp. 110–16.

with scientific thought is misleading. I am thinking here of the contrast between traditional religious thought as 'non-empirical' with scientific thought as 'empirical'. In the first place, the contrast is misleading because traditional religious thought is no more nor less interested in the natural causes of things than is the theoretical thought of the sciences. Indeed, the intellectual function of its supernatural beings (as, too, that of atoms, waves, etc.) *is* the extension of people's vision of natural causes. In the second place, the contrast is misleading because traditional religious theory clearly does more than postulate causal connexions that bear no relation to experience. Some of the connexions it postulates are, by the standards of modern medical science, almost certainly real ones. To some extent, then, it successfully grasps reality.

I am not claiming traditional thought as a variety of scientific thought. In certain crucial respects, the two kinds of thought are related to experience in quite different ways, but it is not only where scientific method is in use that we find theories which both aim at grasping causal connexions and to some extent succeed in this aim. Scientific method is undoubtedly the surest and most efficient tool for arriving at beliefs that are successful in this respect; but it is not the only way of arriving at such beliefs. Given the basic process of theory-making, and an environmental stability which gives theory plenty of time to adjust to experience, a people's belief system may come, even in the absence of scientific method, to grasp at least some significant causal connexions which lie beyond the range of common sense. It is because traditional African religious beliefs demonstrate the truth of this that it seems apt to extend to them the label 'empirical'.

3. *Common sense and theory have complementary roles in everyday life*

In the history of European thought there has often been opposition to a new theory on the ground that it threatens to break up and destroy the old, familiar world of common sense. Such was the eighteenth-century opposition to Newtonian corpuscular theory, which, so many people thought, was all set to 'reduce' the warm, colourful beautiful world to a lifeless, colourless, wilderness of rapidly moving little balls. Not surprisingly, this eighteenth-century attack was led by people like Goethe and Blake—poets whose job was precisely to celebrate the glories of the world of common sense. Such, again, is the twentieth-century opposition to Behaviour Theory, which many people see as a threat to 'reduce' human beings to animals or even to machines. Much recent

Western Philosophy is a monotonous and poorly reasoned attempt to bludgeon us into believing that Behaviour Theory cannot possibly work. But just as the common-sense world of things and people remained remarkably unscathed by the Newtonian revolution, so there is reason to think it will not be too seriously touched by the Behaviour-Theory revolution. Indeed, a lesson of the history of European thought is that, while theories come and theories go, the world of common sense remains very little changed.

One reason for this is perhaps that all theories take their departure from the world of things and people, and ultimately return us to it. In this context, to say that a good theory 'reduces' something to something else is misleading. Ideally, a process of deduction from the premisses of a theory should lead us back to statements which portray the common-sense world in its full richness. In so far as this richness is not restored, by so much does theory fail. Another reason for the persistence of the world of common sense is probably that, within the limits discussed in the last section, common-sense thinking is handier and more economical than theoretical thinking. It is only when one needs to transcend the limited causal vision of common sense that one resorts to theory.

Take the example of an industrial chemist and his relationships with common salt. When he uses it in the house, his relationships with it are governed entirely by common sense. Invoking chemical theory to guide him in its domestic use would be like bringing up a pile-driver to hammer in a nail. Such theory may well lend no more colour to the chemist's domestic view of salt than it lends to the chemically uneducated rustic's view of the substance. When he uses it in his chemical factory, however, common sense no longer suffices. The things he wants to do with it force him to place it in a wider causal context than common sense provides; and he can only do this by viewing it in the light of atomic theory. At this point, someone may ask: 'And which does he think is the real salt; the salt of common sense or the salt of theory?' The answer, perhaps, is that both are equally real to him. For whatever the philosophers say, people develop a sense of reality about something to the extent that they use and act on language which implies that this something exists.

This discussion of common sense and theory in Western thought is very relevant to the understanding of traditional African religions. Early accounts of such religions stressed the ever-presence of the spirit world in the minds of men. Later on, fieldwork experience in African societies convinced most reporters that members of such societies attended to the spirit world rather intermittently.[1] Many modern criticisms of Lévy-Bruhl and other early theorists hinge on this observation. For the modern generation of social anthropologists, the big question has now become: 'On what kinds of occasion do people ignore the spirit world, and on what kinds of occasion do they attend to it?'

In answer we need to recognize the essentially theoretical character of traditional religious thinking. And here our discussion of common sense and theory in European thought becomes relevant.

I suggest that in traditional Africa relations between common sense and theory are essentially the same as they are in Europe. That is, common sense is the handier and more economical tool for coping with a wide range of circumstances in everyday life. Nevertheless, there are certain circumstances that can only be coped with in terms of a wider causal vision than common sense provides. And in these circumstances there is a jump to theoretical thinking.

Let me give an example drawn from my own fieldwork among the Kalabari people of the Niger Delta. Kalabari recognize many different kinds of diseases, and have an array of herbal specifics with which to treat them. Sometimes a sick person will be treated by ordinary members of his family who recognize the disease and know the specifics. Sometimes the treatment will be carried out on the instructions of a native doctor. When sickness and treatment follow these lines the atmosphere is basically commonsensical. Often, there is little or no reference to spiritual agencies.

Sometimes, however, the sickness does not respond to treatment, and it becomes evident that the herbal specific used does not provide the whole answer. The native doctor may rediagnose and try another specific. But if this produces no result the suspicion will arise that 'there is something else in this sickness'. In other words, the perspective provided by common sense is too limited. It is at this stage that a diviner is likely to be called in (it may be the native doctor who started the treatment). Using ideas about various spiritual agencies, he will relate the sickness to a wider range of circumstances—often to disturbances in the sick man's general social life.

What are we describing here is generally referred to as a jump from common sense to mystical thinking. But, as we have seen, it is also,

[1] See for instance E. E. Evans-Pritchard, *Theories of Primitive Religion*, Oxford 1965, p. 88.

more significantly, a jump from common sense to theory. And here, as in Europe, the jump occurs at the point where the limited causal vision of common sense curtails its usefulness in dealing with the situation on hand.

4. *Level of theory varies with context*

A person seeking to place some event in a wider causal context often has a choice of theories. Like the initial choice between common sense and theory, this choice too will depend on just how wide a context he wishes to bring into consideration. Where he is content to place the event in a relatively modest context, he will be content to use what is generally called a low-level theory—i.e. one that covers a relatively limited area of experience. Where he is more ambitious about context, he will make use of a higher-level theory—i.e. one that covers a larger area of experience. As the area covered by the lower-level theory is part of the area covered by the higher-level scheme, so too the entities postulated by the lower-level theory are seen as special manifestations of those postulated at the higher level. Hence they pose all the old problems of things which are at once themselves and at the same time manifestations of other quite different things.

It is typical of traditional African religious systems that they include, on the one hand, ideas about a multiplicity of spirits, and on the other hand, ideas about a single supreme being. Though the spirits are thought of as independent beings, they are also considered as so many manifestations of dependants of the supreme being. This conjunction of the many and the one has given rise to much discussion among students of comparative religion, and has evoked many ingenious theories. Most of these have boggled at the idea that polytheism and monotheism could coexist stably in a single system of thought. They have therefore tried to resolve the problem by supposing that the belief-systems in question are in transition from one type to the other. It is only recently, with the Nilotic studies of Evans-Pritchard and Lienhardt,[1] that the discussion has got anywhere near the point—which is that the many spirits and the one God play complementary roles in people's thinking. As Evans-Pritchard says: 'A theistic religion need be neither monotheistic nor polytheistic. It may be both. It is the question of the level, or situation, of thought, rather than of exclusive types of thought.'[2]

[1] E. E. Evans-Pritchard, *Nuer Religion*, Oxford, 1956; Godfrey Lienhardt, *Divinity and Experience: The Religion of the Dinka*, London, 1961.

[2] Evans-Pritchard, op. cit., p. 316.

On the basis of material from the Nilotic peoples, and on that of
material from such West African societies as Kalabari, Ibo, and Tallensi,[1]
one can make a tentative suggestion about the respective roles of the
many and the one in traditional African thought generally. In such
thought, I suggest, the spirits provide the means of setting an event
within a relatively limited causal context. They are the basis of a
theoretical scheme which typically covers the thinker's own community and immediate environment. The supreme being, on the other
hand, provides the means of setting an event within the widest possible
context. For it is the basis of a theory of the origin and life course of the
world seen as a whole.

In many (though by no means all) traditional African belief-systems,
ideas about the spirits and actions based on such ideas are far more
richly developed than ideas about the supreme being and actions based
on them. In these cases, the idea of God seems more the pointer to a
potential theory than the core of a seriously operative one. This
perhaps is because social life in the communities involved is so parochial
that their members seldom have to place events in the wider context
that the idea of the supreme being purports to deal with. Nevertheless,
the different levels of thinking are there in all these systems. It seems
clear that they are related to one another in much the same way as are
the different levels of theoretical thinking in the sciences. At this point
the relation between the many spirits and the one God loses much of
its aura of mystery. Indeed there turns out to be nothing peculiarly
religious or 'mystical' about it. For it is essentially the same as the
relation between the homogeneous atoms and planetary systems of
fundamental particles in the thinking of a chemist. It is a by-product of
certain very general features of the way theories are used in explanation.

5. *All theory breaks up the unitary objects of common sense into aspects, then
   places the resulting elements in a wider causal context. That is, it first
   abstracts and analyses, then re-integrates*

Commentators on scientific method have familiarized us with the way
in which the theoretical schemas of the sciences break up the world of

[1] Robin Horton, 'The Kalabari World-View: An Outline and Interpretation',
Africa, XXXII, 3, 1962, pp. 197–220; 'A Hundred Years of Change in Kalabari
Religion' (Unpublished paper for the University of Ife Conference on 'The High
God in Africa', December 1964); 'God, Man, and the Land in a Northern Ibo
Village Group', *Africa* XXVI, 1, 1956, pp. 17–28; M. Fortes, *The Web of Kinship
among the Tallensi*, London, 1949, esp. pp. 21–22 and 219.

common-sense things in order to achieve a causal understanding which surpasses that of common sense. But it is only from the more recent studies of African cosmologies, where religious beliefs are shown in the context of the various everyday contingencies they are invoked to explain, that we have begun to see how traditional religious thought also operates by a similar process of abstraction, analysis, and reintegration. A good example is provided by Fortes's recent work on West African theories of the individual and his relation to society. Old-fashioned West African ethnographers showed the wide distribution of beliefs in what they called 'multiple souls'. They found that many West African belief-systems invested the individual with a multiplicity of spiritual agencies. The general impression they gave was one of an unruly fantasy at work. In his recent book,[1] however, Fortes takes the 'multiple soul' beliefs of a single West African people (the Tallensi) and places them in the context of everyday thought and behaviour. His exposition dispels much of the aura of fantasy.

Fortes describes three categories of spiritual agency especially concerned with the Tale individual. First comes the *segr*, which presides over the individual as a biological entity—over his sickness and health, his life and death. Then comes the *nuor yin*, a personification of the wishes expressed by the individual before his arrival on earth. The *nuor yin* appears specifically concerned with whether or not the individual has the personality traits necessary if he is to become an adequate member of Tale society. As Fortes puts it, evil *nuor yin* 'serves to identify the fact of irremediable failure in the development of the individual to full social capacity'. Good *nuor yin*, on the other hand, 'identifies the fact of successful individual development along the road to full incorporation in society'. Finally, in this trio of spiritual agencies, we have what Fortes calls the '*yin* ancestors'. These are two or three out of the individual's total heritage of ancestors, who have been delegated to preside over his personal fortunes. *Yin* ancestors only attach themselves to an individual who has a good *nuor yin*. They are concerned with the fortunes of the person who has already proved himself to have the basic equipment for fitting into Tale society. Here we have a theoretical scheme which, in order to produce a deeper understanding of the varying fortunes of individuals in their society, breaks them down into three aspects by a simple but typical operation of abstraction and analysis.

Perhaps the most significant comment on Fortes' work in this field

[1] Fortes, op. cit.

was pronounced, albeit involuntarily, by a reviewer of 'Oeidipus and Job'.[1] 'If any criticism of the presentation is to be made it is that Professor Fortes sometimes seems to achieve an almost mystical identification with the Tallensi world-view and leaves the unassimilated reader in some doubt about where to draw the line between Tallensi notions and Cambridge concepts!' Now the anthropologist has to find *some* concepts in his own language roughly appropriate to translating the 'notions' of the people he studies. And in the case in question, perhaps only the lofty analytic 'Cambridge' concepts did come anywhere near to congruence with Tallensi notions. This parallel between traditional African religious 'notions' and Western sociological 'abstractions' is by no means an isolated phenomenon. Think for instance of individual guardian spirits and group spirits—two very general categories of traditional African religious thought. Then think of those hardy Parsonian abstractions—psychological imperatives and sociological imperatives. It takes no great brilliance to see the resemblance.[2]

6. *In evolving a theoretical scheme, the human mind seems constrained to draw inspiration from analogy between the puzzling observations to be explained and certain already familiar phenoma*

In the genesis of a typical theory, the drawing of an analogy between the unfamiliar and the familiar is followed by the making of a model in which something akin to the familiar is postulated as the reality underlying the unfamiliar. Both modern Western and traditional African thought-products amply demonstrate the truth of this. Whether we look amongst atoms, electrons, and waves, or amongst gods, spirits, and entelechies, we find that theoretical notions nearly always have their roots in relatively homely everyday experiences, in analogies with the familiar.

What do we mean here by 'familiar phenomena'? Above all, I suggest, we mean phenomena strongly associated in the mind of the observer with order and regularity. That theory should depend on analogy with things familiar in this sense follows from the very nature of explanation. Since the overriding aim of explanation is to disclose

[1] R. E. Bradbury in *Man*, September 1959.
[2] Such parallels arouse the more uncomfortable thought that in all the theorizing we sociologists have done about the working of traditional African societies, we may often have done little more than translate indigenous African theories about such workings.

order and regularity underlying apparent chaos, the search for explanatory analogies must tend towards those areas of experience most closely associated with such qualities. Here, I think, we have a basis for indicating why explanations in modern Western culture tend to be couched in an impersonal idiom, while explanations in traditional African society tend to be couched in a personal idiom.

In complex, rapidly changing industrial societies the human scene is in flux. Order, regularity, predictability, simplicity, all these seem lamentably absent. It is in the world of inanimate things that such qualities are most readily seen. This is why many people can find themselves less at home with their fellow men than with things. And this too, I suggest, is why the mind in quest of explanatory analogies turns most readily to the inanimate. In the traditional societies of Africa, we find the situation reversed. The human scene is the locus *par excellence* of order, predictability, regularity. In the world of the inanimate, these qualities are far less evident. Here, being less at home with people than with things is unimaginable. And here, the mind in quest of explanatory analogies turns naturally to people and their relations.

7. *Where theory is founded on analogy between puzzling observations and familiar phenomena, it is generally only a limited aspect of such phenomena that is incorporated into the resulting model*

Philosophers of science have often used the molecular (kinetic) theory of gases as an illustration of this feature of model-building. The molecular theory, of course, is based on an analogy with the behaviour of fast-moving, spherical balls in various kinds of space. And the philosophers have pointed out that although many important properties of such balls have been incorporated into the definition of a molecule, other important properties such as colour and temperature have been omitted. They have been omitted because they have no explanatory function in relation to the observations that originally evoked the theory. Here, of course, we have another sense in which physical theory is based upon abstraction and abstract ideas. For concepts such as 'molecule', 'atom', 'electron', 'wave' are the result of a process in which the relevant features of certain prototype phenomena have been abstracted from the irrelevant features.

Many writers have considered this sort of abstraction to be one of the distinctive features of scientific thinking. But this, like so many other such distinctions, is a false one; for just the same process is at work in traditional African thought. Thus when traditional thought draws upon people and their social relations as the raw material of its theoretical models, it makes use of some dimensions of human life and neglects others. The definition of a god may omit any reference to his physical appearance, his diet, his mode of lodging, his children, his relations with his wives, and so on. Asking questions about such attributes is as inappropriate as asking questions about the colour of a molecule or the temperature of an electron. It is this omission of many dimensions of human life from the definition of the gods which gives them that rarefied, attenuated aura which we call 'spiritual' But there is nothing peculiarly religious, mystical, or traditional about this 'spirituality'. It is the result of the same process of abstraction as the one we see at work in Western theoretical models: the process whereby features of the prototype phenomena which have explanatory relevance are incorporated into a theoretical schema, while features which lack such relevance are omitted.

8. *A theoretical model, once built, is developed in ways which sometimes obscure the analogy on which it was founded*

In its raw, initial state, a model may come up quite quickly against data for which it cannot provide any explanatory coverage. Rather than scrap it out of hand, however, its users will tend to give it successive modifications in order to enlarge its coverage. Sometimes, such modifications will involve the drawing of further analogies with phenomena rather different from those which provided the initial inspiration for the model. Sometimes, they will merely involve 'tinkering' with the model until it comes to fit the new observations. By comparison with the phenomena which provided its original inspiration, such a developed model not unnaturally seems to have a bizarre, hybrid air about it.

   Examples of the development of theoretical models abound in the history of science. One of the best documented of these is provided by the modern atomic theory of matter. The foundations of this theory were laid by Rutherford, who based his original model upon an analogy between the passage of ray-beams through metal foil and the passage of comets through our planetary system. Rutherford's planetary model of the basic constituents of matter proved extremely useful in explanation. When it came up against recalcitrant data, therefore, the consensus of scientists was in favour of developing it rather than scrapping it. Each of several modifications of the model was a response to the demand for increased explanatory coverage. Each, however, removed the theoretical model one step further away from the familiar phenomena which had furnished its original inspiration.

In studying traditional African thought, alas, we scarcely ever have the historical depth available to the student of European thought. So we can make few direct observations on the development of its theoretical models. Nevertheless, these models often show just the same kinds of bizarre, hybrid features as the models of the scientists. Since they resemble the latter in so many other ways, it seems reasonable to suppose that these features are the result of a similar process of development in response to demands for further explanatory coverage. The validity of such a supposition is strengthened when we consider detailed instances: for these show how the bizarre features of particular models are indeed closely related to the nature of the observations that demand explanation.

Let me draw one example from my own field-work on Kalabari religious thought which I have outlined in earlier publications. Basic Kalabari religious beliefs involve three main categories of spirits: ancestors, heroes, and water-people. On the one hand, all three categories of spirits show many familiar features: emotions of pleasure and anger, friendships, enmities, marriages. Such features betray the fact that, up to a point, the spirits are fashioned in the image of ordinary Kalabari people. Beyond this point, however, they are bizarre in many ways. The ancestors, perhaps, remain closest to the image of ordinary people. But the heroes are decidedly odd. They are defined as having left no descendants, as having disappeared rather than died, and as having come in the first instance from outside the community. The water-spirits are still odder. They are said to be 'like men, and also like pythons'. To make sense of these oddities, let us start by sketching the relations of the various kinds of spirits to the world of everyday experience.

First, the ancestors. These are postulated as the forces underpinning the life and strength of the lineages, bringing misfortune to those who betray lineage values and fortune to those who promote them. Second, the heroes. These are the forces underpinning the life and strength of the community and its various institutions. They are also the forces underpinning human skill and maintaining its efficacy in the struggle against nature. Third, the water-spirits. On the one hand, these are the 'owners' of the creeks and swamps, the guardians of the fish harvest, the forces of nature. On the other hand, they are the patrons of human individualism—in both its creative and its destructive forms. In short, they are the forces underpinning all that lies beyond the confines of the established social order.

We can look on ancestors, heroes, and water-spirits as the members of a triangle of forces. In this triangle, the relation of each member to the other two contains elements of separation and opposition as well as of co-operation. Thus by supporting lineages in rivalry against one another, the ancestors can work against the heroes in sapping the strength of the community; but in other contexts, by strengthening their several lineages, they can work with the heroes in contributing to village strength. Again, when they bring up storms, rough water, and sharks, the water-spirits work against the heroes by hampering the exercise of the village's productive skills; but when they produce calm water and an abundance of fish, they work just as powerfully with the heroes. Yet again, by fostering anti-social activity, the water-spirits can work against both heroes and ancestors; or, by supporting creativity and invention, they can enrich village life and so work with them.

In this triangle, then, we have a theoretical scheme in terms of which Kalabari can grasp and comprehend most of the many vicissitudes of their daily lives. Now it is at this point that the bizarre, paradoxical attributes of heroes and water-spirits begin to make sense: for a little inspection shows that such attributes serve to define each category of spirits in a way appropriate to its place in the total scheme. This is true, for example, of such attributes of the heroes as having left no human descendants, having disappeared instead of undergoing death and burial, and having come from outside the community. All these serve effectively to define the heroes as forces quite separate from the ancestors with their kinship involvements. Lack of descendants does this in an obvious way. Disappearance rather than death and burial performs the same function, especially when, as in Kalabari, lack of burial is almost synonymous with lack of kin. And arrival from outside the community again makes it clear that they cannot be placed in any lineage or kinship context. These attributes, in short, are integral to the definition of the heroes as forces contrasted with and potentially opposed to the ancestors. Again, the water-spirits are said to be 'like men, and also like pythons'; and here too the paradoxical characterization is essential to defining their place in the triangle. The python is regarded as the most powerful of all the animals in the creeks, and is often said to be their father. But its power is seen as something very different from that of human beings—something 'fearful' and 'astonishing'. The combination of human and python elements in the characterization of the water-people fits the latter perfectly for their own place in the triangle—as forces of the extra-social contrasted with and potentially opposed to both heroes and ancestors.

Another illuminating example of the theoretical significance of oddity is provided by Middleton's account of traditional Lugbara religious concepts.[1] According to Middleton, Lugbara belief features two main categories of spiritual agency—the ancestors and the *adro* spirits. Like the Kalabari ancestors, those of the Lugbara remain close to the image of ordinary people. The *adro*, however, are very odd indeed. They are cannibalistic and incestuous, and almost everything else that Lugbara ordinarily consider repulsive. They are commonly said to walk upside down—a graphic expression of their general perversity. Once again, these oddities fall into place when we look at the relations of the two categories of spirits to the world of experience. The ancestors, on the one hand, account for the settled world of human habitation and with the established social order organized on the basis of small lineages. The *adro*, on the other hand, are concerned with the uncultivated bush, and with all human activities which run counter to the established order of things. Like the Kalabari water-spirits, they are forces of the extra-social, whether in its natural or its human form. The contrast and opposition between ancestors and *adro* thus provides Lugbara with a theoretical schema in terms of which they can comprehend a whole series of oppositions and conflicts manifest in the world of their everyday experiences. Like the oddities of the Kalabari gods, those of the *adro* begin to make sense at this point. For it is the bizarre, perverse features of these spirits that serve to define their position in the theory—as forces contrasted with and opposed to the ancestors.

In both of these cases the demands of explanation result in a model whose structure is hybrid between that of the human social phenomena which provided its original inspiration, and that of the field of experience to which it is applied. In both cases, oddity is essential to explanatory function. Even in the absence of more direct historical evidence, these examples suggest that the theoretical models of traditional African thought are the products of developmental processes comparable to those affecting the models of the sciences.

[1] John Middleton, *Lugbara Religion: Ritual and Authority among an East African People*, London, 1960.

In treating traditional African religious systems as theoretical models akin to those of the sciences, I have really done little more than take them at their face value. Although this approach may seem naïve and platitudinous compared to the sophisticated 'things-are-never-what-they-seem' attitude more characteristic of the social anthropologist, it has certainly produced some surprising results. Above all, it has cast doubt on most of the well-worn dichotomies used to conceptualize the difference between scientific and traditional religious thought. Intellectual versus emotional; rational versus mystical; reality-oriented versus fantasy-oriented; causally oriented versus supernaturally oriented; empirical versus non-empirical; abstract versus concrete; analytical versus non-analytical: all of these are shown to be more or less inappropriate. If the reader is disturbed by this casting away of established distinctions, he will, I hope, accept it when he sees how far it can pave the way towards making sense of so much that previously appeared senseless.

One thing that may well continue to bother the reader is my playing down of the difference between non-personal and personal theory. For while I have provided what seems to me an adequate explanation of this difference, I have treated it as a surface difference concealing an underlying similarity of intellectual process. I must confess that I have used brevity of treatment here as a device to play down the gulf between the two kinds of theory. But I think this is amply justifiable in reaction to the more usual state of affairs, in which the difference is allowed to dominate all other features of the situation. Even familiarity with theoretical thinking in their own culture cannot help anthropologists who are dominated by this difference. For once so blinded, they can only see traditional religious thought as wholly other. With the bridge from their own thought-patterns to those of traditional Africa blocked, it is little wonder they can make no further headway.

The aim of my exposition has been to reopen this bridge. The point I have sought to make is that the difference between non-personal and personalized theories is more than anything else a difference in the idiom of the explanatory quest. Grasping this point is an essential preliminary to realizing how far the various established dichotomies used in this field are simply obstacles to understanding. Once it is grasped, a whole series of seemingly bizarre and senseless features of traditional thinking becomes immediately comprehensible. Until it is grasped, they remain essentially mysterious. Making the business of personal versus impersonal entities the crux of the difference between tradition and science not only blocks the understanding of tradition. It also draws a red herring across the path to an understanding of science.

All this is not to deny that science has progressed greatly through working in a non-personal theoretical idiom. Indeed, as one who has hankerings after behaviourism, I am inclined to believe that it is this idiom, and this idiom only, which will eventually lead to the triumph of science in the sphere of human affairs. What I am saying, however, is that this is more a reflection of the nature of reality than a clue to the essence of scientific method. For the progressive acquisition of knowledge, man needs both the right kind of theories *and* the right attitude to them. But it is only the latter which we call science. Indeed, as we shall see, any attempt to define science in terms of a particular kind of theory runs contrary to its very essence. Now, at last, I hope it will be evident why, in comparing African traditional thought with Western scientific thought, I have chosen to start with a review of continuities rather than with a statement of crucial differences. For although this order of procedure carries the risk of one's being understood to mean that traditional thought is a kind of science, it also carries the advantage of having the path clear of red herrings when one comes to tackle the question of differences.

THE 'CLOSED' AND 'OPEN' PREDICAMENTS

Turning, to the differences in African thought and Western science, I start by isolating one which strikes me as the key to all the others, and go on to suggest how the latter flow from it.

What I take to be the key difference is a very simple one. It is that in traditional cultures there is no developed awareness of alternatives to the established body of theoretical tenets; whereas in scientifically oriented cultures, such an awareness is highly developed. It is this difference we refer to when we say that traditional cultures are 'closed' and scientifically oriented cultures 'open'.[1]

---

[1] Philosophically minded readers will notice here some affinities with Karl Popper, who also makes the transition from a 'closed' to an 'open' predicament crucial for the take-off from tradition to science. For me, however, Popper obscures the issue by packing too many contracts into his definitions of 'closed' and 'open'. Thus, for him, the transition from one predicament to the other implies not just a growth in the awareness of alternatives, but also a transition from communalism to individualism, and from ascribed status to achieved status. But as I hope to show in this essay, it is the awareness of alternatives which is crucial for the take-off into science. Not individualism or achieved status: for

One important consequence of the lack of awareness of alternatives is very clearly spelled out by Evans-Pritchard in his pioneering work on Azande witchcraft beliefs. Thus he says:

> I have attempted to show how rhythm, mode of utterance, content of prophecies, and so forth, assist in creating faith in witch-doctors, but these are only some of the ways in which faith is supported, and do not entirely explain belief. Weight of tradition alone can do that. . . . There is no incentive to agnosticism. All their beliefs hang together, and were a Zande to give up faith in witch-doctorhood, he would have to surrender equally his faith in witchcraft and oracles. . . . In this web of belief every strand depends upon every other strand, *and a Zande cannot get out of its meshes because it is the only world he knows. The web is not an external structure in which he is enclosed. It is the texture of his thought and he cannot think that his thought is wrong.*[1]

And again:

> And yet Azande do not see that their oracles tell them nothing! Their blindness is not due to stupidity, for they display great ingenuity in explaining away the failure and inequalities of the poison oracle and experimental keenness in testing it. It is due rather to the fact that their intellectual ingenuity and experimental keenness are conditioned by patterns of ritual behaviour and mystical belief. Within the limits set by these patterns, they show great intelligence, but it cannot operate beyond these limits. Or, to put it in another way; *they reason excellently in the idiom of their beliefs, but they cannot reason outside, or against their beliefs because they have no other idiom in which to express their thoughts.*[2]

In other words, absence of any awareness of alternatives makes for an absolute acceptance of the established theoretical tenets, and removes any possibility of questioning them. In these circumstances, the established tenets invest the believer with a compelling force. It is this force which we refer to when we talk of such tenets as sacred.

A second important consequence of lack of awareness of alternatives is that any challenge to established tenets is a threat of chaos, of the cosmic abyss, and therefore evokes intense anxiety.

there are lots of societies where both of the latter are well developed, but which show no signs whatever of take-off. In the present context, therefore, my own narrower definition of 'closed' and 'open' seems more appropriate.

[1] E. E. Evans-Pritchard, *Witchcraft, Oracles and Magic among the Azande*, Oxford, 1936, p. 194.

[2] Ibid., p. 338.

With developing awareness of alternatives, the established theoretical tenets come to seem less absolute in their validity, and lose something of their sacredness. At the same time, a challenge to these tenets is no longer a horrific threat of chaos. For just as the tenets themselves have lost some of their absolute validity, a challenge to them is no longer a threat of absolute calamity. It can now be seen as nothing more threatening than an intimation that new tenets might profitably be tried. Where these conditions begin to prevail, the stage is set for change from a traditional to a scientific outlook.

Here, then, we have two basic predicaments: the 'closed'—characterized by lack of awareness of alternatives, sacredness of beliefs, and anxiety about threats to them; and the 'open'—characterized by awareness of alternatives, diminished sacredness of beliefs, and diminished anxiety about threats to them.

Now, as I have said, I believe all the major differences between traditional and scientific outlooks can be understood in terms of these two predicaments. In substantiating this, I should like to divide the differences into two groups: those directly connected with the presence or absence of a vision of alternatives; and those directly connected with the presence or absence of anxiety about threats to the established beliefs.[1]

DIFFERENCES CONNECTED WITH THE PRESENCE OR ABSENCE OF A VISION OF ALTERNATIVES

(a) Magical versus non-magical attitude to words

A central characteristic of nearly all the traditional African world-views we know of is an assumption about the power of words, uttered under appropriate circumstances, to bring into being the events or states they stand for.

The most striking examples of this assumption are to be found in creation mythologies where the supreme being is said to have formed the world out of chaos by uttering the names of all things in it. Such mythologies occur most notably in Ancient Egypt and among the peoples of the Western Sudan.

---

[1] In this abridged version of the paper only the former are discussed. For a discussion of differences connected with anxiety about threats to established beliefs the reader is referred to the original version of the paper, in *Africa*, XXVII, No. 2, esp. pp. 167ff.

In traditional African cultures, to know the name of a being or thing is to have some degree of control over it. In the invocation of spirits, it is essential to call their names correctly; and the control which such correct calling gives is one reason why the true or 'deep' names of gods are often withheld from strangers, and their utterance forbidden to all but a few whose business it is to use them in ritual. Similar ideas lie behind the very widespread traditional practice of using euphemisms to refer to such things as dangerous diseases and wild animals: for it is thought that use of the real names might secure their presence. Yet again, it is widely believed that harm can be done to a man by various operations performed on his name—for instance, by writing his name on a piece of paper and burning it.

Through a very wide range of traditional African belief and activity, it is possible to see an implicit assumption as to the magical power of words.

Now if we take into account what I have called the basic predicament of the traditional thinker, we can begin to see why this assumption should be so deeply entrenched in his daily life and thought. Briefly, no man can make contact with reality save through a screen of words. Hence no man can escape the tendency to see a unique and intimate link between words and things. For the traditional thinker this tendency has an overwhelming power. Since he can imagine no alternatives to his established system of concepts and words, the latter appear bound to reality in an absolute fashion. There is no way at all in which they can be seen as varying independently of the segments of reality they stand for. Hence they appear so integrally involved with their referents that any manipulation of the one self-evidently affects the other.

The scientist's attitude to words is, of course, quite opposite. He dismisses contemptuously any suggestion that words could have an immediate, magical power over the things they stand for. Indeed, he finds magical notions amongst the most absurd and alien trappings of traditional thought. Though he grants an enormous power to words, it is the indirect one of bringing control over things through the functions of explanation and prediction.

Why does the scientist reject the magician's view of words? One easy answer is that he has come to know better: magical behaviour has been found not to produce the results it claims to. Perhaps. But what scientist has ever bothered to put magic to the test? The answer is, none; because there are deeper grounds for rejection—grounds which make the idea of testing beside the point.

To see what these grounds are, let us return to the scientist's basic predicament—to his awareness of alternative idea-systems whose ways of classifying and interpreting the world are very different from his own. Now this changed awareness gives him two intellectual possibilities. Both are eminently thinkable; but one is intolerable, the other hopeful.

The first possibility is simply a continuance of the magical world-view. If ideas and words are inextricably bound up with reality, and if indeed they shape it and control it, then, a multiplicity of idea-systems means a multiplicity of realities, and a change of ideas means a change of things. But whereas there is nothing particularly absurd or inconsistent about this view, it is clearly intolerable in the extreme. For it means that the world is in the last analysis dependent on human whim, that the search for order is a folly, and that human beings can expect to find no sort of anchor in reality.

The second possibility takes hold as an escape from this horrific prospect. It is based on the faith that while ideas and words change, there must be some anchor, some constant reality. This faith leads to the modern view of words and reality as independent variables. With its advent, words come 'unstuck from' reality and are no longer seen as acting magically upon it. Intellectually, this second possibility is neither more nor less respectable than the first. But it has the great advantage of being tolerable whilst the first is horrific.

That the outlook behind magic still remains an intellectual possibility in the scientifically oriented cultures of the modern West can be seen from its survival as a nagging undercurrent in the last 300 years of Western philosophy. This undercurrent generally goes under the labels of 'Idealism' and 'Solipsism'; and under these labels it is not immediately recognizable. But a deeper scrutiny reveals that the old outlook is there all right—albeit in a strange guise. True, Idealism does not say that words create, sustain, and have power over that which they represent. Rather, it says that material things are 'in the mind'. That is, the mind creates, sustains, and has power over matter. But the second view is little more than a post-Cartesian transposition of the first. Let me elaborate. Both in traditional African cosmologies and in European cosmologies before Descartes, the modern distinction between 'mind' and 'matter' does not appear. Although everything in the universe is underpinned by spiritual forces, what moderns would call 'mental activities' and 'material things' are both part of a single reality, neither material nor immaterial. Thinking, conceiving, saying, etc. are described in terms or organs like heart and brain and actions like the uttering of words. Now when Descartes wrote his philosophical works, he crystallized a half-way phase in the transition from a personal to an impersonal cosmological idiom. Whilst 'higher' human activities still remained under the aegis of a personalized theory, physical and biological events were brought under the aegis of impersonal theory. Hence thinking, conceiving, saying, etc. became manifestations of 'mind', whilst all other happenings became manifestations of 'matter'. Hence whereas before Descartes we have 'words over things', after him we have 'mind over matter'—just a new disguise for the old view.

What I have said about this view being intellectually respectable but emotionally intolerable is borne out by the attitude to it of modern Western philosophers. Since they are duty bound to explore all the alternative possibilities of thought that lie within the grasp of their imaginations, these philosophers mention, nay even expound, the doctrines of Idealism and Solipsism. Invariably, too, they follow up their expositions with attempts at refutation. But such attempts are, just as invariably, a farce. Their character is summed up in G. E. Moore's desperate gesture, when challenged to prove the existence of a world outside his mind, of banging his hand with his fist and exclaiming: 'It is there!' A gesture of faith rather than of reason, if ever there was one!

With the change from the 'closed' to the 'open' predicament, then, the outlook behind magic becomes intolerable; and to escape from it people espouse the view that words vary independently of reality. Smug rationalists who congratulate themselves on their freedom from magical thinking would do well to reflect on the nature of this freedom!

(b) *Ideas-bound-to-occasions versus ideas-bound-to-ideas*

Many commentators on the idea-systems of traditional African cultures have stressed that, for members of these cultures, their thought does not appear as something distinct from and opposable to the realities that call it into action. Rather, particular passages of thought are bound to the particular occasions that evoke them.

Let us take an example. Someone becomes sick. The sickness proves intractable and the relatives call a diviner. The latter says the sickness is due to an ancestor who has been angered by the patient's bad behaviour towards his kinsmen. The diviner prescribes placatory offerings to the spirit and reconciliation with the kinsmen, and the patient is eventually cured. Now while this emergency is on, both the diviner and the patient's relatives may justify what they are doing by reference to some general statements about the kinds of circumstance which arouse ancestors to cause sickness. But theoretical statements of this kind are very much matters of occasion, not likely to be heard out of context or as part of a general discussion of 'what we believe'.

If ideas in traditional culture are seen as bound to occasions rather than to other ideas, the reason is one that we have already given in our discussion of magic. Since the member of such a culture can imagine no alternatives to his established system of ideas, the latter appear inexorably bound to the portions of reality they stand for. They cannot be seen as in any way opposable to reality.

In a scientifically oriented culture such as that of the Western anthropologist, things are very different. The very word 'idea' has the connotation of something opposed to reality. Nor is it entirely coincidental that in such a culture the historian of ideas is considered to be the most unrealistic kind of historian. Not only are ideas dissociated in people's minds from the reality that occasions them: they are bound to other ideas, to form wholes and systems perceived as such. Belief-systems take shape not only as abstractions in the minds of anthropologists, but also as totalities in the minds of believers.

Here again, this change can be readily understood in terms of a change from the 'closed' to the 'open' predicament. A vision of alternative possibilities forces men to the faith that ideas somehow vary whilst reality remains constant. Ideas thus become detached from reality—nay, even in a sense opposed to it. Furthermore, such a vision, by giving the thinker an opportunity to 'get outside' his own system, offers him a possibility of his coming to see it *as a system*.

(c) Unreflective versus reflective thinking

At this stage of the analysis there is no need for me to insist further on the essential rationality of traditional thought. I have already made it far too rational for the taste of most social anthropologists. And yet, there is a sense in which this thought includes among its accomplishments neither Logic or Philosophy.

Let me explain this, at first sight, rather shocking statement. It is true that most African traditional world-views are logically elaborated to a high degree. It is also true that, because of their eminently rational character, they are appropriately called 'philosophies'. But here I am using 'Logic' and 'Philosophy' in a more exact sense. By Logic, I mean thinking directed to answering the question: 'What are the general rules by which we can distinguish good arguments from bad ones?' And by Philosophy, I mean thinking directed to answering the question: 'On what grounds can we ever claim to know anything about the world?' Now Logic and Philosophy, in these restricted senses, are poorly developed in traditional Africa. Despite its elaborate and often penetrating cosmological, sociological, and psychological speculations, traditional thought has tended to get on with the work of explanation, without pausing for reflection upon the nature or rules of this work. Thinking once more of the 'closed' predicament, we can readily see why these second-order intellectual activities should be virtually absent from traditional cultures. Briefly, the traditional thinker, because he is unable to imagine possible alternatives to his established theories and classifications, can never start to formulate generalized norms of reasoning and knowing. For only where there are alternatives can there be choice, and only where there is choice can there be norms governing it. As they are characteristically absent in traditional cultures, so Logic and Philosophy are characteristically present in all scientifically oriented cultures. Just as the 'closed' predicament makes it impossible for them to appear, so the 'open' predicament makes it inevitable that they must appear. For where the thinker can see the possibility of alternatives to his established idea-system, the question of choice at once arises, and the development of norms governing such choice cannot be far behind.[1]

(d) Mixed versus segregated motives

This contrast is very closely related to the preceding one. The goals of explanation and prediction are as powerfully present in traditional African cultures as they are in cultures where science has become institutionalized. In the absence of explicit norms of thought, however, we find them vigorously pursued but not explicitly reflected upon and defined. In these circumstances, there is little thought about their consistency or inconsistency with other goals and motives. Hence wherever we find a theoretical system with explanatory and predictive functions,

[1] See Ernest Gellner, *Thought and Change*, London, 1964, for a similar point exemplified in the Philosophy of Descartes p.105.

we find other motives entering in and contributing to its development.

Despite their cognitive preoccupations, most African religious systems are powerfully influenced by what are commonly called 'emotional needs'—i.e. needs for certain kinds of personal relationship. In Africa, as elsewhere, all social systems stimulate in their members a considerable diversity of such needs; but, having stimulated them, they often prove unwilling or unable to allow them full opportunities for satisfaction. In such situations the spirits function not only as theoretical entities but as surrogate people providing opportunities for the formation of ties forbidden in the purely human social field. The latter function they discharge in two ways. First, by providing non-human partners with whom people can take up relationships forbidden with other human beings. Second, though the mechanism of possession, by allowing people to 'become' spirits and so to play roles *vis-à-vis* their fellow men which they are debarred from playing as ordinary human beings.

There is little doubt that because the theoretical entities of traditional thought happen to be people, they give particular scope for the working of emotional and aesthetic motives. Here, perhaps, we do have something about the personal idiom in theory that does militate indirectly against the taking up of a scientific attitude; for where there are powerful emotional and aesthetic loadings on a particular theoretical scheme, these must add to the difficulties of abandoning this scheme when cognitive goals press towards doing so. Once again, I should like to stress that the mere fact of switching from a personal to an impersonal idiom does not make anyone a scientist, and that one can be unscientific or scientific in either idiom. In this respect, nevertheless, the personal idiom does seem to present certain difficulties for the scientific attitude which the impersonal idiom does not.

Where the possibility of choice has stimulated the development of Logic, Philosophy, and norms of thought generally, the situation undergoes radical change. One theory is judged better than another with explicit reference to its efficacy in explanation and prediction. And as these ends become more clearly defined, it gets increasingly evident that no other ends are compatible with them. People come to see that if ideas are to be used as efficient tools of explanation and prediction, they must not be allowed to become tools of anything else. (This, of course, is the essence of the ideal of 'objectivity'.) Hence there grows up a great watchfulness against seduction by the emotional or aesthetic appeal of a theory.

DIFFERENCES CONNECTED WITH THE PRESENCE OR ABSENCE OF ANXIETY ABOUT THREATS TO THE ESTABLISHED BODY OF THEORY

(e) Protective versus destructive attitude towards established theory

Both in traditional Africa and in the science-oriented West, theoretical thought is vitally concerned with the prediction of events. But there are marked differences in reaction to predictive failure.

In the theoretical thought of the traditional cultures, there is a notable reluctance to register repeated failures of prediction and to act by attacking the beliefs involved. Instead, other current beliefs are utilized in such a way as to 'excuse' each failure as it occurs, and hence to protect the major theoretical assumptions on which prediction is based. This use of *ad hoc* excuses is a phenomenon which social anthropologists have christened 'secondary elaboration'.[1]

The process of secondary elaboration is most readily seen in association with the work of diviners and oracle-operators, who are concerned with discovering the identity of the spiritual forces responsible for particular happenings in the visible, tangible world, and the reasons for their activation. Typically, a sick man goes to a diviner, and is told that a certain spiritual agency is 'worrying' him. The diviner points to certain of his past actions as having excited the spirit's anger, and indicates certain remedial actions which will appease this anger and restore health. Should the client take the recommended remedial action and yet see no improvement, he will be likely to conclude that the diviner was either fraudulent or just incompetent, and to seek out another expert. The new diviner will generally point to another spiritual agency and another set of arousing circumstances as responsible for the man's condition, and will recommend fresh remedial action. In addition, he will probably provide some explanation of why the previous diviner failed to get at the truth. He may corroborate the client's suspicions of fraud, or he may say that the spirit involved maliciously 'hid itself behind' another in such a way that only the most skilled of diviners would have been able to detect it. If after this the client should still see no improvement in his condition, he will move

---

[1] The idea of secondary elaboration as a key feature of prescientific thought-systems was put forward with great brilliance and insight by Evans-Pritchard in his *Witchcraft, Oracles and Magic*. All subsequent discussions, including the present one, are heavily indebted to his lead.

on to yet another diviner—and so on, perhaps, until his troubles culminate in death.

What is notable in all this is that the client never takes his repeated failures as evidence against the existence of the various spiritual beings named as responsible for his plight, or as evidence against the possibility of making contact with such beings as diviners claim to do. Nor do members of the wider community in which he lives ever try to keep track of the proportion of successes to failures in the remedial actions based on their beliefs, with the aim of questioning these beliefs. At most, they grumble about the dishonesty and wiles of many diviners, whilst maintaining their faith in the existence of some honest, competent practitioners.

In these traditional cultures, questioning of the beliefs on which divining is based and weighing up of successes against failures are just not among the paths that thought can take. They are blocked paths because the thinkers involved are victims of the closed predicament. For them, established beliefs have an absolute validity, and any threat to such beliefs is a horrific threat of chaos. Who is going to jump from the cosmic palm-tree when there is no hope of another perch to swing to?

Where the scientific outlook has become firmly entrenched, attitudes to established beliefs are very different. Much has been made of the scientist's essential scepticism towards established beliefs; and one must, I think, agree that this above all is what distinguishes him from the traditional thinker. But one must be careful here. The picture of the scientist in continuous readiness to scrap or demote established theory contains a dangerous exaggeration as well as an important truth. As an outstanding modern historian of the sciences has recently observed,[1] the typical scientist spends most of his time optimistically seeing how far he can push a new theory to cover an ever-widening horizon of experience. When he has difficulty in making the theory 'fit', he is more likely to develop it in the ways described in Part I of this essay than to scrap it out of hand. And if it does palpably fail the occasional test, he may even put the failure down to dirty apparatus or mistaken meter-reading—rather like the oracle operator! And yet, the spirit behind the scientist's actions *is* very different. His pushing of a theory and his reluctance to scrap it are not due to any chilling intuition that if his theory fails him, chaos is at hand. Rather, they are due to the very knowledge that the theory is not something timeless and absolute.

[1] T. Kuhn, *The Structure of Scientific Revolutions*, Chicago, 1962.

Precisely because he knows that the present theory came in at a certain epoch to replace a predecessor, and that its explanatory coverage is far better than that of the predecessor, he is reluctant to throw it away before giving it the benefit of every doubt, But this same knowledge makes for an acceptance of the theory which is far more qualified and far more watchful than that of the traditional thinker. The scientist is, as it were, always keeping account, balancing the successes of a theory against its failures. And when the failures start to come thick and fast, defence of the theory switches inexorably to attack on it.

If the record of a theory that has fallen under a cloud is poor in all circumstances, it is ruthlessly scrapped. The collective memory of the European scientific community is littered with the wreckage of the various unsatisfactory theories discarded over the last 500 years—the earth-centred theory of the universe, the circular theory of planetary motion, the phlogiston theory of chemical combination, the aether theory of wave propagation, and perhaps a hundred others. Often, however, it is found that a theoretical model once assumed to have universal validity in fact has a good predictive performance over a limited range of circumstances, but a poor performance outside this range. In such a case, the beliefs in question are still ruthlessly demoted; but instead of being thrown out altogether they are given a lesser status as limiting cases of more embracing generalities—still useful as lower-level models as or guides to experience within restricted areas. This sort of demotion has been the fate of theoretical schemes like Newton's Laws of Motion (still used as a guide in many mundane affairs, including much of the business of modern rocketry) and the 'Ball-and-Bond' theory of chemical combination.

This underlying readiness to scrap or demote established theories on the ground of poor predictive performance is perhaps the most important single feature of the scientific attitude. It is, I suggest, a direct outcome of the 'open' predicament. For only when the thinker is able to see his established idea-system as one among many alternatives can he see his established ideas as things of less than absolute value. And only when he sees them thus can he see the scrapping of them as anything other than a horrific, irretrievable jump into chaos.

(f) Protective versus destructive attitude to the category-system

If someone is asked to list typical features of traditional thinking, he is almost certain to mention the phenomenon known as 'taboo'. 'Taboo' is the anthropological jargon for a reaction of horror and aversion to certain actions or happenings which are seen as monstrous and polluting. It is characteristic of the taboo reaction that people are unable to justify it in terms of ulterior reasons: tabooed events are simply bad in themselves. People take every possible step to prevent tabooed events from happening, and to isolate or expel them when they do occur.

Taboo has long been a mystery to anthropologists. Of the many explanations proposed, few have fitted more than a small selection of the instances observed. It is only recently that an anthropologist has placed the phenomenon in a more satisfactory perspective by the observation that in nearly every case of taboo reaction, the events and actions involved are ones which seriously defy the established lines of classification in the culture where they occur.[1]

Perhaps the most important occasion of taboo reaction in traditional African cultures is the commission of incest. Incest is one of the most flagrant defiances of the established catagory-system: for he who commits it treats a mother, daughter, or sister like a wife. Another common occasion for taboo reaction is the birth of twins. Here, the category distinction involved is that of human beings versus animals— multiple births being taken as characteristic of animals as opposed to men. Yet another very generally tabooed object is the human corpse, which occupies, as it were, a classificatory no-man's land between the living and the inanimate. Equally widely tabooed are such human bodily excreta as faeces and menstrual blood, which occupy the same no-man's-land between the living and the inanimate.

Taboo reactions are often given to occurrences that are radically strange or new; for these too (almost by definition) fail to fit in to the established category system. A good example is furnished by a Kalabari story of the coming of the Europeans. The first white man, it is said, was seen by a fisherman who had gone down to the mouth of the estuary in his canoe. Panic-stricken, he raced home and told his people what he had seen: whereupon he and the rest of the town set out to purify themselves—that is, to rid themselves of the influence of the strange and monstrous thing that had intruded into their world.

---

[1] This observation may well prove to be a milestone in our understanding of traditional thought. It was first made some years ago by Mary Douglas, who has developed many of its implications in her book *Purity and Danger*. Though we clearly disagree on certain wider implications, the present discussion is deeply indebted to her insights.

A sort of global taboo reaction is often evoked by foreign lands. As the domains of so much that is strange and unassimilable to one's own categories, such lands are the abode *par excellence* of the monstrous and the abominable. The most vivid description we have of this is that given for the Lugbara by John Middleton.[1] For this East African people, the foreigner is the inverted perpetrator of all imaginable abominations from incest downwards. The more alien he is, the more abominable. Though the Lugbara attitude is extreme, many traditional cultures would seem to echo it in some degree.[2]

Just as the central tenets of the traditional theoretical system are defended against adverse experience by an elaborate array of excuses for predictive failure, so too the main classificatory distinctions of the system are defended by taboo avoidance reactions against any event that defies them. Since every system of belief implies a system of categories, and vice versa, secondary elaboration and taboo reaction are really opposite sides of the same coin.

From all this it follows that, like secondary elaboration, taboo reaction has no place among the reflexes of the scientist. For him, whatever defies or fails to fit in to the established category-system is not something horrifying, to be isolated or expelled. On the contrary, it is an intriguing 'phenomenon'—a starting point and a challenge for the invention of new classifications and new theories. It is something every young research worker would like to have crop up in his field of observation—perhaps the first rung on the ladder of fame. If a biologist ever came across a child born with the head of a goat, he would be hard put to it to make his compassion cover his elation. And as for social anthropologists, one may guess that their secret dreams are of finding a whole community of men who sleep for preference with their mothers!

(g) *The passage of time: bad or good?*

In traditional Africa, methods of time-reckoning vary greatly from culture to culture. Within each culture, again, we find a plurality of time-scales used in different contexts. Thus there may be a major scale which locates events either before, during, or after the time of founding

---

[1] Middleton, op. cit.

[2] This association of foreign lands with chaos and pollution seems to be a universal of prescientific thought-systems. For this, see Mircea Eliade, *The Sacred and the Profane*, New York, 1961, esp. Chapter I.

of the major institutions of the community: another scale which locates events by correlating them with the life-time of deceased ancestors: yet another which locates events by correlating them with the phases of the seasonal cycle: and yet another which uses phases of the daily cycle.

Although these scales are seldom interrelated in any systematic way, they all serve to order events in before-after series. Further, they have the very general characteristic that *vis-à-vis* 'after', 'before' is usually valued positively, sometimes neutrally, and never negatively. Whatever the particular scale involved, then, the passage of time is seen as something deleterious or at best neutral.

Perhaps the most widespread, everyday instance of this attitude is the standard justification of so much thought and action: 'That is what the old-time people told us.' (It is usually this standard justification which is in the forefront of the anthropologist's mind when he applies the label 'traditional culture'.)

On the major time-scale of the typical traditional culture, things are thought of as having been better in the golden age of the founding heroes than they are today. On an important minor time-scale, the annual one, the end of the year is a time when everything in the cosmos is run-down and sluggish, overcome by an accumulation of defilement and pollution.

A corollary of this attitude to time is a rich development of activities designed to negate its passage by a 'return to the beginning'. Such activities characteristically depend on the magical premiss that a symbolic statement of some archetypal event can in a sense recreate that event and temporarily obliterate the passage of time which has elapsed since its original occurrence.[1]

These rites of recreation are to be seen at their most luxuriant in the ancient cultures of the Western Sudan—notably in those of the Bambara and Dogon. In such cultures, indeed, a great part of everyday activity is said to have the ulterior significance of recreating archetypal events and acts. Thus the Dogon labouring in the fields recreates in his pattern of cultivation the emergence of the world from the cosmic egg.

---

[1] In these rites of recreation, traditional African thought shows its striking affinities with prescientific thought in many other parts of the world. The world-wide occurrence and meaning of such rites was first dealt with by Mircea Eliade in his *Myth of the Eternal Return*. A more recent treatment, from which the present analysis has profited greatly, is to be found in the chapter entitled 'Le Temps Retrouvé' in Claude Lévi-Strauss, *La Pensée*.

The builder of a homestead lays it out in a pattern that symbolically recreates the body of the culture-hero Nommo. Even relations between kin symbolize and recreate relations between the primal beings.[1]

One might well describe the Western Sudanic cultures as obsessed with the annulment of time to a degree unparalleled in Africa as a whole. Yet other, less spectacular, manifestations of the attempt to 'get back to the beginning' are widely distributed over the continent. In the West African forest belt, for instance, the richly developed ritual dramas enacted in honour of departed heroes and ancestors have a strong recreative aspect. For by inducing these beings to possess specially selected media and thus, during festivals, to return temporarily to the company of men, such rituals are restoring things as they were in olden times.[2]

On the minor time-scale provided by the seasonal cycle, we find a similar widespread concern for recreation and renewal. Hence the important rites which mark the end of an old year and the beginning of a new one—rites which attempt to make the year new by a thorough-going process of purification of accumulated pollutions and defilements.

This widespread attempt to annul the passage of time seems closely linked to features of traditional thought which I have already reviewed. As I pointed out earlier, the new and the strange, in so far as they fail to fit into the established system of classification and theory, are intimations of chaos to be avoided as far as possible. Advancing time, with its inevitable element of non-repetitive change, is the vehicle *par excellence* of the new and the strange. Hence its effects must be annulled at all costs. Rites of renewal and recreation, then, have much in common with the processes of secondary elaboration and taboo behaviour. Indeed, their kinship with the latter can be seen in the idea that the passage of the year is essentially an accumulation of pollutions, which it is the function of the renewal rites to remove. In short, these rites are the third great defensive reflex of traditional thought.[3]

When we turn from the traditional thinker to the scientist, we find

[1] See M. Griaule, and G. Dieterlen, 'The Dogon', in D. Forde (ed.), *African Worlds*, London, 1954, and M. Griaule, *Conversations with Ogotemmêli*, London, 1965 (translation of *Dieu d'Eau*).

[2] For some interesting remarks on this aspect of West African ritual dramas, see C. Tardits, 'Religion, Epic, History: Notes on the Underlying Functions of Cults in Benin Civilizations', *Diogenes*, No. 37, 1962.

[3] Lévi-Strauss, I think, is making much the same point about rites of renewal when he talks of the continuous battle between prescientific classificatory systems and the non-repetitive changes involved in the passage of time. See Lévi-Strauss, op. cit.

this whole valuation of temporal process turned upside down. Not for the scientist the idea of a golden age at the beginning of time—an age from which things have been steadily falling away. For him, the past is a bad old past, and the best things lie ahead. The passage of time brings inexorable progress. As C. P. Snow has put it aptly, all scientists have 'the future in their bones'.[1] Where the traditional thinker is busily trying to annul the passage of time, the scientist may almost be said to be trying frantically to hurry time up. For in his impassioned pursuit of the experimental method, he is striving after the creation of new situations which nature, if left to herself, would bring about slowly if ever at all.

Once again, the scientist's attitude can be understood in terms of the 'open' predicament. For him, currently held ideas on a given subject are one possibility amongst many. Hence occurrences which threaten them are not the total, horrific threat that they would be for the traditional thinker. Hence time's burden of things new and strange does not hold the terrors that it holds for the traditionalist. Furthermore, the scientist's experience of the way in which successive theories, overthrown after exposure to adverse data, are replaced by ideas of ever greater predictive and explanatory power, leads almost inevitably to a very positive evaluation of time. Finally, we must remember that the 'open' predicament, though it has made people able to tolerate threats to their beliefs, has not been able to supply them with anything comparable to the cosiness of the traditional thinker ensconced amidst his established theories. As an English medical student, newly exposed to the scientific attitude, put it:

> You seem to be as if when learning to skate, trying to find a nice hard piece of ice which you can stand upright on instead of learning how to move on it. You continue trying to find something, some foundation piece which will not move, whereas everything will move and you've got to learn to skate on it.[2]

The person who enjoys the moving world of the sciences, then, enjoys the exhilaration of the skater. But for many, this is a nervous, insecure sensation, which they would fain exchange for the womb-like warmth of the traditional theories and their defences. This lingering sense of insecurity gives a powerful attraction to the idea of progress. For by

[1] C. P. Snow, *The Two Cultures and the Scientific Revolution*, Cambridge, 1959, p. 10.
[2] M. L. Johnson Abercrombie, *The Anatomy of Judgement*, London, 1960, quoted on p. 131.

enabling people to cling to some hoped-for future state of perfect knowledge, it helps them live with a realization of the imperfection and transience of present theories.

Once formed, indeed, the idea of Progress becomes in itself one of the most powerful supports of the scientific attitude generally. For the faith that, come what may, new experience must lead to better theories, and that better theories must eventually give place to still better ones, provides the strongest possible incentive for a constant readiness to expose oneself to the strange and the disturbing, to scrap current frameworks of ideas, and to cast about for replacements.

Like the quest for purity of motive, however, the faith in progress is a double-edged weapon. For the lingering insecurity which is one of the roots of this faith leads all too often to an excessive fixation of hopes and desires on an imagined Utopian future. People cling to such a future in the same way that men in pre-scientific cultures cling to the past. And in doing so, they inevitably lose much of the traditionalist's ability to enjoy and glorify the moment he lives in. Even within the sciences, an excessive faith in progress can be dangerous. In sociology, for instance, it has led to a number of unfruitful theories of social evolution.

At this point, I should like to draw attention to a paradox inherent in the presentation of my subject. As a scientist, it is perhaps inevitable that I should at certain points give the impression that traditional African thought is a poor, shackled thing when compared with the thought of the sciences. Yet as a man, here I am living by choice in a still-heavily-traditional Africa rather than in the scientifically oriented Western subculture I was brought up in. Why? Well, there may be lots of queer, sinister, unacknowledged reasons. But one certain reason is the discovery of things lost at home. An intensely poetic quality in everyday life and thought, and a vivid enjoyment of the passing moment—both driven out of sophisticated Western life by the quest for purity of motive and the faith in progress. How necessary these are for the advance of science; but what a disaster they are when they run wild beyond their appropriate bounds! Though I largely disagree with the way in which the 'Négritude' theorists have characterized the differences between traditional African and modern Western thought, when it gets to this point I see very clearly what they are after.

In modern Western Europe and America the 'open' predicament seems to have escaped precariousness through public acknowledgement of the practical utility of the sciences. It has achieved a secure foothold in the culture because its results maximize values shared by 'closed-' and 'open-' minded alike. Even here, however, the 'open' predicament has nothing like a universal sway. On the contrary, it is almost a minority phenomenon. Outside the various academic disciplines in which it has been institutionalized, its hold is pitifully less than those who describe Western culture as 'science-oriented' often like to think.

It is true that in modern Western culture, the theoretical models propounded by the professional scientists do, to some extent, become the intellectual furnishings of a very large sector of the population. The moderately educated layman typically shares with the scientist a general predilection for impersonal 'it-' theory and a proper contempt for 'thou-' theory. Garbled and watered-down though it may be, the atomic theory of matter is one of his standard possessions. But the layman's ground for accepting the models propounded by the scientist is often no different from the young African villager's ground for accepting the models propounded by one of his elders. In both cases the propounders are deferred to as the accredited agents of tradition. As for the rules which guide scientists themselves in the acceptance or rejection of models, these seldom become part of the intellectual equipment of members of the wider population. For all the apparent up-to-dateness of the content of his world-view, the modern Western layman is rarely more 'open' or scientific in his outlook than is the traditional African villager.

8

The Problem of the Rationality of Magic

I. C. JARVIE AND JOSEPH AGASSI

From Tylor and Frazer to Evans-Pritchard and Beattie anthropologists have tried to explain why someone desiring crops follows up the planting of seeds with the enactment of a magical rite. The problem is why an actor sufficiently rational to know that seeds must be planted bothers with magic. One explanation which was advanced held that magic (or sorcery or witchcraft[1]) was as rational as planting. No one denies that both magic and planting may be performed irrationally, but it is difficult to use irrationality as an explanation of anything.[2] Why, though, was magic problematic and not planting? Why was it taken for granted that planting is rational? Probably because it is relatively easy to explain; although the explanation is seldom stated. Two beliefs we take for granted suffice to explain the planting of seeds to obtain crops. First, the belief that planted seeds grow into crops; second, the belief that crops are highly desirable to those who plant seeds. The planting is thus explained by means of certain beliefs which show it to be conducive to desirable ends, i.e. rational. Can this same pattern of explanation be extended to magical acts? Can they be explained by conjecturing that those who perform them hold beliefs which would show such acts to be conducive to desirable ends? We propose, in this paper, to discuss the problems involved in the attempt, and whether a different kind of explanation is needed.

The first author read a draft of this paper to a colloquium at the University of Minnesota, organized by the Minnesota Center for the Philosophy of Science, and to the staff seminar in philosphy at York University, Toronto, in December 1965. Grateful acknowledgement is made to the discussants on those occasions, and to H. J. Lethbridge and W. W. Bartley III for critical comments. The paper was first published in *The British Journal of Anthropology*, XVIII, 1967, pp. 55–74.

[1] We follow Firth in regarding magic, sorcery and witchcraft as points on a continuous spectrum. See R. Firth, *Human Types*, London, 1957, p. 156. At p. 166ff. Firth suggests the spectrum also includes religion. See also note 29 below.

[2] Cf. I. C. Jarvie, *The Revolution in Anthropology*, London, 1964, p. 218.

It might be as well, before beginning, to make a distinction between rational action and rational belief.[1] Let us attribute rationality to an *action* if there is a goal to which it is directed; let us attribute rationality to a *belief* if it satisfies some standard or criterion of rationality which has been adopted, such as that it is based on good evidence, or is beyond reasonable doubt, or is held open to criticism, etc. When we attribute rationality to a *person* we can mean either: he acts rationally, or he believes rationally, or both. Let us call the rationality that consists in a person acting rationally the *weak* sense or 'rationality'; and the rationality that consists in a person acting rationally on the basis of rationally held beliefs the *strong* sense of 'rationality'.[2] Our thesis in this paper can now be formulated as: the ritual actions of magic are (or can be) rational only in the weak sense; this demarcates them from scientific actions which are (or can be) rational in the strong sense.

II

The well-known theory of magic of Sir James George Frazer will be our starting point because it was his parochial attitude to magic against which later anthropologists reacted strongly. His theory goes roughly like this.[3] The magician performs the magical act because he (mistakenly) believes that that act will bring about the desired effect. Spells invoking things to happen, dances of enactment, are performed because they are thought to have the power of effecting the desired events. Magical acts are the result of false beliefs including the assumptions that:

> first, that by imitating the desired effect you can produce it, and second, that things which have once been in contact can influence each other when they are separated, just as if the contact still persisted (Vol. XIII, p. 1).

[1] This raises the problem of distinguishing action from belief, and of deciding whether rational belief is just a special case of rational action. However, the issue need not be entered here since the argument is not affected by it. See the discussion and references in J. Agassi, 'The Role of Corroboration in Popper's Methodology', *Australasian J. Phil.*, vol. 39, 1961, pp. 82–91.

[2] The rationality that consists in holding certain beliefs rationally but not basing any actions on them is something of a lame duck.

[3] The *locus classicus* is of course his monumental *The Golden Bough*, 3rd edn., London, 1936, in 12 volumes plus *The Aftermath*. The excellent index makes detailed references redundant.

When the hunters enact the chase, or the warriors the victory, Frazer is saying, they do it because they believe this will evoke the desired end: they believe in homeopathic magic, so-called. When the magician casts a spell, when, for instance, he employs finger-nail parings, he likewise does so in the belief that this brings about the desired end; he believes in contagious magic, so-called. In either case—the homeopathic case or the contagious case—the error is the same: the practitioners of magic are victims of a misplaced faith in the association of ideas. They believe, in Freudian language, in the omnipotence of thought. The thought-enactment of the victory, the thought-wish for illness to strike, are considered sufficient, with the right manipulations, to bring about these events. According to Frazer, this fundamental error of all magicians, their misplaced faith, is not an occasional lapse. On the contrary, their magic is an integral part of their whole cosmology; that is to say, magic is part of a theory of the universe according to which given kinds of causes or actions will produce desirable kinds of effects. Frazer's theory that magic is a cosmology, or world-view, explains two things. First, it explains the deep hold of magic on a believer and the wide significance he feels it has, and also the widespread nature of its appeal: it is a complete theory of the universe. Second, it explains how magic can be made more palatable to a Westerner: regarded as a cosmology, magic becomes logically somewhat similar to the world-view of science.

This may require some elucidation. It might help if we add to the comparison between science and magic, a third ingredient, namely religion. Religion seems less primitive than magic. But is it? Is this impression not a sign of our parochialism?

In our society it is no longer controversial to regard religion as irrational; indeed, few people these days bother to claim that religion is rational in either the weak or the strong senses.[1] We should then perhaps be less disturbed by regarding magic as irrational than by

---

[1] We would hold it to be rational in the weak sense: the goal of religious actions is something like the worship of God, or the exorcism of sin, or the survival of life after death. We would however maintain that religion defies most criteria of rational belief and thus is not rational in the strong sense. As an example of the uncontroversial character of the view that religion is irrational take the much-admired recent paper by Robin Horton, a very sophisticated social anthropologist. At pages 222–3 we find him arguing that religion will never be killed off by science because ultimately religion is not rational (in either sense?) and can only be judged by faith, not reason. See 'A Definition of Religion and Its Uses', *J. Roy, Auth. Inst.*, vol. 90, pp. 201–26.

regarding it as rational. Yet it is not as simple as that. Benjamin Franklin attacked religion as irrational, but viewed magic as sheer savagery, as revolting and sub-human. And this feeling is not uncommon today, among religious and non-religious, church-goers and non-church-goers.

But magic *qua* cosmology, as pictured by Frazer, is strikingly different from any religion which pictures the universe as centred on a supreme (and possibly capricious) being; and so, strangely, on Frazer's view belief in magic is nearer to belief in science than to belief in religion and it is less irrational than the latter. Frazer's criterion for rational belief is approximation to the coherence and predictive power of natural science. Religion gives the universe free will; magic (like science) views it as a predictable and manipulable system. On the basis of this logical point, Frazer speculated (mentioning that he had in part been anticipated by Hegel[1]) that human thought might have evolved from a magical stage, through a religious stage, to a scientific stage.[2]

It should be noticed that Frazer's logical distinction between religion and science is very different from widely accepted views of his time, and even of today. Primitive people, it was then supposed, believed in *myths of an historical character*, while rational people believed in *scientific theories of a universal character*. What differentiates the mythical from the scientific is, many people still hold to this day, that myths are stories, they explain by appealing to creations and origins, whereas scientific theories explain by appeal to universal laws.[3,4] Another fashionable

[1] Frazer, op. cit., vol. I, pp. 423ff., Appendix 'Hegel on Magic and Religion'.

[2] The evolution might be reconstructed as follows. At first primitive man superstitiously regarded the world as being dominated by occult forces, and his magic was an attempt to manipulate them; then disappointment at their capriciousness forced a retreat into anthropomorphism, i.e. a belief which explained the capriciousness as caused by gods and goddesses who had to be propitiated; then, finally, a rejection of anthropormorphism and a return to a stable conception of the universe, but this time without the superstitions of the occult and instead the newly refined and tested ideas of empirical science.

[3] Further, it is thought that myths are fantasies, with no relation to facts, while scientific theories are firmly grounded in fact. For an exciting discussion and criticism of this view, see P. K. Feyerabend, *Knowledge Without Foundations*, Oberlin, 1961, esp. paras. 7 et seq.

[4] This view of what constitutes the difference between myths and scientific theories is not new. We find St Augustine arguing against its corollary that Christianity is primitive; and we find St Thomas quoting this theory and its corollary before trying to refute it. His refutation is that since science must be based on relevation the Christian doctrine is scientific *par excellence*, and he

view is that religion is an abstract theology or metaphysics not in competition with science at all. The grounds for this position are often that while religious doctrine is putative history, it is not mythological and does not compete with science because it is not meant to be explanatory—whatever else it may be. Nowadays no one maintains that religion can or should provide answers to questions like why objects fall towards the centre of the earth, or when the next eclipse of the sun will occur. But magic and science both try to explain such things, and once upon a time religion did too.

Frazer not only holds that religion has an explanatory intent but also that it is a very feeble and logically defective competitor to science. He sees magic, religion, and science as three competing systems, one of which is logically defective and one of which is factually defective.

Whatever one may say as to the cogency of Frazer's theory, one must admit that it embodies a certain psychological insight into our parochial attitude towards magic. In spite of all the wars waged between science and religion in the West, in spite of a long and deeply entrenched tradition of hostility, the two now coexist cosily. Magic, however, is still the outcast.[1] The truth is that, for the logical reason Frazer mentioned, science and religion are not intellectual competitors in the same way that science and magic are; religion is a non-starter. Religion, as practised in the West, is not practical but moral; whereas science and magic both claim immense pragmatic value. Hence the seeming irrationality of magic is so much more disturbing to a Westerner than the seeming irrationality of religion. A Westerner may invest much in religion, but unlike the primitive magician he expects no immediate practical returns from his rituals. Once we compare the magical rite not with Western religious rites, but with Western scientific rites, such as decontaminating water by using chlorine rather than holy water, or holding National Productivity Conferences, we see the similarity.

acknowledges this argument to St Augustine. (See *Summa Theologica*, Part I, Question 1, 'The Nature and Extent of Sacred Doctrine. (in ten articles): second article 'Whether Sacred Doctrine is a Science', Objection 2, et. seq.) Nowadays only a very few naïve Catholic teachers and fewer very sophisticated philosophers (notably Polanyi, see *The Logic of Liberty*, Chicago, 1951, esp. pp. 23ff.) advocate views which in any way resemble the ideas of St Augustine and St Thomas.

[1] Or the unrecognized. Instead of casting spells after planting seeds we hold conferences of agriculturists both before and after. Do these not have a strong magical component?

III

In spite of its merit, there is no doubt but that the evolutionist speculation of Frazer may be viewed today with a cautious smile: unlike the
nineteenth century, the twentieth is wary of sweeping historical
schemes. Yet one might also view Frazer's speculation in its nineteenth-
century context, and draw attention to some admirable features of it.
Frazer was anti-religious,[1] yet finally he placed religion a rung higher
up the evolutionary ladder than magic—even though magical causation
appealed to his nineteenth-century 'scientific' mind more than revelation and anthropomorphism. His dislike of religion was characteristic
of the scientific humanism of the nineteenth century; his attempt to be
less parochial about it, the very fact which is so laudable about him,
also shows him to be a man of his time. How different is Frazer from
contemporary social anthropologists, who are no longer bothered by
religion at all, partly because of Frazer himself. It is too early to assess
Frazer's contribution to the fizzling out of the tradition of animosity
between science and religion: but one can say that it is a feature of
twentieth century social anthropologists that they dislike sociological
parochialism and resent the European's ridicule of the aborigines' magic,
yet they are not in the least embarassed by religious parochialism and
do not even notice their own scientific parochialism. They regard the
ridicule of savages as lamentable, but the ridicule of Frazer as a pleasant
pastime and commendable ritual.

Certainly it is not difficult in retrospect to think of criticisms of
Frazer's theory of magic. To begin with, his evolutionary scheme
is very unconvincing. The problem it solves—'why do all human societies have either religion, or magic, or science?'—is a rather poor one.
Magic, religion and science sometimes peacefully coexist in one and
the same society. This makes it harder to show that either one has
'succeeded' or is a 'higher' stage than any other. It could be that they
did evolve the one from the other, or there may have been any number
of intervening stages, but on this question we can learn nothing from

---

[1] His *Golden Bough* is obviously a conscious attempt to discredit religion—
especially Christianity—by tracing its line of descent to primitive superstition.
Dr E. R. Leach has disputed this in his 'Frazer and Malinowski', *Encounter*, vol.
15, November 1965, pp. 24–36. However, he disputes it mainly on the grounds
that Frazer was circumspect in his direct comments on Christianity. Yet Frazer's
circumspection can hardly be interpreted as attempting to conceal his secret
religiosity. See Jarvie's rebuttal 'Academic Fashions and Grandfather Killing—In
Defense of Frazer', *Encounter*, vol. 26, April 1966, pp. 53–5.

the known facts. Even were magic extinct in some society or other, it would still be a very difficult task to argue from that fact to the position that on the evolutionary scale magic is the most primitive of the three. Frazer managed to do so by a psychological explanation of the three stages. He argued that 'magical thinking' gave way to 'religious thinking' which in turn gave way to 'scientific thinking'. This is very unconvincing, too, because Frazer himself admits a closeness between magical thinking and scientific thinking. It is hard to conceive of one way of 'thinking' giving way to another and then reasserting itself, unless it is possible for them also to coexist. But then if they can coexist how can we know in which sequence they were invented? The answer is that magic, religion and science is a logic progression. Yet Frazer offers no reason for the assumption that the course of evolution followed a logical progression; in the nineteenth century it was too easily taken for granted that history followed a pattern of logical development. It is an interesting hypothesis, but a rather doubtful one; even in the history of science, where succession is most likely to be in logical progression, it is very far from being the case that matters have progressed in a logical way.

Leaving Frazer's evolutionary theory and concentrating on his views on magic for a moment, still further criticisms spring to mind. It is not clear that all magic is either homeopathic or contagious, as Frazer seems to have believed. And again, Frazer fails to show that *belief in* magic is any less defensible than *belief in* science. Since he regards these as incompatible ways of thinking he doesn't explicitly face the problem. Moreover to provide a theory explaining why belief in one is more defensible than belief in the other he would have to have a somewhat more sophisticated view of science or 'scientific thinking' than he appears to have. Admittedly, in one passage,[1] he advocates a more sophisticated view of science as the task of offering explanatory hypotheses and improving them by comparing them with, and checking them against, the facts of experience. Yet more often he endorses a naïve view of science as an accumulated mass of empirical observations

---

[1] This redeeming passage is to be found in the summing-up; we find there a most striking and sophisticated picture of science: 'We must remember that at bottom . . . the laws of nature are merely hypotheses to explain that ever-shifting phantasmagoria of thought which we dignify with the high-sounding names of the world and the universe . . . and as science has supplanted its predecessors, so it may hereafter be itself superseded by some more perfect hypothesis . . . of which we in this generation can form no idea.' (*The Golden Bough*, op. cit., vol. XI, p. 306).

from which theories have somehow to be squeezed. Since so much of Frazer's argument turns on comparison and contrast between magic, science and religion, all this has to be reassessed in the light of a more sophisticated view of science.

Granted all these criticisms, then, and granted that the modern strictures about Frazer's work are at least partly justified, there still remains in Frazer's theory of magic an important element which has not thus far been criticized—it concerns the problem 'why do rational people perform magic?' As we recall, Frazer thinks people perform magic because they believe it will realize or help realize, or increase the likelihood of realization of, an end they are aiming at. This is at the very core of our present discussion since, if Frazer is right, then at least in one sense, and a rather central one at that, magic is very rational indeed and even more rational than religion in precisely the logical sense presented by Frazer.

Frazer's theory, as we can see, is on this point a bold and exciting one—and yet one which does not find favour among present-day social anthropologists. The commonest argument given against it is not so much a specific refutation but a general criticism of the entire assumption that people's actions can be explained by their beliefs. Whether explanation of human behaviour should, or may, be in terms of human ends and beliefs is a question which fills a whole literature, and one which we cannot enter here—nor need we. For one of the very few points which are fairly widely agreed upon in the field of philosophy and methodology of the social sciences is this. By definition, a rational action is one based on—amongst other factors—the actor's goals or aims, his present knowledge and beliefs.[1] Thus, to explain magical actions as rational actions presupposes dissent from the belief that belief does not explain action. If one insists that beliefs and ends do not count in the theory of explanation of human behaviour, one cannot formulate the problem of 'why do people we deem to be rational perform magical acts?' but at best 'why do some intellectuals say "magic is not rational" and show signs of displeasure when uttering these words?' To buttress our case we will discuss an influential current view which rejects the use of beliefs in explanations of magic as rational in either the weak or the strong sense, and yet which allows rational or goal-directed explanation in general.

---

[1] For a very clear setting-out of this matter see C. G. Hempel, 'Rational Action', *Proc. and Addresses Amer. Phil. Assn.*, vol. 35, pp. 5–23.

IV

We have selected what might be called the Oxford Theory. It seems to stem from the work of Professor E. E. Evans-Pritchard, especially his Marrett Lecture and *Nuer Religion*,[1] and it is also found in the works of members of his Institute such as G. Lienhardt,[2] and J. H. M. Beattie.[3] We shall draw most heavily on Beattie's *Other Cultures* precisely because it is a general expository work. In fact only in such introductory works does one find systematic attempts to set out and defend current theory. In two chapters of *Other Cultures*, 'Beliefs and Values' and 'Magic', the author expounds a theory he clearly regards as superior to Frazer's. Let us consider Beattie's view of rationality, and how he can impute it to magic without allowing it to be explained as conducive to the realization of certain ends.[4]

Beattie's general theory of beliefs and values seeks to add an extra dimension to the usual view that these are factors which affect people's selection of means and ends. He begins by criticizing the Victorian idea that the thought of primitive people was childish and failed to distinguish between mental associations and causal connections in the real world. With field-work it came to be seen that primitive belief-systems were far from childish. Evans-Pritchard showed in his book on the Azande, according to Beattie, that

> the beliefs of this highly intelligent people . . . are . . . not . . . a set of
> weird and irrational delusions about occult forces, but rather . . . a

[1] Evans-Pritchard's Marrett Lecture 'Social Anthropology Past and Present' is reprinted in his *Essays in Social Anthropology*, London, 1964. Apart from the works mentioned below, the Oxford Theory is also to be found in D. F. Pocock's *Social Anthropology*, London, 1961, and G. Lienhardt's *Divinity and Experience: Religion Among the Dinka*, Oxford, 1961.

[2] See his 'Religion', Chapter XIV in *Man, Culture and Society*, edited by H. L. Schapiro, New York, 1956; and *Social Anthropology*, London, 1964.

[3] *Other Cultures*, London, 1964.

[4] After this paper was written, Dr Beattie's Malinowski Memorial Lecture ('Ritual and Social Change', *Man-J.R.A.I.*, vol. I 1966, pp. 60–74) came into our hands. He there re-argues rather than expands and develops his *Other Cultures* ideas (indeed he refers to the fuller treatment in the latter). Thus our criticisms apply *pari passu*. He ends with the assertion that cargo cults seem more amenable to explanation as proliferations of symbolic representations than as the formulating and testing of hypotheses to explain events. As against Beattie's assertion, see the latest monograph on cargo cults, P. Lawrence, *Road Belong Cargo*, Manchester, 1965, and Jarvie's paper on it 'On the Explanation of Cargo Cults,' *European J. Soc.*, forthcoming.

mode of adjustment to the strains and frustrations of everyday life which, in the whole context of Zande culture, appears as eminently practical and sensible (p. 67).

The modern social anthropologist does not proceed by framing these belief systems into formal propositions about reality and then discussing how a reasonable man could ever have come to believe them—this was the Victorian intellectualist method—instead he attempts to understand the beliefs in the whole context of the culture of which they are a part.

And now Beattie's theory of magic. In non-scientific cultures most thinking about the world is of a symbolic and literary character. The things symbolized are abstract notions like power, group solidarity, and familial or political authority:

> symbolism is essentially expressive; it is a way of saying something important, something which it is impossible or impracticable to say directly (p. 71).

And:

> We sometimes forget that the capacity for systematic analytic thinking about concepts is a product of several millennia of education and conscious philosophizing (p. 70).

It is often difficult in practice to distinguish instrumental (i.e. goal-directed) behaviour from symbolic or expressive behaviour. It is instrumental to try to grow crops or kill one's enemy, but expressive while doing so to chant spells or mutter over finger-nail parings.

> Instrumental behaviour must be understood in terms of the consequences it aims at and achieves; expressive behaviour in terms of the meanings, the ideas, it expresses (p. 72).

Thus:

> Trobriand canoe magic stresses the importance of canoe building for the Trobrianders; blood pact ritual emphasizes the need for mutual support between parties to it; the avoidance ritual asserts the need to maintain good relations between affinally linked groups (p. 210).

All this is very ingenious, but does it explain why the actors perform the rites? Beattie admits that not everyone in the society is aware of the 'importance' of what they are symbolizing, although it is likely that in most societies at least some of the actors will be more or less aware of some of the social implications of their ritual institutions (p. 208).

And besides, Beattie goes on, the symbolic actions themselves come to be thought to have a potency, an ability to bring about the event they are symbolizing. This contradicts Beattie's theory that magic is symbolic rather than instrumental, but he plays the contradiction down by asserting the 'essentially' symbolic character of magic. The social significance of seed sowing, canoe making, etc. is what magical chanting, dancing, etc. come to stress.

First of all, we suggest that Beattie's theory shifts the problem from 'why do people we deem rational perform magical acts?' to 'what do magical acts mean?' We suggest this in order to explain the fact that he insists that perfectly intelligible meaning can be read into the symbolism of magic. Yet he is not interested in the latter question alone; he clearly hopes that the imputation of meaning to magic will defend primitive peoples against Frazer's charge of backwardness and irrationality. In other words, implicit in Beattie's discussion as well as in his very shift from the former problem of giving a rational explanation of magic to the latter problem of whether magic has a meaning—implicit in all this is the view that solving the latter amounts to solving the former. Here, at last, is the kernel of a new theory of rationality—if an act is not sociologically meaningless it is rational. We find a similar theory in Malinowski.[1] Beattie's defence of the rationality of the magician, however, must fail because he is doing two things at once. To put it one way, a believer in the backwardness and irrationality of primitive peoples could easily contend that belief in the potency of symbols was at least as backward and irrational as belief in an occult magical cosmology. To put it differently, when we are faced with the equation of the rationality of an act with its having social meaning, we must first examine this equation against actions we all agree are rational and actions we all agree are not. Only if this equation makes sense of

[1] Malinowski's theory was that magic draws its rationality from the ordered social life of which it was a functioning part. He also argued that magic provided a psychological reassurance, a technique of coping with the unknown and unpredictable. We have not discussed these ideas in the text, partly because of their psychological component, and partly because an excellent discussion of them already exists (see S. F. Nadel, 'Malinowski on Magic and Religion' in R. Firth (ed.), *Man and Culture*, London, 1957, pp. 189–208). Beattie's Malinowski Memorial Lecture, op cit. also has an interesting presentation of Malinowski's views.

uncontroversially rational phenomena, can we use it as an arbiter of sorts concerning a controversial phenomenon like magic. There cannot, after all, be two theories of rationality, one applying only to instrumental actions, the other applying only to symbolic actions. This is where Beattie is trying to get the best of both worlds. He wants to say magic is not a case of a goal-directed rational action but it is rational on some other criterion. But then on that criterion goal-directed actions will have to be rational too. Thus Newton's theory could not be used to decide whether comets belonged to the solar system before it was successfully applied to bodies incontrovertibly belonging to that system. To take another example, when we say that there is no difference between living matter and dead matter and use the crystallizability of viruses as an example, our opponents merely shrug their shoulders and ask for less controversial examples of life than viruses.

Consider Beattie's equation for a moment and see how odd it looks when applied to acts regularly observed in our society, such as celebrating a wedding, standing overnight in a theatre queue, or acts common to all human societies, such as sowing rice and making canoes. These will be accepted as rational only if expressive of social meaning. But however expressive they are, can we explain queueing for Horowitz and sowing seeds without bringing in their goal? And if we can't how far can we get with magic if we refuse to attribute a goal to it? Does Beattie's reading of social values into the symbolism of magic succeed in giving a rational explanation of why people perform magic (even though most of them do not understand what they are doing)? Is there a difference between acts whose social meaning is understood and ones whose social meaning is not? Strictly, if we take Beattie seriously, the answer is 'no' since he is prepared to see magic as rational even though the participants do not know what they are doing. And of course he nowhere denies rationality to actors who do know what they are doing. The trouble is, with these two standards of rationality it is difficult to imagine any act being irrational. Assume however there is a difference between understanding and not understanding the social meaning of one's actions. If so, then those who do not understand the social meaning of what they are doing must be doing it because of some other misunderstanding they have. Is not then the best hypothesis that they do not perform canoe magic because of the social importance of canoe building, they perform it because they think it will help them achieve some end, i.e. sailable canoes?

Beattie's attempt to add an extra (symbolic) dimension to Frazer's 'instrumental' interpretation of magic confuses rather than clarifies the issue, especially when Beattie contradicts himself and allows an instrumental explanation of magic as based on a belief in the potency of symbols. Whether one says with Frazer that the magician believes his spell will invoke an occult force or power that will bring about the desired end; or whether one says with Beattie that magicians believe in the potency of symbols to bring about the desired end; does not make much difference. Both agree that magic is performed to bring about an end. But on the one hand Frazer sees magic as an occult cosmology being applied, whereas on the other hand Beattie's anti-Victorian intellectualism would make him object to the procedure of saying that belief in the potency of symbols is based on some different occult cosmology. To this one could say that either the belief in the potency of symbols is part of a larger cosmology or else it is *ad hoc*. If we have to choose between cosmology and *ad hoc* theory we choose cosmology. If we have to choose between two cosmologies the choice is more difficult, especially since Beattie gives us no clue as to the cosmology behind the belief in the potency of symbols.

What other criticisms can be made of the symbolist view?[1] Mainly, that even if it is true, how the symbolism is interpreted is entirely arbitrary. In order to make his thesis more convincing Beattie tries to say what is being symbolized, he interprets the symbols. He suggests that magic is a substitute—poor substitute may we say, or will this be pressing Beattie too hard on his parochialism?—for 'systematic analytic thinking' about social life and values. Magic may be a substitute in the sense that it is thinking, even 'systematic and analytic' to use Beattie's words, but being not fully articulated it is not sufficiently systematic and analytic. Alternatively, magic may be a substitute in that it is systematically an unanalytic method of destroying all doubts and desire for 'analytic' thinking by intoning impressive mumbo-jumbo. Beattie seems to hold to the second when he says that magical thinking is *assertion* or *affirmation* of social values. What is curious is that he regards this as an alternative way of thinking, not as a precursor; or, at least, so his thesis that magic is perfectly reasonable suggests. Yet on the other hand his mention of millennia of reflection suggests 'systematic and analytic' thinking *is* something better. Again there appears to be some contradiction in his position.

At best, then, Beattie's interpretation of the symbolic thinking of the

[1] For incisive criticisms of the symbolist view by an anthropologist see R. Firth, *Essays in Social Organization and Values*, London, 1964, pp. 235–7.

magician simply involves reading a statement into an act. This move is highly problematic. In the West we are familiar with acts-as-statements. For example flag-semaphore, or the conventions of mime and ballet. The latter are a little vague, the former very precise. Both are quite arbitrary conventions. But the decisive point is that their meaning is intentional: those performing the acts know and need to know what they are doing. A highly technically accomplished dancer unaware of the meaning of what he or she is doing can hardly act the dance in an appropriate way. Just as the uninitiated spectator can hardly react in an appropriate way. There are perhaps a few universals: smiles, tears, etc., but these cannot be grasped out of context. A smile may say 'I am happy' or it may mean 'I am suffering but putting a brave face on it', or it may be a hypocritical smile, etc. It cannot thus be 'read' without the whole context of the conventions. And all this applies to consciously intended meanings. How much more problematic is the reading of meaning into actions which are *not* intentionally meaningful? Of course, it could be said that it is enough that some people know the meaning of what they are doing, they could teach or at least guide the rest. But this does not escape the problem. When we see people performing actions and we ask why and are answered that they are symbolizing something but they don't know it, we are not being told why they are performing the actions they are performing. We are being told how the teachers of the actions they are performing interpret the actions they teach. Perhaps the performers see what they are doing in quite a different light. In a similar way it is a commonplace of criticism of the arts to say that the author's intentions are not necessarily definitive; sometimes one even finds art being judged by the richness of meanings that can be read into it.

Perhaps this point cuts both ways: on the one hand it strengthens the view that imputations of meaning are arbitrary; but it could also be used to separate the 'objective' meaning from the intentional meaning. The intentional meaning is irrelevant to the objective meaning. However, this argument again evades the problem of the explanations of the actions in question. Only the intentional meaning is relevant to why the artist created the work he did. In parallel, only the intentional meaning is relevant to the explanation of why the people are acting as they are.

It is an entertaining game to read meanings into people's actions, just as it is to read symbolism into works of art. Personally we find Freudian analyses of the symbolism of magic somewhat more

entertaining than Beattie's crypto-Durkheimian assertions of its convey-
ing something about social value. But at least we recognize it all as
arbitrary and therefore entirely without power to give a convincing
explanation of the behaviour concerned.

On the basis of his extra dimension, of the social message he reads
into every act of magic, Beattie objects to the parallel Frazer draws
between science and magic. He strongly contrasts symbolic or magical
thinking with scientific thinking. This may sound strange because
Frazer did this too with this parochial view that magical thinking was
an earlier stage than scientific thinking. But here, for a change, Beattie
is consistent. Viewing magic intellectually leads to seeing it as inferior;
viewing it as art of sorts, like a Catholic procession or a ballet performance or poetry, hardly allows of comparison with science, but it
certainly prevents imputations of inferiority.[1] It is perhaps a pity the
symbolist reading of magic does not explain why people do it. Take
Lienhardt's example (1961) of Dinka tying a knot in the grass when
coming home late. This is supposed to express a wish that the women
will delay the dinner. But, not accepting that this ritual action is
sufficient actually to delay the dinner, the Dinka hurries home as well.
Now either: the knotted grass concentrates attention, as Lienhardt
seems to say, in which case it is no more magical than our mnemonic
of tying a knot in a handkerchief; or, it is believed to be efficacious
somehow. But then why does not the Dinka saunter back, confident of
the power of ritual? The answer is the same as when asking why the
farmer plants as well as chants, chases birds away after planting, etc.
The two actions are part of one technique which *we* separate but
which the actors do not.

Evans-Pritchard, at least, is a little clearer on all this. His discussion of
symbolism is concerned with what Nuer mean when they say that
birds are twins, that a sacrificial cucumber is an ox, of a crocodile that it
is spirit, etc. His answer is simple enough, these are poetic modes of
speech, partly theological (spirit is in the sky, birds are in the sky, twins
are spirits and therefore twins are birds), partly symbolic (the cucumber
stands-in for the ox), partly associationist (crocodiles lay eggs, so do
birds, birds are spirit, etc.). But of course Nuer *act* because they believe
all these things. Evans-Pritchard does not say this here, *a propos* of Nuer
religion, which is strange, and perhaps indicative of some hesitation;
after all, in his book on the Azande he stresses that customers test their

[1] This comparison with art is stressed heavily in the Malinowski Memorial
Lecture, op. cit.

magicians and their oracles as severely as they can before submitting to them. Would he now say that they test them though they view them purely symbolically? If not, then the symbolism plays at most a secondary role according to his own views. And so with the Nuer too: They have certain doctrines about spirit that they believe to be *true*. As Lienhardt says (1956):

> If there were no guarantee, for example, that a diviner was permitted an insight into the true grounds of an illness, there would be no means of dealing with that illness. . . .

Only if these 'poetic' ideas are believed will they be acted on, and only if they are being acted on do they explain what people are doing. Beattie, Lienhardt and Evans-Pritchard all confuse the strong and weak senses of rationality. They want to rebut the view that belief in magic and religion is irrational because not strongly rational, and in so doing they undermine the attribution of even weak rationality to religion. If we, the authors of this paper, maintain that *belief* in magic and religion is not rational we would only do so on the basis of a highly sophisticated philosophical argument[1] and we would include the Great Religions. But we still maintain that it is a minimum requirement of explanation that magical *acts* be explained as rational in the weak sense.

It may indeed be 'intellectualist' to explain people's actions by theories which assert that they know what they are doing and act on that knowledge, but it may also be successful to some degree. The question is, whether any other way of explaining human actions is to be found.[2] Moreover, Beattie's discussion of the symbolic or poetic way of thinking as contrasted with 'systematic analytic thinking' accepts implicitly one of the weakest points in Frazer's theory—the view of magic, religion and science are different because different 'ways of thinking' underlie them. Frazer himself confuses his logical distinction between the three (in terms of the manner in which they explain the universe), with a psychological hypothesis about how they were arrived at. But how they were arrived at is a different problem. To explain the behavior concerned it is sufficient to reconstruct beliefs in terms of which the problematic action makes sense.

So, to avoid the psychological parochialism of Frazer's view, which might be formulated as—'scientific thinking is better than erroneous

---

[1] See R. Robinson, *An Atheist's Values*, London, 1964, p. 118ff.
[2] For some discussion of this see *The Revolution in Anthropology*, op. cit., pp. 216ff.

religious thinking which is better than associationist magical thinking'
—Beattie gives us the psychological relativism[1] of 'all humans do some
irrational (poetic, symbolic) thinking'. More schematically, Beattie
replaces Frazer's 'some men's thinking is rational, other men's is not',
with 'all men sometimes think irrationally (i.e. symbolically)'. While
this at first looks like progress away from parochialism, it is no progress
even in that respect: who can say whether it is less parochial to allow
that magic is an inferior substitute for rational thought, or to follow
Frazer who has managed to show it to be rational though erroneous?[2]
Although Beattie's is quite a sophisticated way to avoid parochialism
by viewing magic as a lapse of rational people it is nonetheless very
naïve in another way. Beattie, like Frazer, rejects magic, of course, as
erroneous; unlike Frazer, however, he cannot view error as rational, but
at best as a rationality surrogate. This is the parochialism of the twentieth century in its worst manifestation: science is always right, science
is rational, *ergo* rationality leads to the avoidance of error.[3] This folly
is only partly mitigated by 'all people make some mistakes', which
follows from 'all people are sometimes irrational'. Embedded here is
the incredible idea that there exists something like a rational or scientific
thought process which leads to the discovery of truth and especially
technology.[4] Fundamentally it is Frazer's accusation that primitive
peoples' magic is in error that Beattie is rejecting. Error for Beattie
needs to be explained, especially if it is relinquished slowly; is this because
he associates error with stupidity, irrationality, backwardness?[5] Perhaps

[1] Although there would seem to be some contradiction between his relativism
and his view that primitive peoples are incapable of systematic analytic thinking.

[2] Yet see the puzzling remark of Lienhardt, 'To show a religion to be reasonable
and to suggest that it is the result of reasoning from faulty premisses, as Tylor
and Frazer did, are not the same thing', in 'Religion', op. cit., p. 315.

[3] For a discussion of error see J. Agassi, *Towards An Historiography of Science*,
History and Theory, Beiheft 2, 1963, pp. 54ff.

[4] C. Lévi-Strauss calls it 'theoretical thinking of the highest order' in his
Huxley Memorial Lecture, 'The Future of Kinship Studies', *Proc. Roy. Anth. Inst.*
1965, p. 15. The point arises in the course of his discussion of how involved
rules of marriage preference came to be adopted. He maintains that they are
'true discoveries' by 'a small minority of learned individuals'. He thinks it is
'crude naturalist philosophy' to believe these systems or scientific knowledge in
general could be 'the blind product of a series of trials and errors'.

[5] Lienhardt stresses the point that brilliant minds have believed in magic. He
presumably regards this as a refutation of the theory that magic is a product of
stupid or irrational minds—because, of course, brilliant minds could not embrace
error. But one could just as well say it shows that even clever people make
mistakes. See his *Social Anthropology*, op. cit., p. 149. A much better defence of

this association explains why Beattie accepts Frazer's psychological explanation of the difference between magic and science as a difference between the quality of thought. Why else should Beattie go to great lengths to show that primitive peoples *are* capable of technical-practical thought other than to buttress his claim that they cannot be relegated to an inferior stage? When we examine the content of Beattie's notion of 'rational or scientific thinking' we find he has compounded his error by also swallowing whole Frazer's naïve view of science as accummulated empirical experience from which unquestionably true laws are squeezed by induction.[1] Clearly magic, or symbolic thinking, however it proceeds, does not proceed like inductive or scientific thinking. Here Beattie scores an easy point against Frazer who, as we remember, compares magic with science. We need not labour the obvious point that Frazer does not compare magic and science on all points but only on the point of universality; rather let us continue with Beattie's insight into the contrast between magic and scientific thought. Beattie intimates that in so far as primitive peoples know how and where and when to plant seeds, know how and which trees to carve, know how and where and when to fish, etc., they display a practical mastery of their physical environment similar to that which we base on modern science. They have built this up by steady accumulation of empirical experience.

primitive peoples against charges of 'stupidity and credulity' is to be found in R. Firth's admirable *Human Types*, op. cit., In Chapter VI Firth points out that Polynesian canoe-building is technically admirable as well as dedicated to the gods. Between the poles of magic—irrational because based on false premisses—and science—rational *par excellence*—is a grading where the two phenomena coexist. (Indeed a magical attitude towards science is not unknown.) Both can be closely interwoven into practical affairs, economic wants and the critical periods of human life. On page 161 Firth shows how it remains rational for people to go on believing in failed magic. Close examination, however, reveals that failure is explained by *ad hoc* auxilliary hypotheses which make the magic a reinforced, uncriticizable system. Whether one can entirely clear the natives of the charge of 'stupidity and credulity' as Firth thinks one can, depends on one's criterion of rationality. (Cf. Feyerabend, op. cit., pp. 38–43.) If one does convict the natives of 'stupidity and credulity' one also convicts a great many Westerners, including some religious believers and even some scientifists, Cf. K. R. Popper, *The Logic of Scientific Discovery*, London, 1959, pp. 78–84.

[1] Indeed generally Beattie's attempt in the Malinowski Memorial Lecture to pin down an 'essential' difference between science and expressive actions founders on his misconceptions about science. Most instances of essentially expressive magical behaviour can be matched by examples of expressive scientific behaviour. Beattie, to use his own words, has a 'too exclusive commitment to an instrumentally-oriented' view of science (op. cit. p. 68).

This clinches his point that primitive people are not irrationally incapable of scientific thinking and that all people use both empirical accumulation and symbolic representation in their thinking.

Assume instead a rather more sophisticated view of science as a highly articulated system of explanatory theories which may be tested against the facts. Assume further, that primitive technology is not science in this sense. Agree, still further, with Beattie, that primitive technology is not magic. What, then, is to be made of primitive technology? The question is not only interesting in itself; Beattie would be justified in pressing it on Frazerians like ourselves. For Frazer at times expresses just such a sophisticated view of science, and he surely knew of primitive technology and of the difference between primitive technology and magic.

If a magician is asked why he both plants and chants he will no doubt say that it is the proper procedure to produce crops. If he is asked what would happen if he did not chant he would no doubt answer that if he did not chant the seeds would not grow. If one argued that Westerners grow crops but never chant he would have three alternatives: puzzlement at our success, crowing over our failures, or, more likely, attribution of magic to our ploughing and fertilizer-scattering rituals. This is all commonplace since we know that magic, being a doctrine about the occult, is compatible with all empirical experience and thus cannot be directly refuted.[1] This is an extremely important and puzzling point. It raises the problem of how individuals or communities ever do break out of the magical world-view. Yet those who hold that world-view are surely not in any difficulty with their primitive technology. We believe their explanations of the technology to be false and ours to be true. But explanations are one thing and practical utility is quite another. False technology and even falsly justified true technology can nevertheless work. So the problem of what to make of primitive technology vanishes: primitive people have some technology, that is all. Nothing can be concluded from this about their capacity for science or their freedom from superstition. It is not a question of how people we deem to be rational can perform magical acts, but rather a question of how primitive technology fits into the magical world-view.

---

[1] Cf. J. W. N. Watkins, 'Between Analytic and Empirical', *Philosophy* vol. 32 (1957), pp. 1–20; 'Confirmable and Influential Metaphysics', *Mind*, vol. 67 (1958), pp. 334–65; 'The Haunted Universe', *The Listener*, vol. 57 (1957), pp. 837–8, 883 and 886; and J. Agassi, 'The Nature of Scientific Problems and the i Roots in Metaphysics' in M. Bunge (ed.), *The Critical Approach*, Glencoe, 1964.

V

Examination and discussion of Beattie, then, has forced us to realize, at least, that our original formulation, 'Why do people we deem to be rational perform magical acts?', is question-begging and parochial. It assumes entities, entirely rational persons (Beattie denies their existence), performing what seem at first sight irrational actions, magic (Frazer shows that on deeper examination the first sight impression disappears). How can we formulate the problem so that we neither bifurcate humanity or persons? The question can arise in other fields. Before Jenner, vaccination against smallpox was combined with bleeding, and took five days. Now the vaccination was, of course, rational in the strong sense; can the bleeding be explained as rational in the strong sense? This question improperly separates bleeding and vaccination which, before Jenner, were subsumed under some general theory that explained them as effective in combination (or, perhaps methodologically worse, there may have been two theories of how to prevent smallpox, one by bleeding the other by vaccination, and the purely *ad hoc* hypothesis that two cures is better than one was employed). But in order to explain why doctors did both one must treat the two as one—as they did—and reconstruct their behaviour from that. Similarly, primitive societies have both technology and magic and we should try to explain their behaviour with hypotheses that do not make a separation they do not make. This is very difficult, since we have to overcome our own built-in categories. The problem might become something more like 'is primitive society rational in the weak sense?', i.e. can the actions of people in primitive societies be rationally explained by means of their aims, beliefs and knowledge of their circumstances? There is no doubt about the answer. If we press the point, though, and ask whether primitive people adopt a rational or critical *attitude* to their beliefs and explanations, the issue becomes a little more sensitive. The answer depends upon one's criterion of rationality; and then it becomes a factual question: does or does not such and such a society possess, e.g. the tradition of adopting a critical attitude towards beliefs, values, explanations? This is a question of sociological fact: the presence or absence of a tradition. It reflects in no way upon the intelligence, stupidity, human dignity, or mental capacities of the peoples of the societies in question.

VI

In conclusion, we should remark that our view of magic as cosmology is heavily influenced by Evans-Pritchard. He says the primitive's belief in magic and sorcery plays much the same role as our doctrines of luck and fate.[1] The primitive believes seeds would not grow if he did not chant, if they do not grow anyway he must have chanted wrongly. Good luck will come to him if he does things properly, bad luck is the result of either his own incompetence as a magician, or of malevolent magic performed against him by his enemies. The strength of the magical world-view is that it is a complete world-view, one that explains anything and everything in terms of magic, failed magic, or magical conspiracies. It combines very smoothly with even a sophisticated technology because it explains its success.[2]

What are the consequences of this view of Evans-Pritchard's? First, that in Frazer's sense magic is perfectly compatible with rationally explicable behaviour—it is a world-view, a cosmology, and one with great power to grip. Second, that in Beattie's sense it *is* a substitute for systematic and analytic thinking, it does answer all those difficult questions some of which Western science answers, some of which are ultimate and for which Western science offers no explanation. This result has come about because Beattie has confused rationality in the sense of rational action, with rationality in the sense of rational belief. This is why he criticizes Frazer's 'intellectualism' when Frazer is talking about rational action and not about the way primitives think, and this is why he is caught in a net, in an inconsistency between the non-parochialism of his relativism (all societies have technology which shows they are rational), and the super-parochialism of his assumption that science (equals no error, equals usable technology) is the mark of

[1] E. E. Evans-Pritchard, *Witchcraft, Oracles and Magic Among the Azande*, London, 1937, especially Chapter IV.

[2] It is instructive to compare this with the West where it becomes increasingly difficult for us to accept a world view with no rough edges, one that explains everything. Our own world views no longer do. We allow large roles of coincidence, accident, luck and fate. All of these categories are vague and introduced *ad hoc*; our world-view does not try to explain everything, if it did it would be irrefutable and we have ceased to regard irrefutability as a desirable quality. The unique and disconcerting thing about the western scientific world-view is that it is progressive: it is more interested in the question than the answer; it puts a premium on overthrowing and improving previous answers by means of severe criticisms. Among these severe criticisms is that of irrefutability: immunity to all possible experience.

rationality. The attempt to avoid parochialism is surely laudable; to that end we must first give up scientific parochialism and then view the world as much as possible from the viewpoint of the primitive man, who has no reason to suspect that magic is not as effective as twentieth-century Western technology. We suggest that primitive people do not sow seeds and then perform irrational magic ritual, but that they grow crops in a very inefficient way, having no tractors and not knowing that ritual or no ritual makes no difference. Belief in magic is no better than belief in leeches or in phlogiston. We must assume that believers in either believe it to be true.[1] The problem is not, then, 'how on earth can they believe in magic?'; it is rather 'can people with inefficient magical beliefs come to be critical of them, under what conditions and to what extent?' To us this seems the really urgent sociological problem posed by magic.

[1] Cf. W. R. G. Horton, 'Ritual Man in Africa', *Africa*, XXXIV, 1964, pp. 85–103.

9

Some Problems about Rationality

STEVEN LUKES

In what follows I shall discuss a philosophical problem arising out of
the practice of anthropologists and sociologists which may be stated,
in a general and unanalysed form, as follows: when I come across a set
of beliefs which appear *prima facie* irrational, what should be my
attitude towards them? Should I adopt a critical attitude, taking it as a
fact about the beliefs that they *are* irrational, and seek to explain how
they came to be held, how they manage to survive unprofaned by
rational criticism, what their consequences are, etc? Or should I treat
such beliefs charitably: should I begin from the assumption that what
appears to me to be irrational may be interpreted as rational when
fully understood in its context? More briefly, the problem comes down
to whether or not there are alternative standards of rationality.

There are, of course, a number of different issues latent in the
problem as I have stated it. In particular, it will be necessary to distinguish between the different ways in which beliefs may be said to be
irrational. There are, for example, important differences and asym-
metries between falsehood, inconsistency and nonsense. Also there are
different sorts of belief; indeed there are difficult problems about what
is to count as a belief. Let us, however, leave the analysis of the problem
until a later stage in the argument.

First, I shall set out a number of different answers to it that have
been offered by anthropologists and philosophers with respect to
primitive magical and religious beliefs. In doing so I make no claim to
comprehensiveness. These and related issues have been widely debated
throughout the history of anthropology; all I aim to do here is to
compare a number of characteristic positions. It is, however, worth
stressing at this point that I do not pose the problem as a problem *in*

Originally published in *Archives Européennes de Sociologie*, VIII, 1967, pp.
247–64.

anthropology but rather as a philosophical problem[1] raised in a particularly acute form by the practice of anthropology. It is raised, though in a less clearcut form, by all sociological and historical inquiry that is concerned with beliefs.

Second, I shall try to separate out a number of distinct criteria of rationality which almost all discussions of these issues have confused. Finally, I shall make some attempt at showing which of these criteria are context-dependent and which are universal, and why.

I

Let us compare for plausibility five different answers to the problem.

1. First, there is the view that the seeming irrationality of the beliefs involved in primitive religion and magic constitutes no problem, for those beliefs are to be interpreted as *symbolic*. Take, for instance, the following passages from Dr Leach:

> [. . .] a very large part of the anthropological literature on religion concerns itself almost wholly with a discussion of the content of belief and of the rationality or otherwise of that content. Most such arguments seem to me to be scholastic nonsense. As I see it, myth regarded as a statement in words 'says' the same thing as ritual regarded as a statement in action. To ask questions about the content of belief which are not contained in the content of ritual is nonsense [. . .] In parts of this book I shall make frequent reference to Kachin mythology but I shall make no attempts to find any logical coherence in the myths to which I refer. Myths for me are simply one way of describing certain types of human behaviour.[2]

And again,

> [. . .] the various nats of Kathin religious ideology are, in the last analysis, nothing more than ways of describing the formal relationships that exist between real persons and real groups in ordinary human Kachin society.
>
> The gods denote the good relationships which carry honour and respect, the spooks and the witches denote the bad relationships of jealousy, malice and suspicion. Witchcraft becomes manifest when the

---

[1] Some have argued that its solution bears directly on anthropological practice (see, e.g. P. Winch, Understanding a Primitive Society, *American Philosophical Quarterly* (reprinted above), where Evans-Pritchard's account of witchcraft among the Azande is held to be partly vitiated by his supposedly mistaken answer to it). I agree with this position, but in this paper I do not seek to substantiate it.

[2] E. Leach, *Political Systems of Highland Burma*, London, 1954, pp. 13–14.

moral constraints of the ideally correct social order lose their force.[1]

Professor Firth argues, in a similar fashion, that judgment about the rationality of beliefs is irrelevant to the purposes of the anthropologist. It is, he writes, 'not important for an anthropological study whether witches exist or not [...] we are dealing here only with human relations [...]'.[2] Religious experience

is essentially a product of human problems, dispositions and relationships [. . .] In its own rather different way it is to some extent an alternative to art, symbolising and attributing value to human existence and human endeavour. [. . .] At the level of human dilemma, creative activity and symbolic imagery, indeed, religious concepts and values can be taken as real; they are true in their context. With the claim that their basic postulates have an autonomous, absolute validity I do not agree. But to us anthropologists the important thing is their *affirmation* of their autonomy, their validity, their truth—not the metaphysical question whether they are correct in saying so. Basically, in an anthropological study of religion, as in studies of art, we are concerned with the relevance of such affirmations rather than with their ultimate validity.[3]

The most systematic recent statement of this position is by Dr Beattie.[4] According to Beattie, beliefs associated with ritual are essentially expressive and symbolic. Thus, '[f]or the magician, as for the artist, the basic question is not whether his ritual is true in the sense of corresponding exactly with some empirically ascertainable reality, but rather whether it says, in apt symbolic language, what it is sought, and held important, to say'.[5] More generally,

[1] Ibid., p. 182.

[2] R. Firth, *Essays on Social Organization and Values*, London, 1964, p. 237.

[3] Ibid., pp. 238–39

[4] See J. Beattie, *Other Cultures*, London, 1964, Chapters V and XII, and idem, 'Ritual and Social Change', *Man: The Journal of the Royal Anthropological Institute*, I, 1966, 60–74.

[5] J. Beattie, loc. cit. (1966), p. 68. Thus, magic is 'the acting out of a situation, the expression of a desire in symbolic terms; it is not the application of empirically acquired knowledge about the properties of natural substances' (Beattie, op. cit. (1964), p. 206). Cf. T. Parsons, *The Structure of Social Action*, New York and London, 1937, p. 431 (2nd edition 1949): 'Ritual actions are not[. . .] either simply irrational, or pseudo rational, based on prescientific erroneous knowledge, but are of a different character altogether and as such not to be measured by the standards of intrinsic rationality at all' (cited in Beattie, loc. cit. 1966). Parsons wrongly attributes this position to Durkheim: as I shall show, Durkheim did not see religion as *merely* symbolic.

[. . .] although not all of what we used to call 'primitive' thought is mystical and symbolic, some is, just as some—though less—of 'western' thought is. If it is 'explanatory', it is so in a very different way from science. Thus it requires its own distinct kind of analysis. No sensible person subjects a sonnet or a sonata to the same kind of examination and testing as he does a scientific hypothesis, even though each contains its own kind of 'truth'. Likewise, the sensible student of myth, magic and religion will, I think, be well advised to recognise that their tenets are not scientific propositions, based on experience and on a belief in the uniformity of nature, and that they cannot be adequately understood as if they were. Rather, as symbolic statements, they are to be understood by a delicate investigation of the levels and varieties of meaning which they have for their practitioners, by eliciting, through comparative and contextual study, the principles of association in terms of which they are articulated, and by investigating the kinds of symbolic classifications which they imply.[1]

Thus the first answer to our problem amounts to the refusal to answer it, on the grounds that it is nonsensical (Leach), or irrelevant (Firth), or misdirected (Beattie).[2]

2. The second answer to the problem comes down to the claim that there are certain criteria which we can apply both to modern and to primitive beliefs which show the latter to be quite incomprehensible. (I leave until later the question of whether this claim is itself intelligible.)

As an example, take the following passage from Elsdon Best:

The mentality of the Maori is of an intensely mystical nature [. . .]

[1] Beattie, op. cit. (1966), p. 72. For Beattie magic and religion 'both imply ritual, symbolic ideas and activities rather than practical, "scientific" ones [. . .]' idem (1964), p. 212. For an example of the procedures Beattie advocates, see V. Turner, 'Symbols in Ndembu Ritual' in M. Gluckman (ed.), *Closed Systems and Open Minds*, Edinburgh, 1964, pp. 20–51.

[2] Beattie appeals to the authority of Suzanne Langer (Beattie, 'Ritual and Social Change', loc. cit. p. 66), but I am unsure how far his allegiance to her views goes. I do not know whether he would wish to argue, as she does, that rationality and even logic can be ascribed to expressive symbolism and whether he would subscribe to her general view that ['rationality] is the essence of mind and symbolic transformation its elementary process. It is a fundamental error, therefore, to recognize it only in the phenomenon of systematic, explicit reasoning. That is a mature and precarious product. Rationality, however, is embodied in every mental act [. . .]' (idem *Philosophy in a new Key*, Harvard, 1942, p. 99; 3rd edition 1963. Miss Langer's is in any case a special sense of 'rationality'. As I hope to show, the fundamental meaning of rationality is essentially linked to the phenomenon of systematic, explicit reasoning.

We hear of many singular theories about Maori beliefs and Maori thought, but the truth is that we do not understand either, and, what is more, we never shall. We shall never know the inwardness of the native mind. For that would mean tracing our steps, for many centuries, back into the dim past, far back to the time when we also possessed the mind of primitive man. And the gates have long closed on that hidden road.[1]

A similar view was expressed by the Seligmans about the tribes of the Pagan Sudan:

On this subject [of magic] the black man and the white regard each other with amazement: each considers the behaviour of the other incomprehensible, totally unrelated to everyday experience, and entirely disregarding the known laws of cause and effect.[2]

3. The third answer amounts to the hypothesis that primitive magical and religious beliefs are attempted explanations of phenomena. This involves the claim that they satisfy certain given criteria of rationality by virtue of certain rational precedures of thought and observation being followed; on the other hand they are (more or less) mistaken and to be judged as (more or less) unsuccessful explanations against the canons of science (and modern common sense).

The classical exponents of this position were Tylor and Frazer, especially in their celebrated 'intellectualist' theory of magic. Professor Evans-Pritchard has succinctly summarized their standpoint as follows:

They considered that primitive man had reached his conclusions about the efficacy of magic from rational observation and deduction in much the same way as men of science reach their conclusions about natural laws. Underlying all magical ritual is a rational process of thought. The ritual of magic follows from its ideology. It is true that the deductions of a magician are false—had they been true they would have been scientific and not magical—but they are nevertheless based on genuine observation. For classification of phenomena by the similarities which exist between them is the procedure of science as well as of magic and is the first essential process of human knowledge. Where the magician goes wrong is in inferring that because things are alike in one or more respects they have a mystical link

[1] 'Maori Medical Lore', *Journal of Polynesian Society*, XIII, 1904, p. 219, cited in L. Lévy-Bruhl, *Les fonctions mentales dans les sociétés inférieures*, Paris, 1910, p. 69 (2nd edition 1912).

[2] C. G. and B. Z. Seligman, *Pagan Tribes of the Nilotic Sudan*, London, 1932, p. 25, cited in E. E. Evans-Pritchard, Lévy-Bruhl's Theory of Primitive Mentality, *Bulletin of the Faculty of Arts*, II, 1934, 1–36.

between them whereas in fact the link is not a real link but an ideal connexion in the mind of the magician. [. . .] A casual relationship exists in his mind but not in nature. It is a subjective and not an objective connexion. Hence the savage mistakes an ideal analogy for a real connexion.[1]

Their theory of religion was likewise both rationalistic and derogatory: Frazer in particular held religion to be less rational (though more complex) than the Occult Science of magic because it postulated a world of capricious personal beings rather than a uniform law-governed nature.[2]

There has recently been elaborated a highly sophisticated version of this position on the part of a number of writers, who have stressed the explanatory purport of primitive magical and religious beliefs. In a brilliant paper,[3] Dr Robin Horton treats traditional African religious systems as theoretical models akin to those of the sciences, arguing that many of the supposed differences between these two modes of thought result, more than anything else, from differences of idiom used in their respective theoretical models. His aim is to break down the contrast between traditional religious thought as 'non-empirical' and scientific thought as 'empirical'.

Horton's case is not that traditional magico-religious thought is a variety of scientific thought but that both aim at and partially succeed in grasping causal connexions. He also, of course, maintains that 'scientific method is undoubtedly the surest and most efficient tool for arriving at beliefs that are successful in this respect'[4] and examines the

[1] E. E. Evans-Pritchard, 'The Intellectualist (English) Interpretation of Magic', *Bulletin of the Faculty of Arts*, I, 1933, 282–311. Cf. also idem, *Theories of Primitive Religion*, Oxford, 1965, Chapter II.

[2] Cf. E. Leach, 'Frazer and Malinowski', *Encounter*, XXV, 1965, 24–36: 'For Frazer, all ritual is based on fallacy, either an erroneous belief in the magical powers of men or an equally erroneous belief in the imaginary powers of imaginary deities' (p. 29).

[3] R. Horton, 'African Traditional Thought and Western Science', above pp. 131–171; Cf. also idem, 'Destiny and the Unconscious in West Africa', *Africa*, XXXI (1961), 110–16; 'The Kalabari World View: an Outline and Interpretation', ibid., XXXII, 1962, 197–220; 'Ritual Man in Africa', ibid. XXXIV, 1964, 85–104. (For a symbolist critique of Horton, see Beattie, 'Ritual and Social Change', loc. cit.). For other 'neo-Frazerian' writings, see J. Goody, 'Religion and Ritual: the Definitional Problem', *British Journal of Sociology*, XII, 1961, 142–64; I. C. Jarvie, *The Revolution in Anthropology*, London, 1964; I. C. Jarvie and J. Agassi, 'The Rationality of Magic', above pp. 172–193.

[4] See Horton, above p. 140.

different ways in which traditional and scientific thought relate to experience: his case is that these can ultimately be traced to the differences between 'closed' traditional cultures 'characterized by lack of awareness of alternatives, sacredness of beliefs, and anxiety about threats to them' and 'open' scientifically-orientated cultures 'characterized by awareness of alternatives, diminished sacredness of beliefs, and diminished anxiety about threats to them'.[1]

Thus the third answer to our problem involves the application of given rational criteria to *prima facie* irrational beliefs which shows them to be largely rational in method, purpose and form, though unscientific, and more or less (for Tylor and Frazer, entirely; for Horton, less than we thought) irrational in content. Durkheim put this case, with customary clarity, as follows:

> [I]t is through [primitive religion] that a first explanation of the world has been made possible. [. . .] When I learn that *A* regularly precedes *B*, my knowledge is enriched by a new item, but my understanding is not at all satisfied with a statement which does not appear rationally justified. I commence to *understand* only when it is possible for me to conceive *B* in a perspective that makes it appear to me as something that is not foreign to *A*, as united to *A* by some intelligible relationship. The great service that the religions have rendered to thought is that they have constructed a first representation of what these intelligible relationships between things might be. In the circumstances under which it was attempted, the enterprise could obviously attain only precarious results. But then, does it ever attain any that are definitive, and is it not necessary ceaselessly to reconsider them? And also, it is less important to succeed than to try. [. . .] The explanations of contemporary science are surer of being objective because they are more methodical and because they rest on more rigorously controlled observations, but they do not differ in nature from those which satisfy primitive thought.[2]

4. The fourth position we are to consider is that of Lucien Lévy-Bruhl (until the time of writing *Les Carnets*). This is, as we shall see, crucially ambiguous on the point of concern to us.[3]

Lévy-Bruhl's central theme was to emphasize the differences between the content of two types of beliefs (seen as Durkheimian *représentations*

[1] Ibid. pp. 155–6.

[2] E. Durkheim, *Les formes élémentaires de la vie religieuse*, Paris, 1912, pp. 339–41.

[3] See *Les Carnets de Lucien Lévy-Bruhl*, Paris, 1949, passim., where it is made explicit and partially resolved.

collectives):[1] those characteristic of primitive societies and those characteristic of 'scientific' thinking. He tried to bring out those aspects in which these two types of belief differed: as he wrote 'I intended to bring fully to light the mystical *aspect* of primitive mentality in contrast with the rational *aspect* of the mentality of our societies'.[2] Thus primitive beliefs were characteristically mystical, in the sense of being committed to 'forces, influences, powers imperceptible to the senses, and never the less real'.[3] Indeed,

> [. . .] the reality in which primitives move is itself mystical. There is not a being, not an object, not a natural phenomenon that appears in their collective representations in the way that it appears to us. Almost all that we see therein escapes them, or is a matter of indifference to them. On the other hand, they see many things of which we are unaware.[4]

Furthermore, their thought is (in his confusing but revealing term) 'pre-logical':[5] that is

> [it] is not constrained above all else, as ours is, to avoid contradictions. The same logical exigencies are not in its case always present. What to our eyes is impossible or absurd, it sometimes will admit without seeing any difficulty.[6]

Lévy-Bruhl endorsed Evans-Pritchard's account of his viewpoint as seeking 'to understand the characteristics of mystical thought and to define these qualities and to compare them with the qualities of scientific thought':[7] thus it is 'not in accord with reality and may also

---

[1] It is worth noting that Durkheim differed crucially from Lévy-Bruhl, emphasizing the continuities rather than the differences between primitive and modern scientific thought: see E. Durkheim, *Les formes élémentaires de la vie religieuse*, op. cit. pp. 336–42, and Review of L. Lévy-Bruhl, *Les fonctions mentales dans les sociétés inférieures*, and E. Durkheim, *Les formes élémentaires de la vie religieuse*, in *Année sociologique*, XII, 1913, 33–7.

[2] L. Lévy-Bruhl, 'A Letter to E. E. Evans-Pritchard', *British Journal of Sociology*, III, 1952, 117–23.

[3] L. Lévy-Bruhl, *Les fonctions mentales dans les sociétés inférieures*, Paris, 1910, p. 30.

[4] Ibid. pp. 30–31.

[5] He eventually abandoned it: see *Les Carnets de L. Lévy-Bruhl*, op. cit. pp. 47–51, 60–62, 69–70, 129–35, etc.

[6] L. Lévy-Bruhl, *La mentalité primitive* (Herbert Spencer Lecture), Oxford, 1931, p. 21.

[7] E. E. Evans-Pritchard, 'Lévy-Bruhl's Theory of Primitive Mentality', loc. cit. Lévy-Bruhl's general endorsement of this article is to be found in Lévy-Bruhl, 'A Letter to E. E. Evans-Pritchard', loc. cit.

be mystical where it assumes the existence of suprasensible forces'[1] and is not 'logical' in the sense in which a modern logician would use the term',[2] so that 'primitive beliefs when tested by the rules of thought laid down by logicians are found to contravene those rules'.[3] 'Objects, beings, phenomena' could be 'in a manner incomprehensible to us, at once both themselves and something other than themselves'.[4] Thus according to given criteria derived from 'scientific' thought, 'mystical' and 'pre-logical' thought was to be judged unsuccessful. Yet Lévy-Bruhl also wants to say that there are criteria which it satisfies. Hence, he wants to say that there is a sense in which the suprasensible forces are 'real'. Thus, as we have seen, he writes of mystical forces as being 'never the less real'.[5] (On the other hand, he came to see that the primitive is not uniquely preoccupied with the mystical powers of beings and objects[6] and has a basic, practical notion of reality too). Again, he explicitly endorses Evans-Pritchard's interpretation that 'primitive thought is eminently coherent, perhaps over-coherent. [. . .] Beliefs are co-ordinated with other beliefs and behaviour into an organized system'.[7] Yet he is crucially ambiguous about the nature of this coherence. On the one hand he writes that it is 'logical': '[t]he fact that the "*patterns of thought*" are different does not, once the premises have been given, prevent the "primitive" from reasoning like us and, in this sense, his thought is neither more nor less "logical" than ours'.[8] Yet on the other hand, he appears to accept the propositions that mystical thought is 'intellectually consistent even if it is not logically consistent'[9] and that it is 'organized into a coherent system with a logic of its own'.[10]

Thus Lévy-Bruhl's position is an uneasy compromise, maintaining that primitive 'mystical' and 'pre-logical' beliefs are on our standards

[1] E. E. Evans-Pritchard, 'Lévy-Bruhl's Theory . . . ', loc. cit.
[2] Ibid.
[3] Ibid.
[4] Lévy-Bruhl, *Les fonctions mentales* . . . , op. cit. p. 77.
[5] This position he did not abandon: see *Les Carnets de L. Lévy-Bruhl.*, op. cit. (e.g. pp. 163–98), where it is strongly refirmed.
[6] E. E. Evans-Pritchard, 'Lévy-Bruhl's Theory of Primitive Mentality', loc. cit.
[7] Ibid.
[8] L. Lévy-Bruhl, 'A Letter to E. E. Evans-Pritchard', loc. cit. p. 121.
[9] E. E. Evans-Pritchard, 'Lévy-Bruhl's Theory . . . ', loc. cit.
[10] Ibid. Cf. *Les Carnets* . . . , op. cit. p. 61, where he recalls that he had begun from the hypothesis that societies with different structures had different logics The theory of the 'pre-logical' was a modified version of this hypothesis, which he only finally abandoned much later, when he came to hold that 'the logical structure of the mind is the same in all known human societies' (Ibid, p. 62).

irrational, but that on other (unspecified) standards they are about 'real' phenomena and 'logical'.[1]

5. The fifth answer to our problem asserts that there is a strong case for assuming that, in principle, seemingly irrational belief-systems in primitive societies are to be interpreted as rational. It has been most clearly stated by Professor Peter Winch,[2] and it has been claimed that Evans-Pritchard's book *Nuer Religion* supports it.[3] According to Winch's view, when an observer is faced with seemingly irrational beliefs in a primitive society, he should seek contextually given criteria according to which they may appear rational.

Winch objects to Evans-Pritchard's approach in *Witchcraft, Oracles and Magic among the Azande* on the grounds that the criteria of rationality which he applies there are alien to the context. According to Evans-Pritchard,

> It is an inevitable conclusion from Zande descriptions of witchcraft that it is not an objective reality. The physiological condition which is said to be the seat of witchcraft, and which I believe to be nothing more than food passing through the small intestine, is an objective condition, but the qualities they attribute to it and the rest of their beliefs about it are mystical. Witches, as Azande conceive them, cannot exist.[4]

Winch objects to this position on the ground that it relies upon a notion of 'objective reality' provided by science: for Evans-Pritchard 'the scientific conception agrees with what reality actually is like, whereas the magical conception does not',[5] but, Winch maintains, it is a mistake to appeal to any such independent or objective reality. What counts as real depends on the context and the language used (thus 'it is *within* the religious use of language that the conception of God's reality has its place');[6] moreover, '[w]hat is real and what is unreal shows itself

---

[1] Lévy-Bruhl's final position was as follows: 'there is no primitive mentality which is distinguished from the other by *two* characteristic features (being mystical and pre-logical). There is one mystical mentality that is more marked and more easily observable among 'primitives' than in our societies, but present in every human mind'. (*Les Carnets* . . . , p. 131.)

[2] P. Winch, Understanding a Primitive Society, above pp. 78ff.

[3] E. Gellner, Concepts and Society, above pp. 18ff.; and A. MacIntyre, 'Is Understanding Religion compatible with Believing?' above pp. 62ff.

[4] E. E. Evans-Pritchard, *Witchcraft, Oracles and Magic among the Azande*, Oxford, 1937, p. 63.

[5] P. Winch, Understanding a Primitive Society, loc. cit. p. 81 above.

[6] Ibid. p. 82 above.

in the sense that language has [. . .] we could not in fact distinguish the real from the unreal without understanding the way this distinction operates in the language'.[1] Thus European scepticism is misplaced and (we must suppose) Zande witchcraft is real.

Again, Winch objects to Evans-Pritchard's account of contradictions in the Zande belief-system. The Zande believe that a suspect may be proved a witch by post-mortem examination of his intestines for witchcraft-substance; they also believe that this is inherited through the male line. Evans-Pritchard writes:

> To our minds it appears evident that if a man is proven a witch the whole of his clan are *ipso facto* witches, since the Zande clan is a group of persons related biologically to one another through the male line. Azande see the sense of this argument but they do not accept its conclusions, and it would involve the whole notion of witchcraft in contradiction were they to do so. [. . .] Azande do not perceive the contradition as we perceive it because they have no theoretical interest in the subject, and those situations in which they express their belief in witchcraft do not force the problem upon them.[2]

Winch's comment on this passage is that

> the context from which the suggestion about the contradiction is made, the context of our scientific culture, is not on the same level as the context in which the beliefs about witchcraft operate. Zande notions of witchcraft do not constitute a theoretical system in terms of which Azande try to gain a quasi-scientific understanding of the world. This in its turn suggests that it is the European, obsessed with pressing Zande thought where it would not naturally go—to a contradiction—who is guilty of misunderstanding, not the Zande. The European is in fact committing a category-mistake.[3]

Thus Winch's complaint against Evans-Pritchard's treatment of the Azande is 'that he did not take seriously enough the idea that the concepts used by primitive peoples can only be interpreted in the context of the way of life of these peoples':[4] thus we cannot legislate about what is real for them or what counts as a contradiction in their beliefs.[5] Moreover, Winch goes on to argue, rationality itself is context-

---

[1] Ibid., p. 82.

[2] *Witchcraft* . . . , op. cit. pp. 24–5.

[3] 'Understanding a Primitive Society', above, p. 93.

[4] Ibid.

[5] The philosophical basis for this position is to be found in P. Winch, *The Idea of a Social Science and its Relation to Philosophy*, London, 1958. Cf. in particular

or culture-dependent. 'We start', he writes, 'from the position that standards of rationality in different societies do not always coincide; from the possibility, therefore, that the standards of rationality current in S are different from our own [. . .] what we are concerned with are differences in *criteria of rationality*'.[1] He objects to the view, expressed by Professor MacIntyre, that 'the beginning of an explanation of why certain criteria are taken to be rational in some societies is that they *are* rational. And since this last has to enter into our explanation we cannot explain social behaviour independently of our own norms of rationality'.[2] Winch's case against this is that rationality in the end comes down to 'conformity to norms'; how this notion is to be applied to a given society 'will depend on our reading of their conformity to norms— what counts for them as conformity and what does not'.[3]

Let us see how Evans-Pritchard's *Nuer Religion* could be seen as an exemplification of Winch's approach. In the chapter entitled 'The Problem of Symbols' Evans-Pritchard attempts to show that the Nuer, although they *appear* to say contradictory and inconsistent things, do not really do so. Thus,

> It seems odd, if not absurd, to a European when he is told that a twin is a bird as though it were an obvious fact, for Nuer are not saying that a twin is like a bird, but that he is a bird. There seems to be a complete contradiction in the statement; and it was precisely on statements of this kind recorded by observers of primitive peoples that Lévy-Bruhl based his theory of the prelogical mentality of these peoples, its chief characteristic being, in his view, that it permits such evident contradictions—that a thing can be what it is and at the same time something altogether different.[4]

the following passage: '[. . .] criteria of logic are not a direct gift of God, but arise out of, and are only intelligible in the context of, ways of living and modes of social life. It follows that one cannot apply criteria of logic to modes of social life as such. For instance, science is one such mode and religion is another; and each has criteria of intelligibility peculiar to itself. So within science or religion, actions can be logical or illogical: in science, for example, it would be illogical to refuse to be bound by the results of a properly carried out experiment; in religion it would be illogical to suppose that one could pit one's own strength against God's, and so on [. . .]' (pp. 100–1).

[1] P. Winch, 'Understanding . . .', loc. cit. p. 97.

[2] A. MacIntyre, 'A Mistake about Causality in Social Science', in P. Laslett and W. G. Runciman (eds.), *Philosophy, Politics and Society*, Second Series, Oxford, 1962, p. 61. This formulation suffers from its emphasis on the location of these norms rather than on their nature.

[3] P. Winch, 'Understanding . . .', loc. cit. p. 100.

[4] E. E. Evans-Pritchard, *Nuer Religion*, Oxford, 1956, p. 131.

However,

> no contradiction is involved in the statement which, on the contrary, appears quite sensible and even true, to one who presents the idea to himself in the Nuer language and within their system of religious thought.[1]

According to Evans-Pritchard,

> [. . .] the Nuer do not make, or take, the statement that twins are birds in any ordinary sense. [. . .] in addition to being men and women they are of a twin-birth, and a twin-birth is a special revelation of Spirit; and Nuer express this special character of twins in the 'twins are birds' formula because twins and birds, though for difference reasons, are both associated with Spirit and this makes twins, like birds, 'people of the above' and 'children of God', and hence a bird is a suitable symbol in which to express the special relationship in which a twin stands to God.[2]

Thus, it seems, Evans-Pritchard is claiming that according to Nuer criteria this statement is rational and consistent, indeed 'quite sensible and even true'. As he writes, towards the end of the book,

> It is in the nature of the subject that there should be ambiguity and paradox. I am aware that in consequence I have not been able to avoid *what must appear to the reader to be obscurities, and even contradictions, in my account.*[3]

We shall return below to this example and to the question of whether the fact it is a practical application of Winch's views. Here let us merely restate the fifth answer to our problem: that it is likely in principle that beliefs that appear to be irrational can be reinterpreted as rational, in the light of criteria of rationality to be discovered in the culture in which they occur. (Of course, individual beliefs may fail according to these criteria, but Winch seems to hold that no reasonably large set of beliefs could do so.)

[1] Ibid.
[2] Ibid. pp. 131–2.
[3] Ibid. p. 318. Emphasis mine. Professor Gellner's comment on this approach is that it 'absolves too many people of the charge of systematically illogical or false or self-deceptive thought'. Moreover (E. Gellner, loc. cit. p. 36 above):
'The trouble with such all-embracing logical charity is, for one thing, that it is unwittingly quite *a priori*: it may delude anthropologists into thinking that they had *found* that no society upholds absurd or self-contradictory beliefs, whilst in fact the principle employed has ensured in advance of any inquiry that nothing may count as prelogical, inconsistent or categorically absurd though it may be. And this, apart from anything else, would blind one to at least one socially significant phenomenon: the social role of absurdity.'

II

The use of the word 'rational' and its cognates has caused untold confusion and obscurity, especially in the writings of sociological theorists.[1] This, however, is not the best reason for seeking to break our problem down into different elements. There are strong reasons for suspecting that the first mistake is to suppose that there is a single answer to it; and this suspicion is only reinforced by the very plausibility of most of the statements cited in the foregoing section.

What is it for a belief or set of beliefs to be irrational? A belief may be characterized as a proposition accepted as true.[2] Beliefs, or sets of beliefs, are said to be irrational if they are inadequate in certain ways: (1) if they are illogical, e.g. inconsistent or (self-) contradictory, consisting of or relying on invalid inferences, etc.; (2) if they are, partially or wholly, false; (3) if they are nonsensical (though it may be questioned whether they would then qualify as propositions and thus as beliefs); (4) if they are situationally specific or *ad hoc*, i.e.: not universalized because bound to particular occasions;[3] (5) if the ways in which they come to be held or the manner in which they are held are seen as deficient in some respect. For example:

[a] the beliefs may be based, partially or wholly, on irrelevant considerations; [b] they may be based on insufficient evidence; [c] they may be held uncritically, i.e.: not held open to refutation or modification by experience, regarded as 'sacred' and protected by 'secondary elaboration' against disconfirming evidence;[4] [d] the beliefs may be held unreflectively, without conscious consideration of their assumptions and implications, relations to other beliefs, etc. (though here the irrationality may be predicated of the believer rather than the belief).

In addition, there are other well-used senses of 'rational' as applied

---

[1] I think Max Weber is largely responsible for this. His uses of these terms is irredeemably opaque and shifting.

[2] Philosophers have disputed over the question of whether 'belief' involves reference to a state of mind. I agree with those who argue that it does not; thus I would offer a dispositional account of 'acceptance'. As will be evident, I take it that belief is by definition propositional. As to the philosophical status of propositions, this does not affect the argument.

[3] This is the sense of rationality stressed by Professor Hare. See R. Hare, *Freedom and Reason*, Oxford, 1963.

[4] Cf. R. Horton, 'African Traditional Thought and Western Science', *Africa*, XXXVII (1967), 50–71, and 155–87, especially pp. 167–69 (above, pp. 162–64). For numerous examples of this, see E. E. Evans-Pritchard, *Witchcraft* . . . , op. cit.

to actions, such as (6) the widest sense of simply goal–directed action;[1] (7) the sense in which an action is said to be (maximally) rational if what is in fact the most efficient means is adopted to achieve a given end;[2] (8) the sense in which the means that is believed by the agent to be the most efficient is adopted to achieve the agent's end (whatever it may be); (9) the sense in which an action is in fact conducive to the agent's (expressed or unexpressed) 'long–term' ends; (10) the sense in which the agent's ends are the ends he ought to have.[3]

III

In this section I shall suggest that some criteria of rationality[4] are universal, i.e. relevantly applicable to all beliefs, in any context, while others are context-dependent, i.e. are to be discovered by investigating the context and are only relevantly applicable to beliefs in that context. I shall argue (as against Winch) that beliefs are not only to be evaluated by the criteria that are to be discovered in the context in which they are held; they must also be evaluated by criteria of rationality that simply *are* criteria of rationality, as opposed to criteria of rationality in context [*c*]. In what follows universal criteria will be called 'rational (1) criteria' and context-dependent criteria 'rational (2) criteria'.

Let us assume we are discussing the beliefs of a society *S*. One can then draw a distinction between two sets of questions. One can ask, in the first place: (*i*) what for society *S* are the criteria of rationality *in general?* And, second, one can ask: (*ii*) what are the appropriate criteria to apply to a given class of beliefs within that society?

(*i*) In so far as Winch seems to be saying that the answer to the first question is culture-dependent, he must be wrong, or at least we could never know if he were right; indeed we cannot even conceive what it

[1] See, e.g. I. C. Jarvie and J. Agassi, loc. cit.

[2] Cf. e.g., Parsons, op. cit. pp. 19 and 698–99.

[3] Cf. eg., G. C. Homans, *Social Behaviour: Its Elementary Forms*, London, 1961, p. 60 for senses (9) and (10). It is perhaps worth adding here that I do not find Mr Jonathan Bennett's stipulative definition of rationality germane to the present discussion ('whatever it is that humans possess which marks them off, in respect of intellectual capacity, sharply and importantly from all other known species', in J. Bennett, *Rationality*, London, 1964, p. 5.)

[4] I take 'criterion of rationality' to mean a rule specifying what would count as a reason for believing something (or acting). I assume that it is only by determining the relevant criteria of rationality, that the question 'Why did *X* believe *p*?' can be answered (though, of course, one may need to look for other explanatory factors. I merely claim that one must first look here).

could *be* for him to be right. In the first place, the existence of a common *reality* is a necessary precondition of our understanding *S*'s language. This does not mean that we and the members of *S* must agree about all 'the facts' (which are the joint products of language and reality); any given true statement in *S*'s language may be untranslatable into ours and *vice versa*. As Whorf wrote, 'language dissects nature in many different ways'. What must be the case is that *S* must have our distinction between truth and falsity if we are to understand its language, for, if *per impossibile* it did not, we would be unable even to agree about what counts as the successful indentification of public (spatio-temporally located) objects.[1] Moreover, any culture, scientific or not, which engages in successful prediction (and it is difficult to see how any society could survive which did not) must presuppose a given reality. Winch may write that '[o]ur idea of what belongs to the realm of reality is given for us in the language that we use'[2] and he may castigate Evans-Pritchard as 'wrong, and crucially wrong, in his attempt to characterize the scientific in terms of that which is "in accord with objective reality" '.[3] But, it is, so to speak, no accident that the predictions of both primitive and modern common-sense and of science come off. Prediction would be absurd unless there were events to predict.[4] Both primitive and modern men predict in roughly the same ways; also they can learn each other's languages. Thus they each assume an independent reality, which they share.

In the second place, *S*'s language must have operable logical rules and not all of these can be pure matters of convention. Winch states that 'logical relations between propositions [. . .] depend on social relations between men'.[5] Does this imply that the concept of negation and the laws of identity and non-contradiction need not operate in *S*'s language? If so, then it must be mistaken, for if the members of *S* do not possess even these, how could we ever understand their thought, their inferences and arguments? Could they even be credited with the possibility of inferring, arguing or even thinking? If, for example, they were unable to see that the truth of *p* excludes the truth of its denial,

---

[1] Cf. P. Strawson, *Individuals*, London, 1959, and S. Hampshire, *Thought and Action*, London, 1959, Chapter I.

[2] P. Winch, *The Idea of a Social science*, op. cit. p. 15.

[3] P. Winch, 'Understanding . . .', loc. cit. p. 80.

[4] I owe this argument to Martin Hollis. I have profited greatly
papers, 'Winchcraft and Witchcraft' and 'Reason and Ritual'

[5] P. Winch, *The Idea . . .* , op. cit. p. 126.

how could they ever communicate truths to one another and reason from them to other truths? Winch half sees this point when he writes that 'the possibilities of our grasping forms of rationality different from ours in an alien culture [. . .] are limited by certain formal requirements centering round the demand for consistency. But these formal requirements tell us nothing about what in particular is to *count* as consistency, just as the rules of the propositional calculus limit, but do not themselves determine, what are to be proper values of p, q, etc.'.[1] But this is merely a (misleading) way of saying that it is the content of propositions, not the logical relations between them, that is 'dependent on social relations between men'.

It follows that if S has a language, it must, minimally, possess criteria of truth (as correspondence to reality) and logic, which we share with it and which simply *are* criteria of rationality. The only alternative conclusion is Elsdon Best's, indicated in position (2) of section I above, which seeks to state the (self-contradictory) proposition that S's thought (and language) operate according to quite different criteria and that it is literally incomprehensible to us. But if the members of S really did not have our criteria of truth and logic, we would have no grounds for attributing to them language, thought or beliefs and would *a fortiori* be unable to make any statements about these.

Thus the first two ways that beliefs may be irrational that are specified in section II are fundamental and result from the application of rational (1) criteria. Moreover, it can be shown that the other types of irrationality of belief indicated there are dependent on the use of such criteria. Thus nonsense (3) and the failure to universalize (4) may be seen as bad logic, (e.g.: self-contradiction and bad reasoning). Whether this is the most *useful* way to characterize a particular belief in a given case is another question. Again, the types of irrationality relating to the ways of arriving at and of holding beliefs are dependent on rational (1) criteria. Thus (5) [a]–[d] are simply methodological inadequacies: they result from not following certain procedures that can be trusted to lead us to truths.[2] Again, in the senses of 'rational' relating to actions, senses (7) and (9) require the application of rational (1) criteria.

Thus the general standpoint of position (3) in section I is vindicated. In so far as primitive magico-religious beliefs are logical and follow

'Understanding . . . ', loc. cit. p. 100.
. . . rton shows, they may be unnecessary ('African Traditional . . . p. 140).

methodologically sound procedures, they are, so far, rational (1); in so far as they are, partially or wholly, false, they are not. Also part of Lévy-Bruhl's position is vindicated. In so far as 'mystical' and 'pre-logical' can be interpreted as false and invalid, primitive (and analogous modern) beliefs are irrational (1).

(*ii*) What, now, about the question of whether there are any criteria which it is appropriate to apply to a given class of beliefs within *S*? In the first place, the context may provide criteria specifying which beliefs may acceptably go together. Such criteria may or may not violate the laws of logic. Where they do, the beliefs are characteristically labelled 'mysterious'. Then there are contextually-provided criteria of *truth*:[1] thus a study of Nuer religion provides the means for deciding whether 'twins are birds' is, for the Nuer, to be counted as 'true'. Such criteria may apply to beliefs (i.e. propositions accepted as true) which do not satisfy rational (1) criteria in so far as they do not and could not corres-pond with 'reality': that is, in so far as they are *in principle* neither directly verifiable nor directly falsifiable by empirical means. (They may, of course, be said to relate to 'reality' in another sense;[2] alterna-tively, they may be analysed in terms of the coherence or pragmatist theories of truth.) This is to disagree with Leach and Beattie who seek to discount the fact that beliefs are accepted as true and argue that they must be interpreted metaphorically. But it is also to disagree with the Frazer-Tylor approach, which would simply count them false because they are 'non-objective'.

There are (obviously) contextually-provided criteria of `meaning. Again, there are contextually-provided criteria which make particular beliefs *appropriate* in particular circumstances. There are also con-textually-provided criteria which specify the best way to arrive at and hold beliefs. In general, there are contextually-provided criteria for deciding what counts as a 'good reason' for holding a belief.

Thus, reverting to our schema of way that beliefs can be irrational in section II, it will be seen that, for any or all of a particular class of beliefs in a society, there may be contextually-provided criteria accord-ing to which they are 'consistent' or 'inconsistent', 'true' or 'false', meaningful or nonsensical, appropriate or inappropriate in the circum-stances, soundly or unsoundly reached, properly or improperly held, and in general based on good or bad reasons. Likewise, with respec the rationality of actions, the context may provide crit

[1] Cf. *Les Carnets de L. Lévy-Bruhl*, op. cit. pp. 80–82 and 1
[2] Ibid. p. 194.

which the agent's reason for acting and even the ends of his action may be judged adequate or inadequate.

Thus the first position in section I is largely vindicated, in so far as it is really pointing to the need to allow for contextual (e.g. symbolic) interpretation, but mistaken in so far as it ignores the fact that beliefs purport to be *true*[1] and relies exclusively upon the non-explanatory notion of 'metaphor'.[2] The third position is mistaken (or inadequate) only in so far as it denies (or ignores) the relevance of rational (2) criteria. The fourth position foreshadows that advanced here, but it is misleading (as Lévy-Bruhl himself came to see) in so far as it suggests that rational (1) criteria are not universal and fundamental. The fifth position is ambiguous. In so far as Winch is claiming that there are no rational (1) criteria, he appears mistaken. In so far as he is claiming that there are rational (2) criteria, he appears correct. I take the quotations from *Nuer Religion* to support the latter claim.

One may conclude that all beliefs are to be evaluated by both rational (1) and rational (2) criteria. Sometimes, as in the case of religious beliefs, rational (1) truth criteria will not take the analysis very far. Often rational (1) criteria of logic do not reveal anything positive about relations between beliefs that are to be explicated in terms of 'provides a reason for'. Sometimes rational (1) criteria appear less important than 'what the situation demands'. In all these cases, rational (2) criteria are illuminating. But they do not make rational (1) criteria dispensable. They could not, for the latter, specify the ultimate constraints to which thought is subject: that is, they are fundamental and universal in the sense that any society which possesses what we may justifiably call a language must apply them *in general*, though particular beliefs, or sets of beliefs, may violate them.

If both sorts of criteria are required for the understanding of beliefs (for they enable us to grasp their truth-conditions and their inter-relations), they are equally necessary to the explanation of why they are held, how they operate and what their social consequences are. Thus only by the application of rational (1) criteria is it possible to see how beliefs which fail to satisfy them can come to be rationally criticized, or

[1] Beattie and Firth see the sense of this argument but do not accept its conclusions (see quotations in text above and J. Beattie, *Other Cultures*, London, 1964, 206–7).

Goody, 'Religion and Ritual: the Definitional Problem', *British Journal* 1961, 142–64, especially pp. 156–57 and 161. As Evans-Pritchard says: 'It was Durkheim and not the savage who made *r Religion*, op. cit. p. 313).

fail to be.[1] On the other hand, it is usually only by the application of rational (2) criteria that the point and significance that beliefs have for those that hold them can be grasped. Rational (1) and rational (2) criteria are necessary both to understand and to explain.[2]

[1] Cf. E. E. Evans-Pritchard, *Witchcraft, Oracles and Magic among the Azande*, Oxford, 1937, pp. 475–78, where twenty-two reasons are given why the Azande 'do not perceive the futility of their magic'.

[2] I am most grateful to Martin Hollis, John Beattie, Rodney Needham, Jean Floud, John Torrance and Vernon Bogdanor, among others, for their very kind and helpful criticisms of an earlier draft of this article.

10

The Limits of Irrationality

MARTIN HOLLIS

The anthropologist starts with an empty notebook and it seems that everything he writes in it is discovered empirically. But is it? I shall argue here that the fact that the natives are 'rational' in Mr Lukes first or 'universal' sense is not discovered empirically and that this puts Mr Lukes' philsophical problem in a different light.

To understand native utterances the anthropologist must relate them to one another and to the world. To translate them into, let us say, English, he needs to relate some of them to the world, since, in relating an utterance to others he does not learn what it means, unless he already knows what the others mean. Ultimately, then, he needs a class of utterances whose situations of use he can specify. These situations of use can apparently be specified either as he himself perceives them or as the natives perceive them and it seems that the two specifications might be different. But, if he has to allow for this possibility, he cannot begin at all. For his only access to native perceptions and specifications is by translating what they say about what they perceive. He would therefore have to translate before discovering what they perceive and to know what they perceive before translating. There would be no way in to the circle. The class of utterances which form the bridgehead for his advance must be one for which his specification and his informants' coincide.

His line of attack, then, is that a native sentence can be correctly translated by any English sentence which can be used in the same way in the same situations. Although sentences related like this need not be semantically equivalent, there is no more direct attack on meaning available. In taking this line he makes two crucial assumptions, first that

Originally published in *Archives Européenes de Sociologie* VII, 1967, pp. 265–71. I have profited greatly from reading Mr Luke's paper and should also like to thank him warmly for many earlier discussions of the issues it raises.

the natives perceive more or less what he perceives and secondly that they say about it more or less what he would say. I shall defend my claim that these are assumptions and not hypotheses and then draw some implications for the problem of rationality.

Suppose he gets his bridgehead by pinning down the native counterparts of English sentences like 'Yes, this is a brown cow'. There are no native counterparts to pin down unless the natives perceive brown cows and assert that they do. For, since these are conditions for the English sentence meaning what it does, they are also conditions for any native sentence meaning the same. This is banal enough. But is it not a *hypothesis* that anthropologist and natives share certain percepts and concepts, a hypothesis, moreover, which later successes in translating abundantly confirm?

I suggest not. A hypothesis must be refutable. This one is not. The force of calling a set of utterances a bridgehead is that it serves to define standard meanings for native terms and so makes it possible to understand utterances used in more ambiguous situations. In order to question the perceptual and conceptual basis of the bridgehead, the anthropologist would have to ask the natives what they perceived when confronted with a brown cow and whether their utterances were to be construed as assertions. Also he would have to understand their answers. He can neither ask nor understand, unless he already has a bridgehead. Consequently he cannot refute the 'hypothesis' by establishing a rival one. At most he can merely draw a blank and fail to produce any translations at all. But even this failure would not show that the natives perceived the world after some idiosyncratic fashion or had a language with idiosyncratic functions. It would serve to suggest only that they had no language at all. No successful translation can destroy his bridgehead, since all later translations depend on its being secure.

Nor is the 'hypothesis' confirmed by success. He has indeed discovered what native sentence to pair with 'Yes, this is a brown cow'; but he has not discovered that the natives perceive a brown cow when they utter the native sentence. For, if that were in doubt, so also would the pairing be. And, as has been argued already, if both are in doubt, there is no way in to the circle. Similarly, although it is an empirical matter to discover how the natives signal the difference between assertion and denial, 'yes' and 'no', 'true' and 'false', it is not a *hypothesis* that they have such distinctions. For, to check such a 'hypothesis', the anthropologist would have to establish the meanings of utterances in the bridgehead independently of whether they were used to assert what was taken to be true. But this cannot be done, as their translation depends on what linguistic function they are taken to perform. Consequently the only alternative to finding an overlap in concepts and percepts is to find nothing at all.

If this is right, then the assertions comprising the bridgehead will have to be coherent and, indeed, true. Again it looks as if native notions of coherence and truth need not coincide with the anthroplogist's own. But again, if this is taken as a hypothesis, it generates a vicious circle. For the only way to find native terms for relations among utterances is to translate the utterances and then to interpret the linking terms so that the utterances are linked coherently. Equally the only way to find the native sign of assent is to translate the utterances and then to interpret whatever sign accompanies most of the true ones as assertion. But this makes it impossible for alternative concepts of coherence and truth to show up. If these concepts were in doubt, the anthropologist would have to know what they were, before he could translate the utterances which they linked, and would have to translate the utterances in order to find how they were linked. Again there would be no way in to the circle.

So some overlap in concepts and percepts is a necessary condition of successful translation. The *sine qua non* is a bridgehead of true assertions about a shared reality. But plainly societies differ about what is real and rational and the philosopher's problem is to see where the necessary limits on these divergences lie.

This problem is raised, for example, by belief in agencies and forces which we class as 'supernatural'. It seems that none of the tests for the identification of beliefs in the bridgehead apply the Nuer's *Kwoth* or the Dinka's *Deng*. Utterances expressing the belief that 'twins are birds', for instance, apparently do not have to be translated so as to make the belief true or coherent or even plausible. On the one hand there must be some test of success in identifying 'supernatural' beliefs, otherwise any account would be as good as any other. On the other hand any test proposed looks parochial, in that it forces other cultures to subscribe to a Western and twentieth-century view of what is true, coherent or plausible. So can we hit on a test which is innocent of parochialism?

There seems little point in testing beliefs about *Kwoth* for correspondence with reality. For, unless the anthropologist happens to believe in *Kwoth*, he can report only that they do not correspond with reality. Nor is it yet any help to remark that the natives take beliefs about

Kwoth to be empirically true, since we do not yet know what the beliefs are. Equally, we cannot invoke the notion of a wider reality to give the beliefs something to correspond to, since we can get at the wider reality only through the beliefs.

There is more point in testing the beliefs for coherence. But this cannot be the whole story, since more than one set of beliefs about *Kwoth* may be coherent and since a belief-system may in any case contain incoherences. Incoherence is a *prima facie* reason for rejecting alleged identifications of native beliefs but it can always be removed by showing why the natives do not perceive it. Thus Evans-Pritchard's twenty-two reasons why the Azande fail to perceive the futility of their magic serve to justify his account against a charge of incoherence. The charge would stick only if it were more likely that the natives would notice the contradiction than that it existed. Even if this test eliminates some interpretations, it is still likely to leave more than one. Coherence is at best a necessary condition of success.

A more promising requirement is that the everyday meanings of native words used in utterances expressing 'supernatural' beliefs should have been firmly established. Thus, it might be said, we know that some Australian aborigines believe that the sun is a white cockatoo because we have definitive uses in everyday contexts for terms meaning 'sun', 'is', 'white' and 'cockatoo'. But this is at best inconclusive, since words can bear more than one sense. The anthropologist can invoke the notions of Ambiguity or Metaphor, when he does not wish to be bound by the everyday meanings of native terms. Since one way of putting the question at issue is to ask when an utterance may be given a special or metaphorical interpretation, we cannot rest content with assuming that words always carry the sense they were allotted at the bridgehead.

We must therefore find internal relations among the beliefs which make their identification plausible. Neither deductive nor inductive relations will do. Deductive inference from true premises is bound to give true conclusions and so all beliefs deducible from those in the bridgehead would be true. Besides there is no contradiction in asserting everything the Nuer believe about the everyday world and denying everything they believe about *Kwoth*. Inductive inference proceeds from known cases to unknown cases of the same sort. So it seems that everyday beliefs give the natives inductive grounds for holding 'supernatural' beliefs, in as much as there is no discontinuity in the native thought between natural and supernatural. (If, for instance, lightning and arrows are phenomena of the same sort, then agency in the one gives inductive ground for supposing agency in the other.) But this is of no help in identifying 'supernatural' beliefs, unless the notion of 'the same sort' can be made clearer than I can make it. If we take a scientific criterion of resemblance, we set up an impassible discontinuity between natural and supernatural. But if we accept a loose criterion, then, since everything resembles everything from some point of view, we are left without limits on the supernatural beliefs which might be grounded on the everyday beliefs.

This drives us to testing alleged native beliefs for rational inter-connection. Each new identification of a native belief has to be plausible, given what is already established. In other words, to justify an identification, we must show that a native who believed what we already know he believes would have good reason to believe what we now claim he believes. Here we seem to have met an impasse, since what counts as a good reason appears to be a social matter and so has to be discovered in each case by empirical investigation. This would generate another vicious circle, since we should have to know what the natives believed, in order to find out what was a good reason for what; and we should have to know what the native criteria for rational belief were, before we could find out what they believed. We can avoid the circle, however, if we distinguish between the definition of a concept and examples of its application. It would be fatal to allow that anthropologist and natives might have different concepts of what is meant by saying that one belief gives good reason for holding another. But if we add to the list of necessary conditions for the possibility of anthropology a shared concept of rational belief, then we are free to admit that some societies find rational beliefs which others find irrational.

It is thus the argument of this paper that Mr Lukes' 'rational (1) criteria' are not so much universal as necessary and that his 'rational (2) criteria' are not so much context-dependent as optional. ('Rational (2) criteria' which just happened to apply in all societies would be universal without ceasing to be context-dependent.) If anthropology is to be possible, I have argued, the natives must share our concepts of truth, coherence and rational interdependence of beliefs. Otherwise we are confronted as theorists with vicious circles. In other words Western rational thought is not just one species of rational thought nor rational thought just one species of thought. And if we supposed it was, and so had to discover empirically which societies espoused which brand of rationality, we would destroy our only test for the identification of native beliefs. In this sense 'rational (1) criteria' are necessary. But anthropologists often come across beliefs that seem false, incoherent and unconnected. These beliefs are rendered harmonious by appealing to theoretical options—ambiguity, metaphor and local variations in 'rational (2) criteria'. They are options in the sense that the interpretation to be placed upon native utterances is partly a function of the anthropologist's own view of the possible uses of language and the possible connections among beliefs. If my argument has been sound, the only way to produce justifiable accounts of other cultures is to make the natives as rational as possible.

The argument has been wholly general and applies equally within a single culture, for instance to the study by an Anglican of what other Anglicans believe. If it applies here, where each enquirer is his own bilingual, then it cannot be objected that an anthropologist who works with a native informant by-passes the problems discussed. Equally the behaviourists' contention that we should study causal relations in social behaviour rather than the structure of beliefs is weakened, if theology is from this point of view sacred anthropology. On the other hand the existence of (philosophical) Idealists, with their own concept of Reality, and of Pragmatists, with their own concept of Truth, seems to be an embarrassment. If we can understand their doctrines, does that not show that the arguments here (and in Mr Lukes' paper) are wrong?

I shall not consider here whether these philosophies are true. For the difficulty arises even if they are false. It is that they seem to have their own 'rational (1) criteria' and that, since other philosophers find them intelligible, 'rational (1) criteria' need not be universal and cannot be necessarily so. Now, an Idealist does not deny that everyone perceives the same sort of reality. He does not maintain, for example, that some people perceive cows and others sense-data. Nor does a Pragmatist maintain that some empirical truths correspond with reality, while others are merely useful to believe. Each is, rather, concerned to give his own account of the world we all share. So there is as yet no threat to the thesis that overlap in percepts and concepts is a necessary condition of communication. The difference comes not in concepts but in concepts of concepts. But here, as can be seen by comparing different commentaries on the same thinker, the problem of this paper arises all over again. Like rival anthropologists, rival commentators have to decide what standard of plausibility to set for the identification of their subject's beliefs. Their decision affects their interpretations; and this applies even to the limiting case of a thinker expounding his own thought. So my argument is not, I hope, refuted by this objection alone; and whether it is in general sound must be left to the reader.

The anthropologist emerges as part chronicler, part philosopher and part social theorist. As chronicler he collects observed facts of native behaviour. As philosopher he sets *a priori* limits to the possible interpretations of the facts. As social theorist he decides which of the interpretations consistent with the facts is empirically correct. It has been argued here that relativism, far from being a due recognition of the scope of empirical science, makes anthropology theoretically impossible. We cannot understand the irrational and to suppose that we can is to run into vicious circles.; but we can understand the rational in more than one way.

11

Reason and Ritual

MARTIN HOLLIS

Certain primitive Yoruba carry about with them boxes covered with cowrie shells, which they treat with special regard. When asked what they are doing, they apparently reply that the boxes are their heads or souls and that they are protecting them against witchcraft. Is that an interesting fact or a bad translation? The question is, I believe, partly philosophical. In what follows, I shall propound and try to solve the philosopher's question, arguing that it has large implications for the theory of Social Anthropology.[1]

An anthropologist sets himself to understand a culture which is not his own. He has succeeded when he understands everything the natives say, do and believe. But does he always know that he has understood? What, for instance, would give him the right to be sure that the Yoruba believe boxes covered with cowrie shells to be their heads or souls? It is a curious belief to find among people who are often as rational as we. Yet we claim to know that rational men do sometimes hold curious metaphysical beliefs; so presumably we have some way of identifying such beliefs. On the other hand we sometimes reject proffered accounts of beliefs on the ground that the beliefs are unintelligible. How, then, do we decide when it is more plausible to reject a translation than to accept that a society believes what the translator claims they believe? I shall call those metaphysical beliefs which inform ritual actions 'ritual beliefs'. Our problem is how we know when we have identified a ritual belief.

This looks like an empirical question. For, it might be said, the problem is that of knowing when a language has been correctly

Originally published in *Philosophy*, XLIII, 1967, 165, pp. 231–47.

[1] I am grateful to Prof. F. Willett of Northwestern University for the Yoruba example and the possible explanation of it given later; and to Messrs. S. Lukes, P. M. Hacker and A. Kenny for many helpful discussions of the matters raised.

translated and it is surely an empirical matter what native utterances mean. The anthropologist can learn Yoruba and ask the natives what they believe. Provided that his attempts to speak Yoruba have met with success in everyday contexts, and he has no reason to suppose that the Yoruba are lying about their ritual beliefs, then there is no reason to doubt the resulting translations. Besides, he can always recruit an intelligent bilingual to settle any doubtful points. Admittedly ritual beliefs, like Yoruba boxes, may seem unintelligible in isolation. But this shows only that they should not be taken in isolation. They belong to a ritual context and will be found to make sense when the whole context is grasped. Moreover, ritual is of its essence expressive rather than informative and mystical rather than rational. Consequently a literal translation need not produce a statement which the natives believe literally. Metaphor is to the temple what literal sense is to the market-place. There are, in short, no *a priori* limits on what a society may believe and it is thus an empirical matter whether an anthropologist's account is correct.

If this line of thought is right, there is nothing for a philosopher to discuss. But, I shall argue, far from making anthropology an empirical matter, it makes it instead impossible. If a ritual belief is to be identified after the manner of an everyday belief, then it cannot be identified at all.

The identification of everyday beliefs is indeed (within limits to be discussed later) an empirical matter. The anthropologist learns the native language by discovering the native signs for assent and dissent and the native names for common objects. He then composes statements about objects and elicits assent or dissent from the natives. He thus frames hypotheses by assuming that the natives assent to true statements and dissent from false ones. The exact history of his progress does not concern us but the last assumption is important. For unless the native utterances make sense in simple everyday situations, the anthropologists will not even begin. If the natives made no statements about the cat on the mat and the cow in the corn which can be translated to yield truths, then the anthropologist has no way into the maze. In general identifying an everyday belief involves knowing the truth conditions of the statements which express it. This does not imply that every native belief must, when translated, yield a true statement but it does imply that most of them must. Equally any claim that the natives say something false must be backed by an explanation of why they fail to see that the belief is false. Otherwise the falsity of the belief, as translated, will be a sufficient reason for rejecting the translation. Thus Caesar tells us that some German tribes believe that the elk has no joints in its knees and therefore sleeps leaning against a tree, since, if it lies down, it cannot get up again. Without some explanation of how they manage to believe this taradiddle, we shall have sufficient reason to suppose either that the Germans did not believe it (Caesar's informant was perhaps pulling his leg) or that there had been a mistranslation. In neither case will Caesar have identified a belief which the Germans held. The point is that everyday beliefs have objectively specifiable truth-conditions. That the truth conditions are objective both gives the anthropologist his lead in and, in the absence of a special explanation, provides the tests of his hypotheses.

Ritual beliefs, by contrast, do not have objectively specifiable truth-conditions. To be sure, a Yoruba, who believed a box covered with cowrie shells to be his head or soul, might take that belief to be true. But this is not to say that any fact referred to is objectively specifiable. Consequently the anthropologist cannot use the facts to get at the beliefs: he can, at best, use the beliefs to get at the facts. Here, then, is a first difference between ritual and everyday beliefs.

But this does not dispose of the claim that we are dealing with a wholly empirical question. Is it not an empirical matter what words mean, even in a ritual context? May we not translate ritual literally, marking the fact that we are translating ritual utterances by noting that the statements may be taken metaphorically? Thus we know that some Australian aborigines believe the sun is a white cockatoo, because we have firm everyday translations for 'sun', 'is', 'white' and 'cockatoo' and aboriginal assent to the resulting utterance. Of course the claim would be absurd, if the aborigines were expected to take the belief literally, but it is a ritual belief and they take it metaphorically.

As it stands, this move is useless, since it rests on using the notion of metaphor, without giving it any independent leverage. The notion of metaphor, like that of ritual, must do more than signal a failure to produce sense. If we take a ritual utterance, translate it literally and dub the result 'metaphorical', how do we know that what we now have is equivalent to the original? To put it another way, how do we know what the metaphorical sense of an utterance is, seeing that any utterance might have many metaphorical senses? To put it yet another way, how do we know that words are not used equivocally in ritual contexts? If any piece of literal nonsense can be taken metaphorically, then anthropology rapidly becomes impossible. For there is no way of telling which of rival accounts of ritual beliefs is the right one—the literal nonsense which one anthropologist interprets in one way can always be given a different metaphorical sense by another anthropologist. We need, then, a better test of success than the accuracy of a literal translation.

Let us try next to give the notion of ritual some independent leverage. What is the force of calling something a ritual belief? We have said that ritual beliefs are metaphysical and inform ritual actions (in the sense that ritual actions are identified as the actions which express ritual beliefs). But, so far, this serves merely to sweep them under the rug as beliefs which we have failed to identify by making literal sense of the utterances used to express them. What then is the category of ritual more than a waste bin for unidentified beliefs?

This question has been given an interesting answer by Suzanne Langer in her *Philosophy in a New Key*.[1] Man, she says, is a symbolizing animal and his symbolizing takes two main forms. First there is practical symbolism of the kind used in everyday discourse and in science. Practical symbolism is experience transformed into a form in which it can be talked about, as a means to some practical end. Practical symbolism in effect comprises all and only those utterances which a Logical Positivist would allow to be literally meaningful. Secondly there is expressive or presentational symbolism of the kind found in music or religion. Expressive symbolism is an end in itself and any example of it (like a piece of music) forms a whole, in the sense that its meaning is not a compound of the discrete units which constitute it. Thus language is the best example of practical symbolism, because it is analysable and instrumental; whereas music is the best example of expressive symbolism, because its meaning is total and it is an end in itself. Miss Langer puts the distinction thus:

> It appears then that although the different media of non-verbal representation are often referred to as distinct 'languages' [e.g. the 'language' of painting], this is really a loose terminology. Language in the strict sense is essentially discursive; it has permanent units of meaning which are combinable into larger units; it has fixed equivalences which make definition and translation possible; its connotations are general so that it requires non-verbal acts like pointing, looking or emphatic voice inflections to assign specific denotations to its terms. In all these salient characters it

[1] S. Langer, *Philosophy in a New Key*, Harvard University Press, 1963, (third edition).

differs from wordless symbolism, which is non-discursive and untranslatable, does not allow of definitions within its own system, and cannot directly convey generalisations.[1]

Ritual beliefs, then, if we follow Miss Langer, are the significance of acts of expressive or presentational symbolism. Thus the behaviour of Yoruba towards their boxes covered with cowrie shells may perhaps express a total view of the nature of man, rather as Beethoven's music is sometimes alleged to express a total view about the order of the universe. The reason that Yoruba statements do not make literal sense is that they are, if used to express ritual beliefs, not statements at all and, if used to describe ritual beliefs, not so much statements as clues. Equally if Beethoven was expressing any total belief in his music, then that belief cannot be more than hinted at in words. For, according to Miss Langer, the vehicle of expression is not a means to an end but an unanalysable end in itself. If so, then the reason that ritual statements cannot be taken out of context is that they do not mean anything out of context. Ritual beliefs are the beliefs they are because of their place in a whole. Identification of each depends on the identification of all.

In distinguishing practical and expressive symbolism as she does, Miss Langer is following Carnap, from whom she quotes these remarks:

> Metaphysical propositions—like lyrical verses—have only an expressive function, but no representative function. Metaphysical propositions are neither true nor false, because they assert nothing. . . . But they are, like laughing, lyrics and music, expressive. They express not so much temporary feelings as permanent emotional and volitional dispositions.[2]

When Miss Langer's view of symbolism is added to Carnap's view of metaphysical propositions, the result is a close analogy between ritual and music. This may seem a promising start at characterizing ritual beliefs. But it would be defeat to accept it, as it makes it impossible to identify the ritual beliefs we are characterizing. A ritual belief, on this view, not only lacks a truth-value but also is unanalysable and untranslatable. If this is right, then all we can ever say about two rival anthropologists' accounts of a ritual belief is that they are both wrong. An anthropologist's account of ritual would be limited to what his

---

[1] Ibid., p. 96f.
[2] R. Carnap, *Philosophy and Logical Syntax*, London: K. Paul, Trench, Trubner and Co., 1935, p. 28, quoted by Miss Langer in Chapter IV, p. 84.

camera (equipped for sound) could record: as soon as he told us that the Yoruba believed that their boxes were their souls, he would have tried to translate the untranslatable. His and any rival account, then, would be bound to break down, as soon as they tried to put the significance of the ritual into words.

So far, then, we do not see how to exploit either the fact that natives take their ritual beliefs to be true, or the fact that ritual beliefs can be expressed in words or the fact that ritual has affinities with art, in order to identify these elusive beliefs. But before offering a denouement, I would like to glance at a way of trying to by-pass the problem. We have been assuming that the significance of ritual must lie in the beliefs which it expresses, and this has left us trying to grapple with seemingly untranslatable alien metaphysics. Perhaps, then, the significance of ritual is to be sought strictly in its social effects. Thus Evans-Pritchard found in this studies of the Azande that Zande beliefs in witchcraft, oracles and magic served, *inter alia*, to maintain the power structure of Zande society.[1] It is tempting to argue from this that Zande ritual statements simply are statements 'about' social relations among the Azande. The attraction of such a move is that it gives us something objective for ritual statements to be 'about' and so restores to us objective truth conditions to back our identifications. But in referring ritual beliefs to the social structure, would we be identifying them or would we be, at most, explaining how they come to be held? The latter, I suggest. A Zande, who believes he has been bewitched, surely does not believe that he has offended some social authority or other. If he did, he could perfectly well say so. He surely believes, rather, that he is the victim of supernatural interference. If so, facts about the Zande social structure serve at most to explain why be believes this and perhaps why such a belief is common among the Azande or takes the form it does. But they will not serve to identify the belief, as they do not constitute it. Equally, Catholic beliefs evidenced in the Eucharist might be found to be causally connected with some facts of human social history. But no convinced Catholic would agree that the beliefs were about social facts, if this meant denying them the status of meta-physical truths. Admittedly it might be possible to argue in reply that Azande and Catholics simply did not know what their beliefs were about or even that their beliefs did not exist, being fictions inferred

[1] E. E. Evans-Pritchard, *Witchcraft, Oracles and Magic Among the Azande*, Oxford, 1937. I am not implying that Evans-Pritchard thinks this line to be correct.

from social behaviour.[1] But this takes us outside the scope of the present paper. I shall continue to assume that there are ritual beliefs and that our problem is to show how they can be identified. If this is the problem, then social explanations are not identifications.

So our problem is not to be solved by looking for empirical truth conditions nor by sanctifying a literal translation with the name of Metaphor. Nor is it removed by saying metaphorical propositions are non-assertive and untranslatable. Nor is it by-passed by concentrating on social facts. So how is it possible to identify a ritual belief? The answer is, I believe, to appeal to our own criteria of rationality.

Miss Langer claims that her account of presentational or expressive symbolism has the merit of making it rational. She writes:

> The recognition of presentational symbolism as a normal and prevalent vehicle of meaning widens our conception of rationality far beyond the traditional boundaries, yet never breaks faith with logic in the strict sense.[2]
>
> Rationality is the essence of mind and symbolic transformation its elementary process. It is a fundamental error, therefore, to recognize it only in the phenomenon of systematic explicit reasoning. That is a mature and precarious product.[3]

This will hardly do as it stands. Presentational symbolism, she has just finished saying, 'is non-discursive, untranslatable, does not allow of definitions within its own system and cannot directly convey generalizations'. Its best example is music. Very well then—how can it possibly fail to 'break faith with logic in the strict sense'? Logic in the 'strict sense' (whatever that may be) requires the notions of well-formed formula, truth and falsehood, contradiction and so forth which are notably absent in music. Above all it has criteria of identity for formulae and decision procedures for checking inferences. These notions are, I agree with Miss Langer, what we are looking for. They are not to be found, however, in her presentational symbolism.

It is my thesis that we can identify a ritual belief only if it is rational by our standards of rationality. This will seem parochial: why should the natives share our standards of rationality? In answer I shall try to show that some assumption about rationality has to be made *a priori*,

---

[1] Cf. E. R. Leach, *Political Systems of Highland Burma*, Bell and Sons, 1954, p. 14: 'In sum then, my view here is that ritual action and belief are alike to be understood as forms of symbolic statements about the social order'.

[2] S. Langer, loc. cit., p. 97.

[3] Ibid., p. 99.

if anthropology is to be possible; and that we have no choice about what assumption to make. I begin by arguing that the anthropologist works with a number of *a priori* assumptions, of which rationality is only one.[1]

Let us start with those simple everyday beliefs which the anthropologist shares with the natives. The natives believe that the cat is on the mat and the cow is in the corn. That they hold these particular beliefs is a matter of empirical discovery but the discovery can only be made if some *a priori* assumptions work. The anthropologist begins in earnest by eliciting from a native a true utterance about a common perceived object, or perhaps by eliciting assent to such an utterance. The assumptions here are that the object has properties which they both perceive it to have, that the utterance refers to the object; and that the native believes the utterance to be true. Only if these assumptions are correct, may the native be taken to have said in his language what the anthropologist would have said in his own. I want to insist first that they are *assumptions* and secondly that the anthropologist has no option about making them.

Since the anthropologist knew nothing about the natives when he started, it seems that he discovers everything he knows in the end. Very well; how does he *discover* that the natives sometimes perceive what he perceives? Two possible answers are that he observes their behaviour and that he translates their utterances. But if there is anything to be in doubt about, then observing their behaviour will not help. For he needs to discover that the natives discriminate among phenomena as he does, and this is not guaranteed by outward similarity of reactions to the phenomena. For, until he knows how the natives discriminate, he is imposing his own classification of reactions on their behaviour. And this implies that he is also identifying the phenomena according to his own perceptions, or else simply assuming that the phenomena are common to both parties, which is what he is purporting to discover. To show that he had discovered how they perceived the world, and not merely credited them with his own perceptions, he would have to translate their judgments of perception.

He cannot translate these judgments, however, until he has made

[1] It will be seen that I am much indebted to W. V. O. Quine (especially to the second chapter of *Word and Object*) for several ideas in this paper. But, in virtue of his doctrine that all beliefs are revisable, he is, I think, an empiricist (what C. I. Lewis calls a Conceptual Pragmatist), and I have tried to show that no empiricist can sail so close to the rationalist wind.

some assumption about what the natives perceive. In translating a native word as 'cat', for instance, he is bound to be guided by the fact that it applies only to cats. But now it is too late to discover that they do not perceive what he does when he perceives a cat. He can, of course, be so open-minded that he fails to translate any native word at all. But he cannot first translate the word for 'cat' and then discover that the natives perceive cats. That 'discovery' must come first and the later translation does not confirm it, since the translation depends on it.

The *a priori* element in the process is obscured by some seductive empirical facts. Thus it is an empirical fact that the natives have a word for 'cat', and, indeed, that they have a word for anything. It is also an empirical fact that they react to phenomena and that they make perceptual judgments. All these facts might not have been so; and the anthropologist has *discovered* that they are so. He has not discovered, however, that they perceive phenomena one way and not another way, that they make judgments about phenomena instead of making them only about something else, that they take blue objects to be blue and not pink. Equally, to advance a little further, he has not discovered that when they assent they mean 'yes' or that when they sincerely assent to something they believe it to be true. For he needed this information in order to translate any utterances at all, and it is then too late to discover it false.

This contention floats uneasily between the Scylla of the Whorf hypothesis and the Charybdis of the doctrine of analyticity. I shall next try to avoid both dangers.

The idea common to the many variants of the Whorf hypothesis is that what a man perceives is a function of his language, in the sense that he discriminates among phenomena according to the linguistic categories he has been trained to use. So long as this is a thesis about limited differences in perception embedded in a general agreement in perception, it is an empirical hypothesis, which a philosopher has no business to dispute. But it ceases to be an empirical hypothesis, if it is suggested that two people or societies might have no perceptions in common at all. Such a claim could not be shown empirically false, since there will always be cases uninvestigated. Nor, and this is what counts, can it be shown empirically true. For this would require that the totally different perceptions be the product of a translatable language and translation depends on some apparent agreement of perceptions.

I say 'apparent agreement' advisedly. Let us in a flight of philosophic fancy suppose that a tribe with only the sense of sight meets a tribe with only the sense of touch. Each tribe has a language for describing the world, one without tactual terms, the other without visual. Communication seems impossible, since, without any overlap in perceptions, neither tribe can establish any bridgehead. But now suppose that the tribes inhabit a world where every visual property of objects is, in fact, correlated with just one tactual property, where, for instance, all and only red objects feel square, or, more disingenuously, all and only objects which look square feel square. In these special conditions each tribe could successfully assume that there was overlap in perceptions. While restricted to its peculiar sense, neither could detect or correct the mistake. And so each could chart the other's language to its own satisfaction, provided the languages had the same structure. Now, if this flight of fancy is coherent, it is logically possible for one man to be totally, though systematically, mistaken about the content of another's experience. If the flight of fancy is incoherent, then it is so on *a priori* grounds. In neither case is it an empirical hypothesis that perception is a function of language. Apparent success in translation guarantees identity of the conceptual structure given to experience but not of the experience itself. Identity of content remains, however, a necessary condition of correct translation.

So is it not then analytic that languages are genuinely intertranslatable, only if speakers share experiences and conceptualize them in broadly the same way? That depends, I think, on the sense given to 'analytic'. If 'analytic' is defined broadly and neutrally as *a priori* there is no Charybdis of analyticity to avoid. Indeed, I shall argue later that what is here true of two languages applies equally to one and that we are seeking *a priori* conditions of the possibility of language in general. But 'analytic' is usually given an empiricist definition, whose key idea is that of revisable options. (This may or may not be attached to a sharp analytic-synthetic distinction or one between uninformative and factual.) If the anthropologist's assumptions are *a priori* without being optional, then I suggest that we are committed to some rationalist doctrine about the place of necessary truths in knowledge. With this in mind, I shall first extend the list of assumptions and then continue to argue that we have no option about what to assume.

The assumptions required for identifying everyday empirical beliefs are common perceptions, common ways of referring to things perceived and a common notion of empirical truth.[1] Unless these assumptions work, the anthropologist cannot get his bridgehead—the set of utterances taken as definitive of the meanings of everyday words. Thus to identify the native signs of assent and dissent, he must assume that the natives in the main assent to what is true and dissent from what is false. If his translation has them doing the opposite, that is sufficient reason for rejecting it. If it has them doing something quite different, for example expressing aesthetic reactions to the sound-pattern of the words, then he cannot claim to know what the words mean. Translation is possible only if the natives speak sooth about everyday objects as the anthropologist does and no translation can either verify or falsify this assumption.

The notions of truth and falsehood cannot be separated from the notion of logical reasoning. For they form a pair whose identity depends on the law of contradiction. An anthropologist does not know what he can say in the native language, unless he also knows what he cannot say. (This is why it is much easier to work with a native informant who can say 'No' to a question, than with a set of texts, which cannot.) A language has a word for negation only if its speakers take the truth of a proposition to entail the falsity of a denial of that proposition. A language without a word for negation is translatable only if it is embedded in one which distinguishes what can and cannot be said. The anthropologist must find the word for 'no', and to do so must assume that the natives share (at least partly) his concepts of identity, contradiction and inference.

The case for this needs to be made out with care. The idea of an alternative logic to our own is not obviously absurd and, indeed, it has been claimed that pre-logical peoples actually exist.[2] The right of the law of the Excluded Middle to feature in the corpus of indubitable axioms can certainly be disputed. What, then, is special about Identity, Contradiction and Inference?

The answer is, I believe, that these notions set the conditions for the existence not only of a particular kind of logical reasoning but also of any kind whatever. Let us try to suppose that our natives reason

[1] This might be denied by supposing a tribe which dealt exclusively in imperatives. Here an analogous assumption needs to be made about when an imperative has been put into effect. But, if we stick to imperatives, we shall never get to beliefs at all, much less to ritual beliefs. I shall therefore ignore this enticing alley.

[2] E.g. L. L. Lévy-Bruhl; *La Mentalité Primitive* (Herbert Spencer Memorial Lecture), Oxford, 1931, p. 21. But see also his *Les Carnets*, Paris: Presses Universitaires, 1949, pp. 130f.

logically but not according to the scheme 'If p and if p implies q, then q'. They must reason somehow, however, so let us suppose them to infer something like this:

$$p \star q$$
$$\frac{p}{! \, q}$$

How might we translate this? Well not by 'If p and if p implies q, then q' as that would give us *modus ponens* again. Nor by 'If p and if p implies q, then not q' as that would involve a self-refuting claim that 'p' 'q' '⋆' '!' '—' have the meanings or functions in the native language which 'p' 'q' 'if . . . then' and 'implies' have in English. In general we cannot first identify a native constant as 'if . . . then' and then go on to show that *modus ponens* does not hold, since, if *modus ponens* does not hold, then the constant has been wrongly identified. Nor can we identify a native constant without saying what constant it is, since that gives us no ground for believing it is a constant. Native logic must either turn out to be a version of our own or remain untranslatable.

If this is right, 'p → p', '— (p.p̄)' and '(p.(p → q)) → q' express more than axioms in a particular system or rules in a particular game. They express, rather, requirements for something's being a system of logical reasoning at all. To look for alternatives is like looking for a novel means of transport which is novel not only in that it has no engine but also in that it does not convey bodies from one place to another. Anything which satisfies the latter condition could not be a means of transport at all. If the natives reason logically at all, then they reason as we do.

I suggest, then, that what sentences mean depends on how the beliefs which they express are connected, and that to justify a claim to have identified a belief one must show the belief is connected to others. Logical connection is not the only kind and to identify ritual beliefs we need to introduce the notion of rational connection. I shall try to show that a ritual belief p can be identified only if there is a belief q which supplies the holder of p and q with a reason for believing p.

Let us return for a moment to the Yoruba and their boxes. One possible explanation which has been put forward is that these Yoruba believe each man to have a spiritual counterpart in heaven, who is susceptible to witchcraft. Witchcraft can be fended off by ritual treatment of the box, which represents the spiritual counterpart of the owner. Thus, when the Yoruba say the boxes are their heads or souls, they are using 'are' of symbolization and not of identity. In this explanation a pattern of behaviour is referred to a set of ritual beliefs and some of the beliefs are used to determine the translation of sentences expressing others. In seeing why the explanation has any force, we may perhaps answer our original question about the identification of ritual beliefs.

Are we to test Yoruba beliefs for rationality at all and, if we do, are we to pronounce them rational or irrational? As ritual beliefs rarely entail each other and are sometimes contradictory and as they do not correspond to objective facts, they will be unidentifiable, unless connected according to some notion of rationality. Besides we must surely allow for the fact that the Yoruba think their beliefs (whatever they are) true; and whatever the Yoruba take to make them true will make them *pro tanto* rational, from a Yoruba point of view. But this is not yet to say that we and they must have our concept of rationality and we may be reluctant to do so, as that might oblige us to believe in witchcraft too. So I shall consider next whether Yoruba beliefs may be rational by their standards but irrational by ours.

It may seem irrational to hold as true a belief which corresponds to no empirical reality. Ritual beliefs, as defined in this paper, are certainly of this sort. Equally ritual beliefs can be incoherent, and this might also seem to make them irrational. But this is not to say that we can accept identifications which make the empirical falsity and logical incoherence explicit, general and recognized. For that would give us sufficient reason to reject the identification on the grounds that, given this degree of laxity, we no longer have any way of deciding between rival translations. A man may believe a contradiction but, if he were also to believe that it was a contradiction, he might believe anything and neither we nor he could identify what he did believe. The only relevant fact about someone's ritual beliefs cannot be that we find them irrational.

Perhaps, however, the natives find rational what we find irrational, in the sense that they have a different notion of 'being a reason for'. We could discover this only if we could first identify the beliefs and then see how they were connected. In other words, we must be able to reach a partial translation of the form 'I believe p * I believe q' without translating '*' and then go on to translate '*' without making it our own (rational) 'because'. But now we are stuck. We could take '*' as 'although'; but this would leave us with our concept of rational connection. There is no English word, however, for an alternative to our (rational) 'because'; and, if there were, the native language would again turn out to be a version of ours. Moreover, without a translation of '★', how do we know that we have identified p and q? If p is 'this box is my soul', what makes that a correct translation? Why not 'this box is my spiritual identity card'? I contend that, without a translation of '★', the only answers are those mentioned at the beginning of this paper, and I would hope that the argument has by now advanced beyond them.

It may be well to disentangle the *a priori* and empirical elements here. It is an empirical matter what ritual beliefs the natives hold, what sentences they express them in and how they express the connection between them. It is *a priori*, however, that any ritual beliefs which we can identify form a related set whose members supply reasons for each other. This is *a priori* in the sense that it is an assumption which determines the translation of native sentences and so cannot be shown to be false. It is not optional, in the sense that, if we try to make any other assumption, we cannot identify any native ritual beliefs at all.

An anthropologist is thus obliged, I suggest, to remove obvious incoherences, if he is to give his readers better reason to accept his account than to reject it. It may be of interest to note how Evans-Pritchard does so in his *Witchcraft, Oracles and Magic among the Azande*. He writes:

> Azande see as well as we that the failure of their oracle to prophesy truly calls for explanation, but so entangled are they in mystical notions that they must make use of them to account for the failure. The contradiction between experience and one mystical notion is explained by reference to other mystical notions.[1]

Thus, for instance, an oracle can be bewitched and so its failure will reinforce beliefs about witchcraft. The connectedness of Zande thought is crucial to Evans-Pritchard's account. He finds that:

> Witchcraft, oracles and magic form an intellectually coherent system. Each explains and proves the others. Death is a proof of witchcraft. It is avenged by magic. The achievement of vengeance-magic is proved by the poison-oracle. The accuracy of the poison-oracle is determined by the king's oracle, which is above suspicion.[2]

[1] E. E. Evans-Pritchard, loc. cit., p. 338 (Pt. 3, Chapter IV, Section viii).
[2] Ibid., p. 476. This is one of 22 reasons cited to account for the failure of the Azande to perceive the futility of their magic.

Elsewhere in the book he says:

> In this web of belief every strand depends on every other strand and a Zande cannot get out of its meshes because it is the only world he knows. The web is not an external structure in which he is enclosed. It is the texture of his thought and he cannot think that his thought is wrong.[1]

Although Evans-Pritchard may have changed his philosophical ground in later works, here he takes the line that Zande beliefs are empirically false but rational both for them and for us. If my argument is sound, this approach is the only one which allows the identification of ritual beliefs. Recently a belief in 'Interpretative Charity' has found general favour.[2] If Interpretative Charity means merely making the native society as rational as possible, I have no objection. But if it means making the notions of Reality and Rationality relative to the native conceptual scheme, in the belief that we should not claim the monopoly of these notions, then I maintain that anthropology is in consequence impossible. Without assumptions about reality and rationality we cannot translate anything and no translation could show the assumptions to be wrong.

In agreeing with Miss Langer that ritual beliefs are to be identified by treating ritual utterances as acts of expressive, rather than presentational, symbolism, I am taking rationality as a relation between beliefs. A ritual belief p is rational if and only if there is a belief q such that q supplies a reason for holding p and p does not entail the falsity of q. This, I hope will 'extend the concept of rationality without breaking faith with logic in the strict sense'. In other words, since the Correspondence Theory of Truth is beside the point, we must make use of the Coherence Theory. To explain this, I shall next draw an analogy between an anthropologist and an unbelieving theologian.

Most theologians are believers and hold their own religions to be internally rational. They may take religion to begin with faith and end with mystery but they also hold that every belief which can be made explicit either makes rational another belief or is made rational by another belief or both. An unbelieving theologian can take the same line. He can certainly judge that the system is in sum irrational but he may (and, I contend, must) hold that most individual beliefs are connected rationally. In short, he may disagree totally with a believing

[1] Ibid., p. 195.
[2] E.g. Peter Winch, 'Understanding a Primitive Society', above pp. 78ff., and the references cited in that article.

theologian, but he must also agree with him in most particulars. Otherwise the believer will be entitled to claim that the unbeliever does not understand what he is disagreeing about. Mystery is divine truth to the believer and human nonsense to the unbeliever. But both can agree where it sets in. A mysterious belief is presumably one for which some other (non-mysterious) beliefs supply reasons but which does not in turn supply reasons for other beliefs. This is, at least, as far into the unknown as I can stretch the notion of identifying a ritual belief. Here, however, both theology and my analogy stop: a complete mystery is unintelligible to all.

The analogy between anthropologist and unbelieving theologian may be missed, because it is easy simply to credit the theologian with an understanding of the language of the faithful. The theologian, in other words, is his own bilingual. If so, the price of drawing the analogy seems to be the collapse of my thesis, since, as remarked at the beginning, an articulate and intelligent bilingual can apparently make the anthropologist a gift of all the natives' ritual beliefs. But this presupposes that the bilingual has already identified the ritual beliefs and can present them in English sentences intelligible to the anthropologist. The conceptual problem, however, remains the same whether it is stated for two men and two languages or for one man and one language. It is that of putting ritual beliefs into a form in which they can be classed as rational without ceasing to be the beliefs in question. This is one task of theology.

As proof of the pudding, let me offer as a model piece of anthropology a quotation from the Greek Cardinal Bessarion:

> In the sacrament of the Eucharist there is one thing which is merely a sign, namely, the visible species of bread and wine; and another thing which is the reality signified, namely, the true body and blood of Our Lord, which he took from the pure flesh of the Blessed Virgin. But the body and blood of Christ, while it is a reality pointed to by the sign of the bread and wine, as we shall shortly show, nevertheless is, itself, the sign of another reality, since its points to the Mystical Body of Christ, and the Unity of the Church in the Holy Ghost. This Mystical Body, however, and this unity do not point beyond themselves to any other reality, but are only themselves pointed to.[1]

[1] *De Sacramento Eucharistiae*, P. G. 161, 496. The passage is quoted and discussed by Fr. Bernard Leeming, S.J., in his *Principles of Sacramental Theology*, London: Longmans Green and Co., 1956, p. 256.

Bessarion is a believing theologian. How is the unbeliever to understand his account, without becoming a convert? He should, I suggest, take it literally and test it for rationality, in order to understand it, and then deny that it corresponds to anything, in order to disagree with it. For, if it is taken as simply metaphorical or false or without truth-value or irrational, then it is unintelligible, and, if it is taken not to make any empirical claims, then there is nothing to disagree with.

Unless we take the expression of some ritual beliefs literally, we shall again make anthropology impossible. I said earlier that a ritual belief p could be identified only if it was rational and that it was rational if and only if there was a belief q which supplied a reason for holding it. If q is itself a ritual belief then we need a further belief r which supplies a reason for holding q. In other words, if ritual beliefs form an autonomous system, we cannot understand one without understanding many or many without understanding one. We need, then, a belief Z which is expressed in practical, and not in expressive, symbolism and which supplies a reason for holding some ritual beliefs. Moreover Z must itself be identified and so must either be true or be traceable in the same way to some further empirical belief which is true.[1] For, as has been argued all along, understanding is only possible if it advances from a bridgehead of true and rational empirical statements. Literal sense is as important to the temple as it is to the market place.

But, it will be objected, people speak in metaphors, especially in ritual. The objects used in sacraments may be everyday things, like bread, blood and water, but they are used symbolically. If the upshot of this paper is that metaphor is impossible or unintelligible, so much the worse for the paper. My answer is that some metaphors are unintelligible, in the way that some mysteries are.

> 'Life like a dome of many-coloured glass
> Stains the white radiance of eternity.'

This is what Carnap would call a Metaphysical Proposition and only a rash man would claim to know what it means. At any rate, since the claim is undemonstrable, we are free to reject it. Here, I think, we can at last settle for Miss Langer's analogy between ritual and music. Shelley's metaphors cannot be rendered discursive.

Not all metaphors are so resistant. Some can be cashed (only indirectly, perhaps) in terms which can be understood literally. Thus the

---

[1] Mr. Hacker has pointed out that the argument, if sound, should hold against Intuitionist Theories of Ethics.

metaphor in 'He makes my blood boil', like the symbolism in the Statue of Liberty, is easily dissected. Metaphor, while it is still alive and not dead, is a new and self-conscious way of conceptualizing experience and, although not purely descriptive, can be traced to descriptive statements. But this makes it a civilized phenomenon; a savage who says 'He makes my blood boil', is likely to mean exactly what he says.[1] I am not saying here that there is no difficulty about metaphor. Indeed, I would agree that many metaphors have to be construed by analogy with music, and this requires a sense of 'understanding' which I do not pretend to grasp. I am saying only that claims to have identified the metaphorical uses of words and gestures must be rationally justified. This involves cashing the metaphors and therefore the notion of 'metaphorical use' never has any explanatory force.

This paper stands or falls with the claim that a theorist of social anthropology must budget for *a priori* elements which are not optional. It may be as well to finish by rehearsing the claim. The *a priori* elements are those notions which the natives must be assumed to have, if any identification of their ritual beliefs is to be known to be correct. To get at ritual beliefs, the anthropologist works from an understanding of the native language in everyday contexts. To establish a bridgehead, by which I mean a set of utterances definitive of the standard meanings of words, he has to assume at least that he and the native share the same perceptions and make the same empirical judgments in simple situations. This involves assumptions about empirical truth and reference, which in turn involve crediting the natives with his own skeletal notion of logical reasoning. To identify their ritual beliefs he has to assume that they share his concept of 'being a reason for'. There will be better reason to accept his account than to reject it, only if he makes most native beliefs coherent and rational and most empirical beliefs in

[1] It is important also that a similar 'civilized' distinction between instrumental and symbolic behaviour does not always hold in primitive thought. Thus Evans-Pritchard remarks of the Azande:

'When a man chooses a suitable tree and fells it and hollows its wood into a gong his actions are empirical, but when he abstains from sexual intercourse during his labour we speak of his abstinence as ritual, since it has no objective relation to the making of gongs and since it involves ideas of taboo. We thus classify Zande behaviour into empirical and ritual, and Zande notions into common sense and mystical, according to our knowledge of natural processes and not according to theirs. For we raise quite a different question when we ask whether the Zande himself distinguishes between those techniques we call empirical and those techniques we call magical.' Loc. cit., p. 492. The passage does not imply relativism.

addition true. These notions are *a priori* in the sense that they belong to his tools and not to his discoveries, providing the yardsticks by which he accepts or rejects possible interpretations. They are not optional, in that they are the only conditions upon which his account will be even intelligible. In short, although it is an empirical fact that the natives hold any beliefs and have any language at all, and although it is a matter of hard work and huge expertise to discover what forms they take, the anthropologist needs conceptual tools before he can even begin. When packing his tool box, he is a philosopher.

Evans-Pritchard ends his book on Nuer Religion with these words:

> Though prayer and sacrifice are exterior actions, Nuer religion is ultimately an interior state. This state is externalized in rites which we can observe, but their meaning depends finally on an awareness of God and that men are dependent on him and must be resigned to his will. At this point the theologian takes over from the anthropologist.[1]

The theologian seems already to have taken over from the anthropologist. But why not? Sacred anthropology is sceptical theology.

[1] E. E. Evans-Pritchard, *Nuer Religion*, Oxford, 1956, Chapter XII, p. 322.

12

On Understanding Ritual

J. H. M. BEATTIE

I

In my 1965 Malinowski Lecture[1] I developed the theme that the ideas and procedures which we generally call 'ritual' differ from those which we call 'practical' and scientific (or 'proto-scientific') in that they contain, or may contain, an expressive, symbolic quality, which is not found in technical thought or activity as such. I argued that even though both expressive and 'practical' modes may be and often are combined in the same course of thought or action, we need to distinguish them, for they imply different attitudes to experience, and call for different kinds of understanding. 'Practical', empirically-based procedures are essentially understood when the ends sought and the techniques used by the actor are grasped. The understanding of ritual acts, however, requires in addition the comprehension of the meanings which the participant's ideas and acts have, or may have, as symbolic statements; the kinds of mental associations they involve; and the types of symbolic classifications they imply. Thus, following Raymond Firth, Leach, and others, I argued that understanding religious and magical rites[2] is in these respects more like understanding art than it is like understanding modern science. I went on to suggest that the belief in the efficacy of

I am grateful to Professor E. E. Evans-Pritchard, to Dr Godfrey Lienhardt, and to the members of a graduate seminar at the University of Manchester, for helpful comments on this paper.

[1] 'Ritual and Social Change', *Man* (N.S.), 1, 1966, pp. 60–74.

[2] I should perhaps say here that when in this paper I use the terms 'religion' and 'religious' I refer to what used to be called 'primitive' religion, that is to the belief, widespread in all cultures, in individual and 'personalized' gods and other non-human spirit powers, who can influence and be influenced by human beings, and to the rites associated with this belief. I do not intend to refer to the vastly more sophisticated and abstract theological concepts of, for example, some kinds of modern Western Christianity.

ritual (where, as is usually the case, it is believed to produce results) is not, like the belief in 'science', however prototypical, based on experience and hypothesis-testing, but is rather founded in the imputation of a special power to symbolic or dramatic expression itself.

In the course of this discussion I made some criticism of the views of Jack Goody, who had suggested that ritual could only be defined as the irrational or non-rational,[1] of Robin Horton, who had interestingly argued that African religious systems are the outcome of a model-building process which can usefully be compared with that found in modern science,[2] and of I. C. Jarvie, who had claimed that the ritual response to social change exhibited in Melanesian cargo cults was the result of 'a purely intellectual craving'.[3] It seemed to me that all of these views were defective in that they either denied or ignored ritual's symbolic component, the quality which (I had argued) makes it what it is and not something else, and which gives rise to the characteristic problems of understanding it.[4]

If ambiguity is to be avoided, a word must first be said about the meanings of the terms 'ritual', 'expressive' and 'symbolic'. By 'ritual' I mean, following the *Shorter Oxford English Dictionary*, 'pertaining or relating to, connected with, 'rites', and by 'rite' I mean any 'formal procedure or act' of the kind which we generally call religious or magical. I realize that the problem of identifying what is religious or magical (or magico-religious) is not a simple one, though I do not think that it usually offers any very great difficulty in practice. For my present purpose I take both religious and magical acts to be those which involve, either explicitly or implicitly, a reference to a power, whether 'personalized' or not, belief in which is based not on 'scientific' procedures of formulating hypotheses and testing them against experience, but on 'faith', revelation, or (as I have argued) ultimately on the imputation of causal efficacy to the symbolic expression itself.[5]

[1] Jack Goody, 'Religion and ritual: the definition problem', *The British Journal of Sociology*, 12, 1961, pp. 142–64, esp. p. 159.

[2] Robin Horton, 'The Kalabari world-view: an outline and interpretation', *Africa*, XXXII, 1962, pp. 197–220.

[3] I. C. Jarvie, *The Revolution in Anthropology*, London: Routledge, 1964, p. 166.

[4] The essays in this volume by Horton and by Jarvie and Agassi are at least in some part responses to some of my arguments, as also is the paper by Steven Lukes. I am therefore grateful for the opportunity to continue here this in many respects fruitful dialogue.

[5] In fact, of course, as far as individuals are concerned, the validity of most beliefs, whether 'practical' or magico-religious, derives from custom and precedent, not from the individual's attempts at epistemological analysis. But this

It is important to bear in mind that what are being distinguished are, usually, not so much actions as *aspects* of actions; the same pattern of behaviour may have both empirically-grounded and symbolic components, and the way in which we classify it will reflect the aspect which predominates. There are certainly borderline cases (for example, alchemy, and astrology and some other forms of divination), but usually the distinction is evident enough. Even where it is not, these separate aspects must be distinguished analytically; our analytic categories are intended to resolve the confusions of reality, not merely to reproduce them.

Thus, as Leach has put it, 'Almost every human action that takes place in culturally defined surroundings ... has a technical aspect which does something and an aesthetic, communicative aspect which says something'.[1] But it is not enough to define ritual as 'expressive', and to leave it at that. Ritual certainly does, or may, 'say something', in so far as it is symbolic. But not everything that expresses something is symbolic, at least in the sense in which most social anthropologists have found it useful to use the term. In *Other Cultures* (pp. 69–71) I suggested that when we speak of symbols we refer to comprehensible (i.e. 'graspable') entities, whether objects, ideas or patterns of behaviour, which represent, by means of an underlying rationale, some more or less abstract notion (power, social or group unity, 'maleness' and 'femaleness', life, the dangerous and unfamiliar, are examples), to which social or cultural value, either positive or negative, is attached. These qualifications enable us to use the term 'symbol' with something approaching precision, and to exclude from our consideration the wide field of mathematical symbolism, communication theory, etc., which do not deal with symbols in our sense of the term (though of course the entities they deal with may come to be so regarded). It follows, also, that whether or not an object, act or idea is 'symbolic' depends on how it is thought about; symbolism may degenerate into 'empty ceremonial', and the same thing may be symbolic for some people and not for others, or symbolic for different people in different ways. These facts give rise to problems for the investigator,[2] but I do not believe that is not incompatible with the assertion that ritual beliefs and 'scientific' ones can be seen to differ in their nature when they are deeply thought about (as they rarely are).

[1] E. R. Leach, 'Ritual', *International Encyclopedia of the Social Sciences*, Volume 13, New York: Macmillan and The Free Press, 1968, pp. 520–26. This quotation is from p. 523.

[2] Some of them are discussed in Beattie, 'Ritual and Social Change', pp. 66–70.

they are insuperable, or that they invalidate the usefulness of this approach, or diminish the importance of the kinds of analysis to which it gives rise.

Jarvie and Agassi set out to discuss the problems involved in the attempt to explain magical acts 'by conjecturing that those who perform them hold beliefs which would show such acts to be conducive to desirable ends', and to consider 'whether a different kind of explanation is needed'.[1] They do not say who has ever attempted to explain magical acts by pointing out that the people who practise them believe that they will produce desired ends. If people did not believe this, one might have thought, they would hardly practise magic. The fact that they do believe it, and act accordingly, can hardly be an explanation: rather, as a statement of what people do, it is itself what needs to be explained.

But we can hardly set about explaining magical acts until we have some notion of what we mean by them, as distinct from non-magical ones. I had argued that in so far as they involve ritual they are essentially expressive and symbolic (though of course they are believed to be instrumentally effective as well), and I had suggested that it is the presence of this quality, conceived of as causally effective, that we indicate by calling such acts 'magical'. Later in their paper Jarvie and Agassi attack this view, but if they have an alternative one (other than that magic is not based on 'rational' belief—and, as they say, 'it is difficult to use irrationality as an explanation of anything'[2]), they do not reveal in this paper what they think it might be.

They do however tell us what they mean by 'rational'. An *action* is rational if it is goal-directed. A *belief* is rational 'if it satisfies some standard or criterion of rationality which has been adopted, such as that it is based on good evidence, or is beyond reasonable [*sic*] doubt, or is held open to criticism etc.' (p. 55). Leaving aside the question in what sense, if any, being 'beyond reasonable doubt' (whose doubt?) can be held to be a standard or criterion of rationality, presumably most—or all—accepted and firmly-held beliefs in any culture could be

[1] Above p. 172.
[2] Above, loc. cit. Cf. also Talcott Parsons, *The Structure of Social Action*, Glencoe: The Free Press, 1949, p. 431 (quoted in Beattie op. cit.):
'Ritual actions are not . . . either simply irrational, or pseudo-rational, based on pre-scientific erroneous knowledge, but of a different character altogether and as such not to be measured by the standards of intrinsic rationality at all'. Cf. also M. Hollis in this volume (p. 244), 'the only relevant fact about someone's ritual beliefs cannot be that we find them irrational'. This was the point of my criticism of Goody (Beattie, ibid., p. 63).

held to be rational in this sense. And a *person* is rational, they go on, if he either 'acts rationally, or he believes rationally, or both'.

In this sense, since a 'primitive' magician seeks specific goals in terms of beliefs held, in his society, to be beyond reasonable doubt, he is as rational as anybody else, and there is no problem to solve. But the authors go on to distinguish 'the *weak* sense of "rationality" ' ('a person acting rationally'), and 'the *strong* sense of "rationality" ' ('a person acting rationally on the basis of rationally held beliefs'). They then formulate the 'thesis' of their paper: 'the ritual actions of magic are (or can be) rational only in the weak sense; this demarcates them from scientific actions which are (or can be) rational in the strong sense' (p. 173). That is, scientists act on beliefs which satisfy some (vaguely specified) criterion of 'rationality'; magicians don't. As a thesis this is hardly startling: we all know that magical behaviour is not rational in the sense of being scientific (though it might well be held to be 'strongly' rational in Jarvie's and Agassi's sense of that term); the question, then, is, how are we to make sense of it, if we are to do so at all? Frazer gave one answer to this question; I and others have proposed another.

In the second section of their paper, Jarvie and Agassi discuss Sir James Frazer's 'well known theory of magic'. According to them, this theory holds that 'the magician performs the magical act because he (mistakenly) believes that that act will bring about the desired effect' (p. 173). It did not need a Frazer to tell us this. 'Magical acts', they continue, 'are the result of false beliefs' (the beliefs that like produces like, and that things once in contact can continue to influence each other after they are separated).

So far so good, but their conclusion, that according to Frazer 'the practitioners of magic are victims of a misplaced faith in the association of ideas', or 'in Freudian language, in the omnipotence of thought', could hardly misrepresent Frazer's view more completely. Far from imputing to 'savage' magicians a belief in the power of their own thinking to bring about results (a position which, if acting and thinking be taken together, is very much nearer to that of Frazer's critics than to that held by Frazer himself), Frazer saw magic as 'a set of precepts', which are 'implicitly believed' by the magician to be 'of universal application, and . . . not limited to human action'.[1] The 'misplaced faith' which Frazer imputes to magicians is not in the association of ideas, or in 'the omnipotence of thought'; it is in 'a spurious system of

[1] Sir James Frazer, *The Golden Bough* (third edition), Part I, *The Magic Art*, vol. I, London, 1926, p. 53.

natural law'; that is, 'a faith, implicit but real and firm, in the order and uniformity of nature'.[1] According to Frazer this view of the natural order is based on a 'misapplication of the association of ideas', but it is quite plain that according to him the magician's 'faith' is not in the latter, but in the former. There is a great difference between believing in a system of natural law, independent of man, and in believing in the power of human thinking. It is the first of these beliefs and not the second that Frazer is imputing to the magician.

It was of course this notion of magic as involving the idea of 'natural law' that Evans-Pritchard criticized in his paper 'The Intellectualist (English) Interpretation of Magic' (a paper which Jarvie and Agassi seem either not to have read or not to have understood).[2] In it Evans-Pritchard shows clearly that a world in which everybody believed, implicitly or not, that the 'Law of Similarity' and the 'Law of Contact' were, in Frazer's words, of 'universal application', would be chaotic and nonsensical. The 'crude intelligence ... of the savage' was not as crude as Frazer thought it was; he knew better than Frazer did (and, apparently, than Jarvie and Agassi do) that when he was making magic he was performing a rite, not applying laws of nature, however dimly apprehended. It was, of course, because Frazer conceived of magic as 'a false science as well as an abortive art' that he thought ('strangely', in Jarvie's and Agassi's view) that 'belief in magic is nearer to belief in science than to belief in religion'.[3]

In their Section III Jarvie and Agassi engage in the diverting but doubtfully useful exercise of setting up and then attacking a position never held by anybody. They begin by contrasting Frazer, to his advantage, with 'contemporary social anthropologists', on the curious ground that unlike him, they 'are no longer bothered by religion at all' (p. 177). If by bothered they mean *worried*, they may be right (but was Frazer?); if they simply mean 'concerned', then they are plainly wrong: it would be easy to name a dozen or more recent books by social anthropologists which are centrally concerned with religion.[4]

---

[1] Frazer, op. cit., p. 220.

[2] *Bulletin of the Faculty of Arts*, Egyptian University, Cairo, vol. 1, 1933. See also E. E. Evans-Pritchard *Theories of Primitive Religion*, Oxford: Clarendon Press, 1965, p. 29.

[3] Frazer, op. cit., pp. 53 and 57.

[4] To name only a few: M. Douglas, *Purity and Danger*, London, 1966; E. E. Evans-Pritchard, *Nuer Religion*, Oxford, 1956 and *Theories of Primitive Religion*, Oxford, 1965; M. Fortes, *Oedipus and Job in West African Religion*, Cambridge, 1959; C. Geertz, *The Religion of Java*, Glencoe, 1960; J. Goody, *Death, Property*

Then, after accusing anthropologists of regarding 'the ridicule [*sic*] of Frazer as a pleasant pastime' (p. 177: they seem unable to distinguish ridicule from criticism), they go on to criticize him on their own account, on the just and familiar grounds that his evolutionary scheme, in which religion replaces magic and is in its turn replaced by science, is undemonstrable (and anyway most societies have some of all three); that not all magic is either homeopathic or contagious; and that his notion of science was rather unsophisticated.

But despite these criticisms they think that Frazer's theory of why rational people perform magic is 'a bold and exciting one' (p. 179). This bold and exciting theory has been disclosed to us already; it is that 'people perform magic because they believe it will realize or help realize, or increase the likelihood of realization of, an end they are aiming at.' It can hardly be conceived that anyone who has reflected, even for a moment, upon what magicians do would think of denying this proposition; yet Jarvie and Agassi make the astonishing assertion that 'it does not find favour with present-day social anthropologists!' Of course no present-day social anthropologist denies so obvious a truism. What some of them, including myself, *have* been concerned with are the different, more difficult, and very much more interesting questions, just what are the kinds of symbolism involved in magical thought and action, what are the rationales that underlie them?, and how is it, in terms of what kinds of representations, that people believe that their magic will be effective? The problem is about the nature of magical thought and behaviour, not about whether or not people make magic to bring about desired ends; one might have thought that that could be taken for granted.

Jarvie and Agassi go on to explain that the reason for this extraordinary (and of course non-existent) scepticism on the part of social anthropologists is that they are critical of 'the entire assumption that people's actions can be explained by their beliefs'. I do not think that any anthropologist has ever denied that belief may 'explain' action, at least some action, or that the practice of magic involves certain beliefs; I certainly know of none who does.

and the Ancestors, London, 1962; G. Lienhardt, *Divinity and Experience*, Oxford, 1961; J. Middleton, *Lugbara Religion*, London, 1960; S. F. Nadel, *Nupe Religion*, London, 1954; M. Wilson, *Rituals of Kinship among the Nyakyusa*, London, 1957. See also M. Banton (ed.), *Anthropological Approaches to the Study of Religion*, London, 1966; D. Forde (ed.), *African Worlds*, London, 1956; M. Fortes and G. Dieterlen (eds.), *African Systems of Thought*, London, 1965; J. Middleton (ed.), *Gods and Rituals*, New York, 1967.

In Section IV they go on to discuss this 'influential current view which rejects the use of beliefs in explanation of magic as rational in either the weak or the strong sense', christening it 'the Oxford Theory', and associating it with the names of Evans-Pritchard, Godfrey Lienhardt and myself. They honour me by singling out Chapters 5 and 12 of my *Other Cultures* as a representative exposition of this 'theory', and Section IV of their essay is almost all a criticism of what they take to be my views.[1]

They begin by attributing to me 'a view of rationality' which imputes it to magic 'without allowing it [i.e. the magic] to be explained as conducive to the realization of certain ends' (p. 180). What they mean, presumably, is '*thought* to be conducive to the realization of certain ends'; even they, I suppose, are not suggesting that magic should be 'explained' as conducing to ends to which in fact it does not conduce. As I have said, I have never at all disputed the self-evident fact that people practise magic because they want results; on the contrary, I have explicitly stated that they do.[2] Obviously part of the fieldworker's task is to record the goals which people seek by means of their rites. But this is the beginning, not the end, of his analysis. It is only *after* we have recorded the facts, including the fact that the magician is trying to kill an enemy, make rain, or whatever it may be, that the interesting problems in the analysis of ritual thought and action arise: I have referred to some of them above.

Jarvie and Agassi then assert that my thesis (of course not only mine) that, as they put it, 'the symbolic actions themselves come to be thought to have a potency, an ability to bring about the event they are symbolizing[3] ... contradicts [my] theory that magic is symbolic rather than instrumental' (p. 182). Of course it does not. There is no contradiction in asserting that like other ritual magic is symbolic, and at the same time that it is thought by its practitioners to be instrumentally

[1] They refer also to Beattie 'Ritual and Social Change', in which some of the themes considered in *Other Cultures* are further considered, but this essay only came into their hands after their paper was written. They claim that their criticisms apply to it *pari passu*.

[2] *Other Cultures*, London: Cohen and West, 1964, pp. 204 and 234: 'Ritual and Social Change', op. cit., p. 68.

[3] This is not quite what I said, but it will do. I did not say that symbols *come to* be thought casually effective (which suggests that people had symbols first and only later developed the idea that they might be casually effective); what I said was that 'fundamentally ritual's effectiveness is thought to lie in its very expressiveness' ('Ritual and Social Change', p. 69).

effective.[1] The first of these propositions would only be contradicted by the statement that magical actions do not involve symbolism (which is evidently untrue); the second by the statement that symbolism is never believed to be causally effective (which also is demonstrably untrue). The 'contradiction' which Jarvie and Agassi impute to me does not exist.

At this point their criticism of the position they attribute to me becomes increasingly difficult to follow. First they suggest that 'Beattie's theory shifts the problem from "why do people we deem rational perform magical acts?" to "what do magical acts mean?" ' As is I hope already sufficiently plain, if the first of these two problems is to be solved, as Jarvie and Agassi suggest, simply by enunciating the truism that people perform magical acts to produce results, then indeed I think the second problem is the more significant. Next they claim that I 'insist that perfectly intelligible meaning can be read into the symbolism of magic'. Of course I have nowhere claimed that the symbolism of magic, or of ritual generally, is always 'perfectly intelligible': what I have asserted is simply that it has, or may have, a rationale, which it is the anthropologist's business to try to discover.

They go on to impute to me (of course without evidence) the hope 'that the imputation of meaning to magic will defend primitive peoples against Frazer's charges of backwardness and irrationality' (p. 182). Really, nothing was further from my thoughts; I had not supposed that it was necessary nowadays, at least in the context of scholarly discourse, to 'defend primitive [sic] peoples' against such charges. Everybody acts

[1] Of course I am very far from being the first to stress that magic is both expressive *and* thought to be effective. Cf. R. R. Marett, 'Magic (Introductory)', *Encyclopaedia of Religion and Ethics*, vol. VIII, Edinburgh 1915, pp. 245–52. On pages 247–8 he writes:

'It is putting the cart before the horse to say, as Frazer seems to do, that the belief that "like produces like", or what not, generates symbolic ritual. It is, on the contrary, symbolic ritual—i.e. a ritual that involves a more or less realistic reproduction of some practical activity—that generates the doctrine of "sympathetic" causation in one or another of its forms.' And 'It is just this faith in their [ritual practices'] efficacy that distinguishes nascently religious practices from such as are merely aesthetic' (loc. cit.). See also Leach, op. cit., p. 524, where he asks: 'if ritual be that aspect of customary behaviour that "says things" rather than "does things", . . . how is it that, in the view of the actors . . . , ritual may "do things" as well as "say things" '? And he answers, following Robertson Smith (and Marett), that 'the rite is prior to the explanatory belief', and involves the imputation of power either to the rite itself (magic) or to an external agent (religion). He makes the further important point—here following Hume—that 'power' is itself not observed in any context, but inferred. We impute it to the phenomenal world on the basis, in the last resort, of our own experience.

rationally in Jarvie's and Agassi's 'strong' sense some of the time, and in their 'weak' sense some of the time. But, as has often been pointed out, lack of technical knowledge (not the same thing as 'irrationality') renders preliterate and technologically less advanced peoples more dependent on ritual than members of modern, Western societies, though of course they always have some technology as well.

'Here at last', Jarvie and Agassi go on, 'is the kernel of a new theory of rationality—if an act is not sociologically meaningless it is rational'. But this is just playing with words. Evidently the activity of a magician (or a poet) is not 'rational' in the sense that it is based on premises derived from controlled observation and empirically tested hypotheses. But this is not to say that it is 'meaningless', sociologically or otherwise. The point of my argument, which I should have thought straightforward and intelligible enough, was that magical behaviour, irrational though it is in Jarvie's and Agassi's 'strong' sense of the term, may none the less have a rationale, that is, a meaning (or meanings) in terms of the symbolic ideas of the people concerned. These meanings are not the same as their explicit aim in performing the magic act, and they are a legitimate and important subject for study. I nowhere suggest that ritual, symbolic behaviour is as 'rational' a means of seeking results as empirically-based, 'practical' behaviour; obviously it isn't. The 'theory that magic is perfectly reasonable' (p. 184) is nowhere propounded by me—or, so far as I know, by anyone else.

'There cannot, after all, be two theories of rationality, one applying to instrumental actions, the other only to symbolic actions', Jarvie and Agassi continue. Leaving aside the important point, already stressed, that the same action may have both instrumental and symbolic aspects, the truth of this proposition depends entirely on what one chooses to mean by 'rationality'. As Martin Hollis remarks in his essay on 'Reason and Ritual', 'logical connection is not the only kind, and to identify ritual beliefs we need to introduce the notion of rational connection';[1] 'rationality' in this context meaning any kind of intelligible relation between beliefs.[2] Whether Jarvie and Agassi want to call the symbolic associations involved in ritual (or, for that matter, in art, music or literature) rational or irrational is of course their affair, but they can hardly deny that they are or may be meaningful.

[1] Above, p. 232.
[2] Above, p. 235. The difference approximates to that made by Langer between 'presentational' and 'discursive' symbolism (or 'language' proper). See Suzanne Langer, *Philosophy in a New Key*, Harvard, 1942, Chapter 4.

Their ensuing criticisms are similarly misconceived. Of course I have never asserted that acts are 'rational only if expressive of social meaning' (p. 183); what I have said is that one way of understanding ritual is by regarding it as (possibly) symbolizing socially recognized values. Nor have I ever 'refused to attribute a goal' to magic; on the contrary I have frequently referred to the magician's overt intentions.[1] Of course Trobriand canoe builders perform magic 'because they think it will help them to achieve some end, i.e. sailable canoes'; this is a platitude which no one denies. But the symbolism their magic involves has other important significances too; if it were simply mistaken technology it would be incredible that the Trobriand Islanders should have either evolved it or retained it. Apart from the fact that the position Jarvie and Agassi are attacking has never been held by anyone, their whole approach is vitiated by their unstated assumption that there can only be *one* way of understanding any phenomenon, so that once the 'right' one has been identified, all the others can be rejected out of hand.

Next (p. 184) Frazer is represented as seeing magic 'as an occult cosmology being applied', whereas my 'anti-Victorian intellectualism' makes me 'object to the procedure of saying that belief in the potency of symbols is based on some different occult cosmology'. Whether Frazer's theory that underlying magic is a faith in 'the order and uniformity of nature' (a theory quite unsupported by ethnography) may properly be described as an account of an occult cosmology is perhaps open to doubt. In any case, the reason why 'Beattie gives no clue as to the cosmology behind the belief in the potency of symbols' is simply that as far as magic is concerned usually there is no evidence that there is any cosmology behind it. And even where there is the 'cosmology' is based on the belief in the potency of symbols, not *vice versa*. It may reasonably be argued (as Marett argued more than fifty years ago) that a belief in the power of symbolic action *underlies* the collective representations about magic held in many, perhaps all, societies; it certainly cannot be argued on the basis of ethnographic evidence that the belief itself derives from some pre-existent cosmology, occult or otherwise, in the sense of some 'theory of the universe as an ordered whole and of the general laws which govern it' (*Shorter Oxford English Dictionary*). It would no doubt be very convenient if all so-called 'primitive' beliefs could be so deduced, but they cannot.

---

[1] For example, 'The sorcerer *intends* to injure his enemy (not just to relieve his feelings); the rainmaker *intends* to make rain; the sacrificer *intends* to avert a spirit's wrath. (Beattie, 'Ritual and Social Change', p. 68.)

Jarvie's and Agassi's next criticism of what they call 'the symbolist view' is that 'how the symbolism is interpreted is entirely arbitrary' (p. 184). To this sweeping judgement one can only reply by pointing to the work of numerous contemporary social anthropologists whose careful analyses of the symbols of the peoples whose cultures they have studied are very far from arbitrary.[1]

Then, once again, 'some contradiction' is attributed to my position, apparently on the ground that I suggest that 'magical' thinking may sometimes be an 'alternative' to 'systematic and analytic thinking', and has its own rationale, while at the same time I agree that the latter kind of thinking is instrumentally more effective. Of course I have never argued that 'magical' thinking (or the action associated with it) is effective at all, at least in the ways in which its practitioners think it is. But it is evident that as scientific understanding of and control over the physical world increase, people will tend to rely less on ritual as a means of attempting to cope with it. It would indeed be curious, as Jarvie and Agassi remark, if I regarded magical thinking as 'an alternative way of thinking, not as a precursor' to 'systematic and analytic thinking'; like most people, I regard it as both. Here again they seem unable to see that sometimes propositions put forward as alternatives can both be true.

Apparently with the object of showing once again that 'the symbolist reading of magic does not explain why people do it', Jarvie and Agassi refer to the Dinka practice of tying a knot in the grass when returning home late, in order to delay the dinner. They ask why, if this rite is believed to be effective as well as expressive, the Dinka hurries home as well. I find it hard to see what their difficulty is; as well as expressing his desire to delay the meal, the rite may (it is thought) help. That is why they do it, but it is certainly desirable to run too. They then refer to Evans-Pritchard's discussion of the symbolic meanings sometimes attached by the Nuer to birds, cucumbers, etc., and ask (turning to the Azande), who sometimes test their magicians and oracles, if they would do this if they viewed them 'purely symbolically'. The answer to this has been suggested already. The total procedures which we label 'magical' need not be, and often are not, viewed by their practitioners as purely symbolic (or even as symbolic at all). They are ways of getting what they want, what is done in such and such a situation in a given culture. But although they certainly have, as Leach puts it, a 'technological aspect', nevertheless they involve—even, usually, in such

[1] As even the most superficial study of any of the works listed in note 4 on pp. 245–6 above would amply demonstrate.

borderline cases as divination and omen-reading—'a symbolic element, in which something is standing for something else'.[1] This aspect, the characteristic feature of magical behaviour, calls for its own kind of investigation. The matter is as simple as that.

'Beattie, Lienhardt and Evans-Pritchard all confuse the strong and weak sense of rationality', they go on, because 'they want to rebut the view that belief in magic and religion is irrational because not strongly rational' (p. 187). Beattie, Lienhardt and Evans-Pritchard (if I may speak also for my two colleagues) are quite as capable of distinguishing Jarvie's and Agassi's 'strong' and 'weak' senses of rationality as they are. They are quite aware that magic is 'irrational' in the sense that it is not based on trial and error, the testing of hypotheses, and so on, as 'science' is. The fact that the two ways of thinking about and coping with reality may be combined in the same activity (as in Trobriand canoe building) is no ground for confusing them in analysis. 'We still maintain', Jarvie and Agassi go on, 'that it is a minimum requirement of explanation that magical acts be explained as rational in the weak sense' (p. 187). No one has ever denied it. Further, as they say, 'it may indeed be "intellectualist" to explain people's actions by theories which assert that they know what they are doing and act on that knowledge, but it may also be successful *to some degree*' (my italics). Indeed it may; again, who has ever denied it? But is it enough? The question is whether ritual is sufficiently explained when we understand what the people who do it are aiming at. Jarvie and Agassi apparently think it is (though the words italicized above suggest that they are beginning to have doubts); like most social anthropologists I think it is not.

They go on to describe the assertion, attributed to me, that 'all men sometimes think irrationally (i.e. symbolically)' (which, granted the equation—which I would not accept—of symbolic thought with irrationality, I should have thought an obvious truism), as 'psychological relativism'. If by this they mean that I suppose the processes of thought to be fundamentally the same for everyone, I freely admit the charge. Do they hold a different view?[2] This position implies, they

---

[1] Beattie, *Other Cultures*, p. 203.

[2] On p. 181, footnote 1 they suggest that 'there would seem to be some contradiction' between this 'relativism' and my 'view that primitive peoples are incapable of systematic, analytic thinking'. Of course I hold no such view; in the passage to which I suppose they are referring (*Other Cultures*, p. 70) I said that 'the capacity for systematic analytic thinking *about concepts* [italics added] is a product of several millennia of education and conscious philosophizing'. I should have thought it was now accepted (it has certainly been pointed out often enough) that

continue, that Beattie 'cannot view error [i.e., in this context, magic] as rational, but at best as a reality surrogate'. If by this they mean that I view magic (or the magical component in behaviour) as being based not upon observation, experiment, etc., but upon symbolism, and that I hold that at some times and places magical procedures have played a role largely taken over in technologically more advanced societies by empirically-based, 'scientific' procedures, then this is indeed my view, and, I think, that of most social anthropologists. But the conclusion they draw from this is puzzling. The 'folly', as they call it, of supposing that 'rationality' (in the sense of a scientific, empirically-grounded approach to reality) 'leads to the avoidance of error' is 'the parochialism of the twentieth century in its worst manifestation' (p. 188). 'Embedded here', they go on, 'is the incredible idea that there exists something like a rational or scientific thought process which leads to the discovery of truth and especially technology'.

Do Jarvie and Agassi really mean this remarkable observation seriously? One wonders what can have been the nature of the thought process which led them to write their article if it was neither rational nor scientific. How do they suppose that man's present knowledge was acquired if not through 'something like a rational or scientific thought process'? If Jarvie and Agassi propose to deprive us altogether of the tool of rational thinking, then indeed further discourse becomes impossible.[1]

All 'scientific' procedures, whether sophisticated or proto-scientific, and whether directed to the making of a hydrogen bomb or to the building of a grass hut, involve the formulation of hypotheses (no

---

the thought of 'primitive' peoples about their environment is systematic and 'scientific' in numerous practical contexts, though not usually to the extent of formulating explicit metaphysical systems. I might, perhaps have made my position on this matter clearer in the passage I have quoted, though so far as I know it has not been misunderstood by anybody else.

[1] Of course I do not 'swallow whole Frazer's naïve view of science as accumu-lated empirical experience from which unquestionably true laws are squeezed by induction', as they assert on p. 189, and I have written nothing to suggest that I did. In fact I have explicitly criticized this view, from which Radcliffe-Brown never quite freed himself (Other Cultures, pp. 55–56, 38; Beattie, 'Radcliffe-Brown', in T. Raison (ed.) Founding Fathers in Social Science, Penguin 1969, p. 181). I should have thought that nowadays most people accepted as commonplace Jarvie's and Agassi's 'rather more sophisticated view of science as a highly articulated system of explanatory theories which may be tested against the facts'. But don't they think that the formulation of these hypotheses is 'something like a rational and scientific thought process'? If not, what is it?

doubt of very different levels of abstraction and complexity), and their testing against experience. The intellectual procedures this involves differ in some important and obvious respects from those involved in symbolism and analogy, whether in the context of magic, religion or art. It is because these two modes of thinking have to be understood in different ways that it is important to distinguish them. Nothing in Jarvie's and Agassi's long and discursive argument effectively criticizes this position.[1]

In the fifth section of their essay Jarvie and Agassi conclude that 'primitive societies have both technology and magic' (so magic is not after all the same as technology, misguided or otherwise?). But they think it wrong to allow the distinction between the two to enter into their explanation of magic: 'we should try to explain their behaviour with hypotheses that do not make a separation they [i.e. 'primitive' people] do not make' (p. 191). As I have said, I hold this restriction unacceptable; it is indeed a most important part of the social anthropologist's job to try to understand the distinctions consciously made by the people whose culture he is studying, but evidently his analysis may, and indeed must, go further.[2] In the last resort their categories must be conceived in terms of ours, if they are to be intelligible to us at all.

In their final section Jarvie and Agassi assert that their view of 'magic as cosmology' owes much to Evans-Pritchard. Evans-Pritchard does indeed present the magical beliefs of the Azande as forming a coherent system, but he does not claim, as Jarvie and Agassi state, that they explain 'anything and everything' in magical terms. Azande know as well as anyone else that a pot may crack because of defective workmanship, or a meal be spoiled by a wife's carelessness.[3] Further, magical

[1] Jarvie and Agassi end this section with a curious distinction between 'false technology' and 'true technology' (which can be 'falsely justified'), and they claim that both can 'work' (p. 190). But they leave unanswered the interesting question by what criteria a 'false technology' which works can be judged to be false.

[2] Here Jarvie and Agassi are joining hands with Winch, who has argued 'that the concepts used by primitive peoples can only be interpreted in the context of the way of life of those peoples' (p. 24). As Hollis and Lukes have shown in their contributions to this volume, this argument would, by depriving us of a 'bridgehead' (to use Hollis's term) into that other culture, make any understanding of ways of thought other than our own impossible. The problem of how we may impute to a culture concepts which are not explicitly formulated by all the individual members of that culture is briefly discussed in Beattie, 'Ritual and Social Change', pp. 66–68.

[3] Witchcraft, Oracles and Magic Among the Azande, Oxford: Clarendon Press, 1937, pp. 74–80.

beliefs are found in many societies, including modern Western ones, in which they do not form a 'cosmology' in any sense of that term (the authors acknowledge as much on p. 192, footnote 2). How then would Jarvie and Agassi explain them? Their paper offers no answer.

In their last paragraph, they appear to draw two conclusions. The first is that 'in Frazer's sense magic is perfectly compatible with rationally explicable behaviour—it is a world-view, a cosmology, and one with great power to grip' (p. 192). The answer to this is that if in some cultures it may, in a sense, be said to be so, in others it certainly may not. And even where it may, it still needs to be understood; it is not explained simply by calling it a cosmology. The explanation that Jarvie and Agassi *do* offer, the truism that people practise magic in order to realize ends, hardly advances our understanding of magical behaviour.

Their second conclusion, if I understand them correctly, is that 'in Beattie's sense' magic '*is* a substitute for systematic and analytic thinking'. This is the view which they dismissed as 'folly' only three pages back. They then, incredibly, ascribe their change of heart on this matter to *my* 'confusion', once again attributing to me views which I have never expressed and do not hold.

They end their paper with a final and egregious *non sequitur*, 'The problem is not, then, 'how on earth can they [i.e. 'primitive' people] believe in magic?''; it is rather "can a people with inefficient magical beliefs come to be critical of them, under what conditions and to what extent?" To us this seems the really urgent sociological problem posed by magic.'[1] This question certainly raises valid problems, but it is not what Jarvie's and Agassi's paper, or the discussion to which it is presumably intended as a contribution, is about. And in any case it can hardly be dealt with unless we know first of all what magical beliefs and actions (or rather aspects of actions) are, that is, how we are to distinguish them from non-magical ones. Like Frazer, Jarvie and Agassi appear to hold that they are simply errors, based on a mistaken view of nature. I hope I have said enough to show that this view is inadequate.

---

[1] If Jarvie and Agassi are in doubt as to the answer to the first part of their question, they may be assured that people *can* come to be critical of their magical beliefs, though they usually retain a few.

II

It is a relief to turn to Lukes's concise and well-argued paper. With Horton, he is more concerned with the status of religious and magical beliefs than with the nature of magical acts. His central question is the philosophical one: how are we to understand 'beliefs which appear *prima facie* irrational?' He distinguishes two senses of the ambigious term 'rational'. 'Rational (1) criteria' are 'those that simply *are* criteria of rationality', shared as such by all men as rational beings, and 'rational (2) criteria', are those 'context-dependent' ones which involve the particular world view or symbolic system of a specified culture.[1] He agrees with Hollis (as against Winch) that without 'rational (1) criteria' in the sense, for example, of 'the concept of negation, and the laws of identity and non-contradiction', we could never understand other cultures at all.

Lukes discusses five answers given by social anthropologists and philosophers to the question how seemingly irrational beliefs are to be understood. With most of his observations I am in full agreement, but I do not think that he does full justice to the 'symbolist' position, which he attributes to Leach, Firth and myself, or that he sees as clearly as he might that Lévy-Bruhl's views, certainly his later ones, may be interpreted as merging very closely with that position. I develop these two points briefly.

First, Lukes attributes to Leach, Firth and myself 'the view that the seeming irrationality of the beliefs involved in primitive religion and magic [why only 'primitive'?] constitutes no problem, for these beliefs are to be interpreted as symbolic' (p. 195). This seems to me to be something of a *non sequitur*; far from constituting no problem, the symbolic and metaphorical character of such beliefs raises a range of extremely interesting and complex problems, which are of central concern to a number of modern social anthropologists. The structure, in the context of specific cultures, of the symbolism involved in belief and rite; the types of symbolic classification implied; the kinds and levels of meaning of symbolic procedures; the grounds upon which the beliefs concerned come to be held; the reasons why rites are thought to be causally effective; the ways in which the symbolic notions involved

---

[1] Above p. 208. This is a much more useful (because more precisely defined) distinction than Jarvie's and Agassi's distinction between the 'strong' and the 'weak' senses of rationality.

are related to other representations current in the culture: these problems and many more arise if, and only if, ritual is understood as symbolic. Far, then, from implying that the 'seeming irrationality' of ritual constitutes no problem, the 'symbolist' interpretation of ritual has permitted the formulation and investigation of a wide range of important questions.

So this approach hardly amounts to a 'refusal to answer' the questions Lukes asks about how we should regard *prima facie* irrational beliefs. My answer was, I thought, quite explicit. It was that while we may regard such beliefs as irrational in the sense that they are not of the same order as the empirically-grounded and testable hypotheses of science (or 'common sense'), they are by no means irrational in the sense that they lack coherent organization or a rationale. The associations and classifications which they involve, like those in music, drama and the other arts, may make perfectly good sense—though not 'scientific' sense—when they are understood.[1]

It should perhaps be made plain that not all of the five answers which Lukes cites to the question how irrational-seeming beliefs are to be understood are mutually exclusive (though certainly some are). In particular, as he himself concludes, magico-religious beliefs may be both symbolic *and* explanatory (in the sense that they may sometimes aim at 'grasping causal connections'). As he says, there is a need for 'contextual (e.g. symbolic)' intrepretation, as well as an obligation to examine such beliefs as attempts to understand causes. Lukes's assertion that I (and Leach) 'seek to discount the fact that beliefs are accepted as true and argue that they must be interpreted metaphorically' (p. 212) seems to me to imply this unnecessary disjunction. It is perfectly possible for beliefs to be accepted as true (and indeed I have never denied that people believe their beliefs) and even as 'explanatory', and at the same time for them to be interpreted metaphorically. I have been concerned to stress their symbolic content, and to emphasize that where they do explain, they do not do so through empirically testable hypotheses comparable with those of modern science, but through systems of symbolic, even dramatic representations. The point is simply that we need to distinguish between the 'truths' of practical experience (whether 'science' or 'common sense'), and those, also 'true'

---

[1] On Luke's ancillary questions, how such beliefs can come to be held and to survive, and what consequences they may have, a good deal has been written by modern social anthropologists from Evans-Pritchard onwards, and there is no need to discuss them here.

but in a different way, of religion, myth and poetry, even though both may be accepted on the same ground of 'custom' by the less reflective members of all cultures.

Beliefs may be accepted and held on various grounds, and one reason, though not the only one, why magico-religious beliefs continue to be held is that in so far as they are understood, even implicitly, as symbolic statements it would be irrelevant, even absurd, to attempt to falsify them by regarding them as assertions of 'fact' and then confronting them with contrary evidence. As Evans-Pritchard has said, a Nuer is quite aware that human twins do not fly, have feathers, etc.; nevertheless twins are birds, in a meaningful though symbolic way. As Lukes and Hollis recognize, all 'truth' is not to be assimilated to scientific explanation.

Further, to interpret a ritual belief as symbolic is rather more than to interpret it merely 'metaphorically', as Lukes suggests (p. 212). Symbols are more than metaphors because, as has often been pointed out, they frequently come to be imbued with a special potency. As Edwin Smith put it, 'the symbol melts into the talisman'.[1] How and under what conditions this comes about are valid and important questions, but they cannot even be formulated, let alone investigated, until the symbolic, 'metaphorical' element in ritual is recognized.

My second general comment on Lukes's essay relates to his statement of Lévy-Bruhl's position. This he described as an 'uneasy compromise', since he (Lévy-Bruhl) maintains 'that primitive "mystical" and "pre-logical" beliefs are on our standards irrational, but that on other (unspecified) standards they are about "real" phenomena and "logical"' (pp. 202-3). It is easy to see how much depends on the meanings attributed to the several highly ambiguous words which this statement contains. I certainly do not wish to attempt a reassessment of Lévy-Bruhl's position; on the whole I accept Lukes's statement of it. But I would suggest, without attempting to develop any of these points, that if the terms 'mystical' and 'pre-logical' are interpreted as applying respectively to beliefs, not founded in experience, in the potency of symbols and symbolic procedures, and to the association of ideas in terms of metaphor rather than of real identity; if the concept of the rational be taken to include also the concept 'rationale'; and if, finally, the development of Lévy-Bruhl's thought as revealed in his *Carnets* be also taken

[1] 'African Symbolism', *Journal of The Royal Anthropological Institute*, 82, Part I, 1952, pp. 13-37 (p. 33). In this connection see also the interesting paper by S. J. Tambiah, 'The Magical Power of Words', *Man* (N.S.) 3, 2, 1968, pp. 175-208, especially pp. 185-8. Cf. also Beattie, 'Ritual and Social Change', pp. 68-9.

into account; then he may not unreasonably be represented as holding, or at least foreshadowing, the position held by those of us who assert that the symbolic, and the practical, 'scientific' ways, or aspects, of thinking may usefully be distinguished.[1]

I agree with Lukes and with Hollis that rationality and the rules of inference it implies are fundamental and universal. But this is not to say that all thinking about symbols is irrational. When conclusions are drawn from religious or magical premises they are drawn *logically*; they could not be drawn in any other way. And even though these premises are founded in metaphor and drama rather than in the controlled hypothesis-testing of science, they have, or may have, their own order. When the principles of this ordering are understood, the notions involved can be seen to make sense. If this were not so, social anthropologists could not even begin either to understand them or to explain them, and in fact they try, not wholly unsuccessfully, to do both.

III

Robin Horton's 'African Traditional Thought and Western Science' is a clear and stimulating exposition of the ways in which, in his view, traditional African thought, especially in the sphere of religion and cosmology, and modern 'scientific' thought as found in Western science, resemble each other, and of the ways in which they differ from each other. He here takes very much further some ideas already propounded in earlier articles,[2] and, I think, a little modifies others, as well as adding some important new ones. In my Malinowski Lecture I criticized his approach on the ground that it represented the kind of thinking involved in religion as very much closer to the kind of thinking involved in modern science than it really is.[3] This seemed to

---

[1] As Evans-Pritchard has pointed out, Lévy-Bruhl's error was to compare 'mystical and prelogical' ways of thought in 'primitive' societies with rational and scientific ways of thought in 'modern' ones, rather than each type of thought with the other in the context of the same culture.

[2] Especially 'A definition of religion and its uses', *Journal of the Royal Anthropological Institute* 90, 1960, pp. 201–26; 'The Kalabari world-view' op. cit.; and 'Ritual Man in Africa', *Africa*, XXXIV, 1964, pp. 85–104.

[3] Beattie, 'Ritual and Social Change', p. 64. In particular, it appeared to me that his claims that ' "Ritual Man" is really a sub-species of theory-building man', and that African religious systems 'can be seen as the outcome of a model-building process which is found *alike* [my italics] in the thought of science and in that of pre-science' (Horton 'Ritual Man . . . ', op. cit. pp. 96 and 99), clearly implied that the thinking involved in 'primitive' religion and magic is quite similar to that found in modern science. I thought, and still think, this view mistaken.

me to obscure what appear to be very crucial differences between them.

Horton now says that some of his critics (including me) have mis-understood him; he had not intended to present traditional thinking as 'a species of science', only to show the 'continuities' between the two kinds of thought. In fact I find very much more to agree with than to disagree with in his present paper; indeed most of the differences now remaining between us appear to be of emphasis rather than of substance. But there are a few points in his essay on which further brief comment may be useful.

First, an initial and rather important source of possible confusion should be cleared up. It is plain from the way in which Horton uses the term 'African traditional thought' that what he means by it is 'African traditional religious or mystical thought', as expressed, for example, in the Kalabari or Lugbara spirit worlds. He is *not* referring to the processes of thought, often no less traditional, involved in the practical side of such activities as house-building, crop rotation or boatmaking. And it is not immediately obvious why African, rather than Western, religion should be compared with Western science. If religious beliefs are to be compared with 'scientific' ones, it might be thought more instructive to compare them in the same cultural context rather than in different ones.

This of course was the point of Evans-Pritchard's criticism of Lévy-Bruhl, referred to above. The effect of this cross-cultural comparison, Horton's as well as Lévy-Bruhl's, is inevitably to represent 'primitive' people as more mystical than they really are, and modern Westerners as more 'scientific' than they really are. We have noted that pre-literate, technologically undeveloped peoples are likely to be more dependent on ritual as a way of attempting to cope with their environment than members of industrialized Western societies are. But the matter is one of degree: both 'scientific' ideas and procedures and 'magical' ones are found in all societies.

However if the comparison is cautiously used it may be illuminating, and in the first part of his paper, as a preliminary to investigating the acknowledged differences between traditional religious thought and the theoretical thinking involved in modern science, Horton sets out to show what they have in common. In the course of this demonstration, he draws some interesting and original analogies. But a few of them seem to me to be rather strained, others to be little more than glimpses of the obvious. No doubt, as he says, traditional religion, like science, 'explains' by elaborating 'a scheme of entities or forces operating "behind" or "within" the world of common-sense observations' (p. 132). But both the entities themselves and the procedures by which the idea of them is reached are so very different in the two cases that it is not easy to see what new light the comparison between them can throw on either.

I argued that while science analyses experience, myth, magic and religion dramatize it.[1] The myth-makers, I suggested, are on the side of the poets, not of the scientists; both find 'order underlying apparent disorder', but they find very different kinds of order, and they seek them by very different means. I pointed out that one consequence of this is that mythical agencies, unlike scientific ones, tend to proliferate. Horton ingeniously counters this by pointing out that Western cosmology does the same thing in giving us 'a myriad molecules' for every common-sense object, and, further, that if it is *kinds* of entity or process we are concerned with, 'then the picture becomes very different' (p. 133). Thus among the Kalabari there are only three principal kinds of mystical forces; ancestors, heroes and water spirits.

In a sense Horton is right. Like everything else, gods and spirits may be classed in a few broad categories, and they do indeed introduce a kind of order into the phenomenal world, and so far explain it. But they have their disorderly side too. And, unlike the concept of the molecule, the gods and spirits of the Kalabari and of other African cultures are the product of the poetic (rather than the scientific) imagination. As such, however and whenever they were developed and elaborated, they are unfettered by the demand, which even the most imaginative scientific hypothesis must acknowledge, that they should submit themselves to rigorous testing against experience. Thus, through a wide range of symbolic and ever-proliferating images, they can express a variety of aspects of the human character and condition. As individual quasi-persons, they are in these respects quite opposite to the neutral, impersonal and relational constructs of the physical sciences.[2]

Again, to claim as Horton does (p. 136) that the diviner who attributes disease to a spirit and the Westerner who attributes an explosion to nuclear fusion are both explaining 'by reference to theoretical entities'

[1] 'Ritual and Social Change', p. 65.

[2] Bronowski among many others has put the point well. 'The Greeks,' he writes, 'peopled nature with a rowdy, happy-go-lucky train of gods and spirits. Science arrived like an Old Testament prophet, with a puritan and obsessed vision of single-minded coherence, to sweep that pagan plenty out of the window and put in its place the Jehovah who orders all things under laws.' J. Bronowski 'The Machinery of Nature', *Encounter*, November 1965, p. 53.

is to use the last two words so imprecisely as to render them hardly more meaningful than the term 'something' would be. The two forces concerned (whether the Westerner understands nuclear physics or not) are so different in conception as to be scarcely comparable. The fact that the unscientific Westerner may regard the achievements of science as 'mystically' as the pre-literate tribesman regards the spirits is not really relevant, since what we are comparing are 'mystical' and scientific representations, not the states of mind of the uninformed in either context.

But with a great deal that Horton says in this part of his essay about gods and spirits and the 'jobs' they do, about the 'psychosomatic insight' of traditional healers, and about the analogy between psychoanalytic ideas and traditional African ones I am in full agreement, as I am with much else in both parts of his paper.

Again, Horton's arguments that 'abstraction is as essential to the operation of traditional African religious theory as it is to the thought of modern Western theory', that both involve the assimilation of the unfamiliar, and that only 'limited aspects' of a given phenomenon can be taken into account at one time (his fifth, sixth and seventh points on pp. 144–8), can really hardly advance our understanding of either science or traditional religion, for evidently all three processes are essential to any thinking about anything. Taking, lastly, Horton's eighth and final point of comparison between traditional African thought and Western science, it is indeed a scientific fact that 'a theoretical model, once built, is developed in ways which sometimes obscure the analogy on which it was founded' (p. 148). As he points out, Rutherford's planetary model, 'when it came up against recalcitrant data', was subject to 'constant modification'. But this can hardly be said to be true of the traditional African 'models' which Horton goes on to describe. The bizarre, paradoxical attributes of Kalabari heroes and water spirits, like those of Lugbara *adro* spirits (which are split down the middle, walk about upside down, etc.), far from being the result of constant modification, are, as Horton puts it, 'integral to the definition' of them. There is no evidence at all that these bizarre qualities were added later, one by one, in order to provide for recalcitrant data. As Horton himself says p. 68*),[1] they are a 'graphic expression of their [the spirits'] general perversity', not a theory which might explain it.

Horton concludes the first part of his article by claiming that his

[1] Starred page numbers here and on pp. 265 and 266 below give references to the original pagination of Horton's 'African Traditional Thought and Western Science', op. cit.

treatment of 'African religious systems as theoretical models akin to those of the sciences' removes obstacles to understanding; for until this 'underlying similarity' is recognized, anthropologists 'can only see traditional religion as wholly other' and 'essentially mysterious' (p. 152).[1] But, ingenious though Horton's analogy between traditional African religion and modern scientific thought is, it is perfectly possible to make sense of traditional (or for that matter non-traditional) religious and magical acts and beliefs without regarding them as being in any significant respect 'like' science. Indeed it seems to me that Horton's analogy, if pressed, is likely to obscure rather than to advance understanding. The 'bizarre and senseless features' of such beliefs do not become immediately comprehensible, to me at any rate, when they are seen as the product of a model-building process comparable with that of modern science. If they were this, their presence and persistence would indeed be inexplicable. On the contrary, they make sense when they are regarded very differently, that is, as symbolizing certain important aspects of the physical and socio-cultural environment. It is exactly by this sort of understanding that, only a few pages earlier in his essay, Horton has himself so illuminatingly explained the more bizarre aspects of Kalabari and Lugbara representations.

However Horton now says quite explicitly that 'traditional thought' is *not* a kind of science. But since he represents it as a means of explaining things which is based on procedures comparable to scientific ones, it is not yet very clear how he thinks they differ. In the second Part of his article he tackles this question.

IV

The 'key' difference between 'the religious thinking of traditional Africa and the theoretical thinking of the modern West',[2] Horton now states, is that 'in traditional cultures there is no developed awareness of alternatives to the established body of theoretical tenets; whereas in scientifically oriented cultures, such an awareness is highly developed. It is this difference we refer to when we say that traditional cultures

[1] Though he admits 'playing down' the difference between 'personal and non-personal theory', Horton regards it as 'a surface difference concealing an underlying similarity of intellectual process', in short, 'more than anything else a difference of idiom' (p. 69). I think it is plain that it is a good deal more than this.

[2] Again, this formulation seems to me to convey the quite false impression that there are two different kinds of thinking which are found respectively in 'traditional' Africa and in the modern West. I would stress that both 'kinds' are found in both contexts, though certainly in differing proportions.

are "closed" and scientifically oriented cultures "open".' (p. 153).

Now this is certainly a very valuable observation, and although, as has been pointed out, whether a society is 'open' or 'closed' is very much a matter of context and degree,[1] it certainly does point to an important difference between traditional and 'modern' societies. The tradition of questioning accepted beliefs is indeed a part of the modern scientific tradition (though, as Horton realizes, by no means as widely or firmly established as we may like to think), as it is not of more traditionally-minded cultures. But it is possible to exaggerate the degree of 'absence of any awareness of alternatives' (p. 154) in traditional societies; the distinction is relative. It is certainly difficult, even dangerous, to question accepted beliefs in such societies, as Socrates and many after him have found, but it is not impossible. If it were, 'awareness of alternatives' could never have developed at all.

Further, as far as 'traditional' African beliefs are concerned, is it in fact true that for their adherents there is a 'lack of awareness of alternatives'? In most of Africa south of the Sahara Christianity has been well established for several generations, yet traditional African beliefs continue to thrive, in some areas even to gain ground. And hosts of separatist movements, about which there is now a substantial literature, have grown up in many areas, combining aspects of both Western Christianity and traditional belief. There can be very few Africans today, even among the most traditionally-minded, who are not 'aware of alternatives'. The necessity for choice between these may, and sometimes does, give rise to stress and conflict, but both traditional and Western standards may, and do, coexist in Africa, as they do almost everywhere. Religion in one form or another is by no means dead in the 'open' societies of Western Europe, nor is the belief in magic.[2] And in Europe as elsewhere they both involve ways of thinking about and dealing with experience which are very different from those involved in the scientific outlook.

So although Horton is certainly right in suggesting that in a broad sense the magico-religious attitude is characteristic of the 'closed' society, the scientific attitude of the 'open' one (for reasons which can be and have been elaborated), this cannot constitute the 'key' difference between the two attitudes, for both of them are found (though in

[1] See Dorothy Emmet's useful critique of Popper's distinction in D. Bidney (ed.) *The Concept of Freedom in Anthropology*. The Hague: Mouton, 1963.

[2] For a recent colourful illustration of this see two articles by Richard Cavendish in *The Observer* (colour supplement) of November 24 and December 1, 1968.

different proportions and at different levels of development) in both kinds of societies. The key difference is not to be found in the distinction between whether alternative systems of belief are conceivable or whether they are not: if it is to be discovered at all it must be found in the nature and grounds of the beliefs themselves.

The rest of Horton's essay seems to support this view of the matter, rather than his own. The principal difference between us now seems to be that while I find it useful to regard the scientific and the 'traditional' as two approaches representing fundamentally different and mutually irreducible ways of looking at the world, Horton thinks that they can be understood in terms of the difference between 'closed' and 'open' societies.

First, he stresses the fact that in 'traditional' thinking a special power is ascribed to symbols, preeminently to words, but also to other things 'verbally designated as such' (p. 158*).[1] This ascription is not of course based on hypothesis or experiment: in this context the idea of testing is, as he correctly remarks, 'beside the point', for it implies an attitude 'quite opposite' to that of the scientist. Here indeed Horton has put his finger on what I (and others) have argued to be ritual's essential quality, namely its expressive character. I have argued that it is from this quality, not from any kind of 'scientific' process, that the belief in its causal efficacy (where it is believed to have such efficacy) is fundamentally derived.

His next two points, that in a 'traditional' culture ideas are seen as bound to particular contexts rather than (as in scientifically oriented cultures) to other ideas, and that a concern with the nature and rules of logical inference is characteristic of the scientific rather than of the 'traditional' outlook (together with his claim that both of these differences are associated with the 'lack of alternatives' characteristic of the 'closed' predicament), are reasonable enough. So is his next claim, which is (if I have understood him correctly) that in 'scientific' cultures the aims of scientific enquiry, especially 'the quest for "objectivity"' (p. 165*), are specific and explicit, whereas in 'traditional' thought a variety of ends, 'not explicitly reflected upon or defined', may be

---

[1] This point is made in the full version of Horton's paper, in *Africa*, XXXVII, 2, 1967, pp. 158ff. Horton's explanation of the grounds for the belief in the power of verbal symbols, that the words through which man makes contact with reality 'appear bound to reality in an absolute fashion', is not convincing. No traditionalist, however 'primitive', believes that words always affect the reality they stand for. Only some words do, and even these, usually, only sometimes. Here Horton is reviving Lévy-Bruhl's idea of 'mystical participation' in a new dress.

sought at the same time (p. 162*).[1] His argument here interestingly shifts the emphasis from the 'explanatory' to the expressive. There is in traditional thought, he writes, 'a gradual shading of the cognitive into the aesthetic' (p. 163*); 'dramatic representations of the gods' are thought to be both causally effective in influencing them, and 'enjoyable' for their own sakes (p. 164*); and we end up with 'a rich encrustation of cultural growths whose underlying motives have little to do with explanation or prediction' (p. 165*).[2] In this respect traditional (ritual) thought differs radically from 'the scientific ideal', whose primary canon is that 'every new theory be subjected to the widest possible testing and criticism' (p. 164*). One could hardly agree more, but all this seems hardly consistent with Horton's original contention that both traditional (ritual) and scientific thought share a common 'model-building process'.[3]

Referring to Mary Douglas,[4] Horton contrasts the traditional view of the anomalous and exceptional as something dangerous (since they defy established lines of classification), and the scientist's view of them —to him the anomalous offers an intriguing challenge. Thus (Horton does not say this explicitly although Douglas does) 'taboo', a characteristic concept of 'traditional' thinking, essentially implies symbolizing; for the ground of avoidance lies not in the experienced qualities of the object itself, but in what it represents. Finally, Horton brilliantly argues that for 'traditional' thought the passage of time ('the vehicle *par excellence* of the new and the strange') is dangerous and unwanted, and attempts are made to annul it through rites of renewal and recreation. To the scientist, on the other hand, the temporal process, with the associated—and now rather threadbare—idea of progress, is welcome and indispensable.

[1] However, I do not believe that, as Horton claims, 'the goals of explanation and prediction are as powerfully present in traditional African cultures as they are in cultures where science has become institutionalized' (p. 162). As he himself remarks a few pages later, divination is 'concerned with discovering the identity of the spiritual forces responsible for particular happenings', and the reasons for their action, rather than with prediction. Also, in a 'closed' society where things could not be conceived to be otherwise than they are there could hardly be much concern with explanation as a goal pursued for its own sake.

[2] It was of course precisely this 'rich encrustation' that I had in mind when I referred to ritual's 'proliferating tendency' ('Ritual and Social Change', p. 65). Earlier in his essay Horton has argued that this tendency is *not* distinctive of traditional (ritual) thought (cf. p. 23 above).

[3] Horton 'Ritual Man . . . ', op. cit., p. 99.

[4] *Purity and Danger*, London: Routledge 1966.

If, with Horton, we mean by traditional thought the ideas involved in magical and religious ritual in (mostly) small-scale societies, then he and I would seem now to be in pretty close agreement both that performing rites is not really very like acting scientifically, and that where religious and magical beliefs 'explain', they do so by procedures very different from those of science. But I think that perhaps we still disagree as to what the basic difference between the two approaches is.

For Horton, the key is 'the concept of the "closed" predicament'. Now there is no doubt that explanations in terms of religious and magical beliefs are characteristic of small-scale, preliterate, technologically simple societies (though they are by no means confined to them), and that modern science is a product of literate, complex, more or less 'open' societies. But this in itself tells us nothing about the difference (if, as seems now to be conceded, there is one) between the mythical and the scientific world views; it only tells us in which kind of society each is likely to be dominant. I had attempted in my Malinowski lecture to identify this difference, and the second half of Horton's essay seem to me to be almost wholly consistent with the distinctions I proposed.

I think it is likely—and indeed Horton has suggested as much to me in a personal communication—that his earlier emphasis on the explanatory aspect of religion and myth stems from his concern with belief and cosmology; my emphasis on the expressive and symbolic aspects of magic and religion from my interest in ritual as a way of acting as well as (or rather than) a way of thinking. I am very willing to agree with him that theologies and cosmologies, whatever their level of sophistication, are explanatory as well as expressive. Although I had explicitly acknowledged this, it may well be that I paid less attention to this aspect than I would have done if I had been more concerned with mythical ideas and less with magical acts. For, as a system of interconnected concepts, a religious myth gives an *account* of the matters it is concerned with (as of course Malinowski in particular stressed): thus it is explanatory almost by definition. In this it differs from magic, which, as Marett saw, need imply no articulate cosmology, only an inchoate 'faith' that performing it will somehow be effective. But, whether all of their adherents are aware of it or not, both religious myth and magical performance do, I believe, involve an underlying but indispensable expressive and symbolic component. If they did not, we should not call them magical or religious, but something else.

So, taking the term 'ritual' in its very broadest sense (i.e. as including beliefs as well as rites), there is no reason why both its explanatory and its expressive, symbolizing aspects should not be acknowledged and investigated. Symbolism and ritual in all their variety attach to a vast range of human thought and behaviour, and it is entirely to be expected that, in the context of belief, cognitive (and so explanatory) aspects will be stressed; in the context of rites the emphasis will be on the expressive, the symbolic and the putatively causal. Ritual may be many things to the people who practise it and have faith in it, and a monolithic type of explanation is as misleading in the attempt to understand it as it is in other contexts of understanding human behaviour.

BIBLIOGRAPHY

An extensive literature on the philosophy of the social sciences exists. The works in this bibliography are those that have most relevance for the subjects raised in the articles in this volume. The various works in anthropology and sociology to which particular writers make allusion are not included here: details are given in the appropriate footnotes.

Abel, T. in E. Feigel and M. Brodbeck (Eds.) *Readings in the Philosophy of Science*, New York: Appleton-Century-Crofts, 1953.

Albert, H. 'Der Mythos der totalen Vernunft', *Kölner Zeitschrift für Sociologie und Sozialpsychologie*, 16, 2, 1964, pp. 225–6.

Ayer, A. J. *The Problem of Knowledge*, London: Macmillan, 1956.

— 'Can There be a Private Language?' *Proceedings of the Aristotelean Society* Supplement XXVIII.

Bartley, W. W. 'Achilles, the Tortoise and Explanation in Science and History', *British Journal of the Philosophy of Science*, 13, 1963, pp. 15–33.

— *The Retreat to Commitment*, New York: Knopf, 1963.

Beattie, J. H. M. 'Ritual and Social Change', *Man: The Journal of the Royal Anthropological Institute*, I, 1966, pp. 60–74.

Bendix, R. 'Concepts and Generalizations in Comparative Sociological Studies', *American Sociological Review*, 28, 4 August 1963, pp. 532–539.

Bennett, Jonathan. *Rationality*, London: Routledge, 1964.

Braithwaite, R. B. 'An Empiricist's View of the Nature of Religious Belief', The Eddington Memorial Lecture, Cambridge: University Press, 1955.

Brown, R. R. *Explanation in Social Science*, Chicago:Aldine, 1963.

Chambers, F. P. *Perception, Understanding and Society: A Philosophical Essay on the arts, sciences and human studies*, London: Sidgwick and Jackson, 1961.

Claessens, D. 'Rationalität revidiert', *Kölner Zeitschrift für Soziologie und Sozialpsychologie*, 17, 3, 1965, pp. 465–76.

Cody, A. B. 'Can a single action have many different descriptions?', *Inquiry*, 10, 2, Summer 1967, pp. 164–80.

Cunningham, F. 'More on Understanding in the Social Sciences', *Inquiry*, 10, 3, Autumn 1967, pp. 321–8.

Evans-Pritchard, E. E. 'Lévy-Bruhl's Theory of Primitive Mentality', *Bulletin of the Faculty of Arts* (Alexandria), II, 1934, pp. 1–36.

— 'The Intellectualist (English) Interpretation of Magic', *Bulletin of the Faculty of Arts* (Alexandria), I, 1933, pp. 282–311.

— *Theories of Primitive Religion*, Oxford: Clarendon Press, 1965.

Ferber, C. von. 'Zur Werturteilsfrage in der Soziologie', *Zeitschrift für die gesamte Staatswissenschaft*, 120, 1, Jan. 1964, pp. 144–9.

Feyerabend, P. K. *Knowledge without Foundations*, Oberlin/Ohio, 1961.

Garfinkel, H. 'The rational properties of scientific and common sense activities', *Behavioral Science*, 5, 1, Jan. 1960, pp. 72–83.

Gellner, Ernest. *Thought and Change*, London: Weidenfeld, 1964.

Gibson, Q. B. *The Logic of Social Enquiry*, London: Routledge, 1960.

Goody, J. 'Religion and Ritual: the Definitional Problem', *British Journal of Sociology*, XII, 1961, pp. 142–64.

Gross, L. 'An Epistemological View of Sociological Theory', *American Journal of Sociology* 65, 5, March 1960, pp. 441–8.

Gruner, R. 'Understanding in the Social Sciences and in History', *Inquiry*, 10, 2, Summer 1967, pp. 151–63.

Habermas, J. 'Gegen einen positivistisch halbierten Rationalismus', *Kölner Zeitschrift für Soziologie und Sozialpsychologie*, 16, 4, 1964, pp. 635–59.

Hartnack, J. 'Remarks on the Concept of Knowledge', *Inquiry*, 4, 4, 1961, pp. 270–4.

Hempel, C. G. 'Rational Action', *Proceedings and Addresses of the American Philosophical Association*, 35, . . . pp. 5–23.

Hick, John (Ed.). *Faith and the Philosophers*, London: Macmillan, 1964.

Langer, S. *Philosophy in a New Key*, Cambridge, Mass.: Harvard University Press, 1942.

Leach, E. R. *The Political Systems of Highland Burma*, London: Bell, 1954.

— 'The Epistemological Background to Malinowski's Empiricism', in R. Firth, *Man and Culture*, London: Routledge, 1957.

— 'Ritual', *International Encyclopaedia of the Social Sciences*, vol. 13, New York: Macmillan and The Free Press, 1968.

Lévy-Bruhl, L. *Les fonctions mentales dans les societies inferieures*, Paris: Presses Universitaires de France, 1910. English translation: *How Natives Think*, London: Allen & Unwin, 1926.

— *Les Carnets de Lucien Lévy-Bruhl*, Paris: Presses Universitaires de France, 1949. English translation in preparation (Oxford: Blackwell).

Louch, A. R. *Explanation and Human Action*, Oxford: Blackwell, 1966.

MacIntyre, Alasdair. 'The Logical Status of Religious Beliefs', in *Metaphysical Beliefs*, London: S.C.M. Press, 1957.

— 'A Mistake about Causality in Social Science', in Peter Laslett and W. G. Runciman, *Philosophy, Politics and Society* (Second Series), Oxford: Blackwell, 1962.

McEwen, W. P. *The Problem of Social-Scientific Knowledge*, Totowa, N.J.: Bedminster Press, 1963.

Nielsen, K. 'Appealing to Reason', *Inquiry*, 5, 1, 1962, pp. 65–85.

Popper, K. R. *The Logic of Scientific Discovery*, London: Hutchinson, 1959.

Topitsch, E. (ed.). *Logik der Socialwissenschaften*, Berlin: Kiepenheuer, 1965.

Toulmin, Stephen. *Foresight and Understanding*, London: Hutchison, 1961.

Wax, M. L. 'On Misunderstanding Verstehen: a Reply to Abel', *Sociology and Social Research*, 51, 3, April 1967, pp. 323–33.

Weber, Max. *Theory of Social and Economic Organization* (Part I of *Wirtschaft und Gesellschaft* translated by A. R. Henderson and Talcott Parsons), London: Hodge, 1947.

INDEX OF NAMES